Hokkaido

Aomori

Akita   Iwate

Yamagata   Miyagi

Niigata   Fukushima

Ishikawa   Tochigi

Gumma

Toyama   Ibaraki

Nagano   Saitama

Fukui   Yamanashi   Tokyo

Kyoto   Gifu   Kanagawa   Chiba

Tottori   Shiga   Aichi

Shimane   Hyogo   Shizuoka

Okayama   Osaka   Mie

Yamaguchi   Hiroshima   Kagawa   Nara

Fukuoka   Ehime   Tokushima

Saga   Wakayama

ıgasaki   Oita   Kochi

umamoto   Miyazaki

Kagoshima

Okinawa

Lectures on Modern Japanese Economic History 1926–1994

LTCB International Library Selection No. I

LECTURES ON MODERN JAPANESE ECONOMIC HISTORY 1926–1994

NAKAMURA TAKAFUSA

Professor Emeritus
The University of Tokyo

LTCB International Library Foundation

Transcription of names

The Hepburn system of romanization is used for Japanese terms, including the names of persons and places. Long vowels are not indicated. Chinese terms are romanized using the pinyin system. The Wade-Giles system is used, however, for certain place-names outside mainland China. As for the romanization of Korean terms, the McCune-Reischauer system is used.

With regard to Japanese, Chinese, and Korean personal names, we have followed the local custom of placing the family name first.

This book was originally published in 1986 by Iwanami Shoten Publishers under the title *Showa Keizai Shi*.
English translation rights reserved by LTCB International Library Foundation under contract with Nakamura Takafusa and through the courtesy of Iwanami Shoten Publishers.
© 1994 by LTCB International Library Foundation

Published November 1994 by LTCB International Library Foundation
1-8, Uchisaiwaicho 2-chome, Chiyoda-ku, Tokyo 100, Japan
Tel: 03-5223-7204   Fax: 03-5511-8123

Translation and production by Simul International, Inc., Tokyo

Printed in Japan
ISBN 4-924971-00-6 C1333 P3300E

All photographs courtesy of Kyodo Press.

CONTENTS

The LTCB International Library Foundation:
Statement of Purpose

PREFACE TO THE
ENGLISH-LANGUAGE EDITION

I am delighted that this work, which first appeared under the title *Showa Keizai Shi*, has been translated into English and made available to overseas readers thanks to the LTCB International Library Foundation. I hope that it will present overseas readers with a balanced picture of Japan's modern economic history and encourage a fair perspective on Japan.

The Japanese-language edition presents seven lectures that I gave at a seminar series sponsored by the prestigious publishing house Iwanami Shoten Publishers. The lectures, given in March and April 1985, were transcribed in shorthand, and after some editing and rewriting, the volume appeared in February 1986. The title *Showa Keizai Shi* (Economic History of the Showa Era) was adopted because the seminar sponsors and I felt that it would be a valuable exercise to commemorate the 60th of the reign of the Showa Emperor by undertaking a retrospective of the economic events and development of this turbulent era. Chapter 7 of the English-language edition, however, differs significantly from that in the Japanese edition. In order to take into account the dramatic changes that have occurred since 1985, the text of that chapter is based on a talk that I presented to the Planning Division of the Long-Term Credit Bank of Japan, Ltd., and covers events up to 1994.

Showa refers to a reign period, a method of reckoning dates that was adopted and adapted in Japan from Chinese usage. Nowadays the practice is to assign a new reign period when a new emperor ascends the throne. This year, 1994, is the sixth year of the Heisei reign period. The term Showa was adopted in December 1926, when the Showa Emperor came to the throne, and was employed for 64 years until his death in January 1989. The Showa period thus accounts for half of Japan's modern history, as dated from the opening of Japanese ports in 1854.

The Showa era began in recession and saw Japan embark on the path of steady recovery and growth, only to have these destroyed by eight years of senseless war. The period of the late 1940s and early 1950s was one of economic recovery, followed by over a decade of dramatic growth that lasted up to about 1970 and changed Japan's economy and society in every imaginable way. The oil crisis of 1973–74 drew the final curtain on the era of rapid growth, which was followed by a period of stable growth in which Japan's economy began to internationalize and Japan found itself having to meet new responsibilities to the global economy.

This volume attempts to recount Japan's economic history from the 1920s to the present day in a way that is accurate and, hopefully, easy to comprehend. Economic history relates to obvious events, such as depressions and wars, but it also must deal with less visible, continuous, but no less definitive processes, such as changes in industrial structure and movements of population among regions. I hope that I have been able to convey both aspects as objectively as possible in this work.

I would like to take this opportunity to thank the many people who made this English-language edition possible. First, my gratitude goes to Messrs. Uehara Takashi and Ito Yoshiaki, of the LTCB International Library Foundation, who first proposed the translation project. I would like to thank the many staff members at Simul International, Inc., for their efficient teamwork in translating, revising, and producing the English-language text and especially Dr. Chris Brockett, of the University of Washington, who undertook the translation of the entire Japanese text into English with enthusiasm. In addition, I would like to acknowledge the immense effort of Messrs. Takeda Koshi and Sugita Tadashi, of Iwanami Shoten Publishers, in bringing about the publication of the original Japanese-language edition. To all these individuals, I would like to extend my appreciation.

Transformation amid Crisis: The 1920s

It is 1927 and crowds are rushing the banks as scandal surrounding government earthquake notes shakes depositor confidence. Many banks will close their doors in the following days

1926	December	Emperor Taisho dies. Emperor Showa ascends the throne, and a new era is proclaimed.
1927	March	The bank panic (triggered by an ill-advised statement by Finance Minister Kataoka).
	April	The Privy Council rejects a proposed imperial order for the rescue of the Bank of Taiwan. Prime Minister Wakatsuki Reijiro and his cabinet resign. Tanaka Giichi becomes prime minister and ends the crisis with a three-week bank moratorium.
1928	June	The Chinese Nationalists crush the northern warlords and reunify China. Zhang Tsolin is assassinated by Japanese forces.
1929	July	Tanaka and his cabinet resign. Hamaguchi Osachi becomes prime minister with an agenda of naval disarmament and of lifting the gold embargo.
	October	The New York Stock Exchange crashes, triggering global panic and recession.
	November	Japan's Ministry of Finance orders the ban on gold exports lifted, to be implemented in January the following year.
1930		The recession deepens in agriculture. The Showa depression is in full swing.
	November	Prime Minister Hamaguchi is assassinated. Wakatsuki becomes prime minister again.
1931	March	Mid-ranked army officers unsuccessfully plot overthrow of the government.
	April	The important Industries Control Law is promulgated.
	September	Crisis in Manchuria. Great Britain goes off the gold standard. Dollar purchases soar; the government responds aggressively.
	December	Wakatsuki and his cabinet resign. Inukai Tsuyoshi becomes prime minister. Takahashi Korekiyo is appointed minister of finance and abandons the gold standard.

Lecture 1

TRANSFORMATION AMID CRISIS: THE 1920S

INTRODUCTION

This year, 1985, marks the 60th year of the Showa era, which has thus completed one full cycle of the old Chinese calendar. Half of Japan's modern history has been in the Showa era. Since the 60th year of Showa is 118 years after the Meiji Restoration, the Showa era has lasted slightly longer than the preceding Meiji and Taisho eras combined. The first year of Showa, 1926, marked the midway point between the beginning of modern Japan and the present day. Moreover, since 40 years have now elapsed since Japan's defeat in World War II, one-third of Japan's modern history has taken place in the postwar period.

The Showa era has not just been of long duration, but it has been an age of tumultuous change seldom matched in other modern nations. Nowadays we hear a good deal about the newly industrializing economies (NIEs), whose number in Asia includes South Korea, Taiwan, Singapore, and Hong Kong. Future generations may argue that the changes that have taken place in these countries have been more rapid than those that took place in Japan, but Japan's transformation, I am convinced, has been the most dramatic in modern history. If you will look at figure 1.1, I have presented the changes that have taken place since 1920 in terms of population employed and income, broken down by industrial sector. Between 1925, the year before Emperor Showa ascended the throne, and 1980, the working population almost exactly doubled. In 1925, primary industries—in other words, agriculture, forestry, and fisheries—still accounted for half of the working population. Secondary industries, which include con-

3

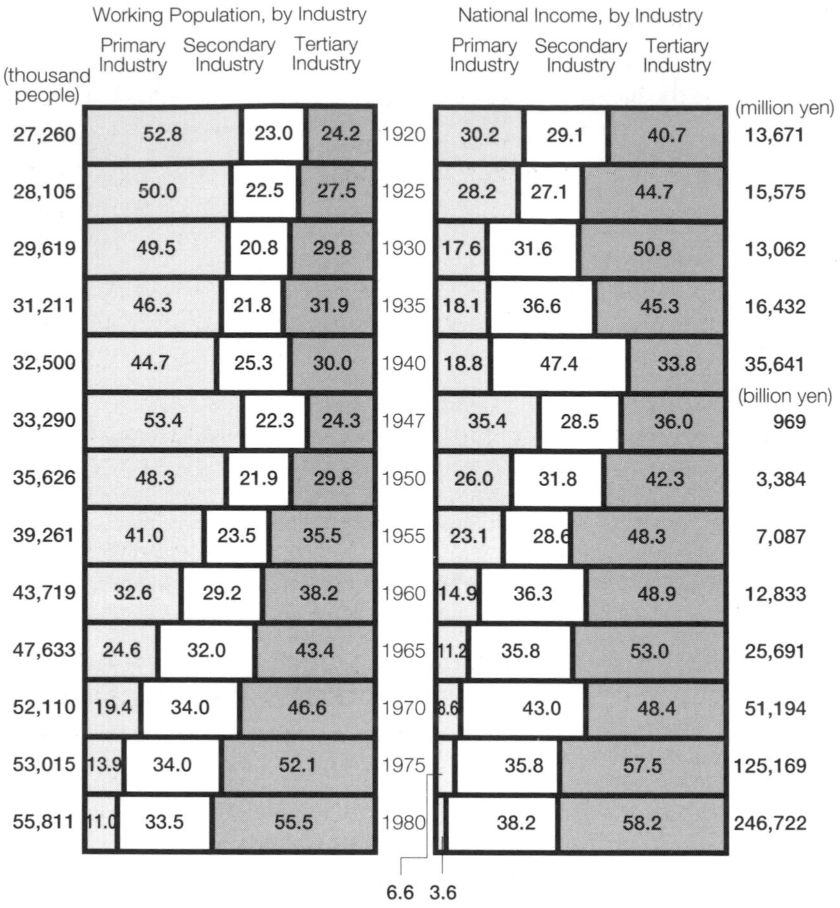

Working Population, by Industry					National Income, by Industry			
(thousand people)	Primary Industry	Secondary Industry	Tertiary Industry		Primary Industry	Secondary Industry	Tertiary Industry	(million yen)
27,260	52.8	23.0	24.2	1920	30.2	29.1	40.7	13,671
28,105	50.0	22.5	27.5	1925	28.2	27.1	44.7	15,575
29,619	49.5	20.8	29.8	1930	17.6	31.6	50.8	13,062
31,211	46.3	21.8	31.9	1935	18.1	36.6	45.3	16,432
32,500	44.7	25.3	30.0	1940	18.8	47.4	33.8	35,641
								(billion yen)
33,290	53.4	22.3	24.3	1947	35.4	28.5	36.0	969
35,626	48.3	21.9	29.8	1950	26.0	31.8	42.3	3,384
39,261	41.0	23.5	35.5	1955	23.1	28.6	48.3	7,087
43,719	32.6	29.2	38.2	1960	14.9	36.3	48.9	12,833
47,633	24.6	32.0	43.4	1965	11.2	35.8	53.0	25,691
52,110	19.4	34.0	46.6	1970	8.6	43.0	48.4	51,194
53,015	13.9	34.0	52.1	1975	6.6	35.8	57.5	125,169
55,811	11.0	33.5	55.5	1980	3.6	38.2	58.2	246,722

Fig. 1.1. Working Population and National Income by Industry

Sources: Working population figures are from census data. National income data are from Okawa Kazushi, et al. *Kokumin Shotoku* (National Income) in *Choki Keizai Tokei* (Long-term Economic Statistics), Toyo Keizai Shinpo Sha, 1974 and Economic Planning Agency estimates.

struction and mining in addition to manufacturing, accounted for a total of 22.5 percent, while tertiary industries, such as transportation, communications, electric power, gas, water supply, finance, commerce, services, and public administration, totaled 27.5 percent altogether.

Changes between 1925 and 1985

The proportion of the population working in primary industries declined up to the end of World War II, when the numbers jumped 10 percent in 1947 to nearly 18 million, with the proportion working in secondary and tertiary industries declining proportionately for a time. After that, the changes came fast and furious. The working population grew by approximately 22 million. The agricultural population, after decreasing moderately up to 1955, subsequently plunged 11 percent, or to about 6 million today in 1985. Meanwhile, the number of workers in secondary and tertiary industries increased. Secondary industries in particular grew rapidly to 1970, but after that only the tertiary industries continued to expand, growing to the point where they employed over half the working population.

Income statistics indicate that in 1925 primary industries supplied 28 percent of all income, secondary industry 27 percent, and tertiary industries 45 percent. Incomes from primary industries then declined as a percentage in the period up to World War II, while secondary industries showed atypical growth owing to demand for military materiel, something that is strikingly apparent from the 1940 statistics. Income from tertiary industries shrank temporarily during the same interval. After Japan's defeat, the percentage of income from primary industries rose for a brief period beginning in 1947, but later plunged, while the shares of secondary and tertiary industry, especially tertiary, surged ahead. The shifts reflect the immense transformation that took place in the Japanese economy in the Showa era.

I should also add that in the 1860s, at the beginning of the Meiji era, about 80 percent of the population was engaged in agriculture, an indication of just how completely Japan's economic structure has changed in the 118 years since the Meiji Restoration.

ECONOMY AND SOCIETY IN THE EARLY SHOWA YEARS

Let me begin by sketching the shape of the Japanese economy in the early years of the Showa era, that is, the latter half of the 1920s. Japan was already a well-established capitalist society. There is much debate as to when the capitalist society became established; I myself date it to the 1890s and to the latter part of the 1890s in particular.

The Japanese economy enjoyed a period of prosperity during World War I, but in 1920, two years after the war ended, the country was plunged into recession. Since economies around the world were in protracted recession, a somber economic mood prevailed in Japan. Nonetheless, by this stage the Japanese economy now featured a full range of industries, and the top companies, notably in the textile industry, were already dominating the economic picture.

Old-fashioned capitalism

There were, however, some major differences between the industries of the time and the industries of today. The 1920s was an age in which old-style capitalists still existed in some number, and the gap between rich and poor was far wider than today. Japanese society of the time, as indeed did other societies around the world, still retained something of the nineteenth-century capitalism of the age of Marx and Engels. In America, the great capitalists—Rockefeller, the oil king; Carnegie in steel; Harriman and Vanderbilt in railroads; Ford in automobiles; and Morgan, who single-handedly dominated the banking industry—and their families held sway over American society. Japan also had its great capitalists: there were the big *zaibatsu* conglomerates of Mitsui, Mitsubishi, Sumitomo, and Yasuda and the second-tier zaibatsu of Furukawa, Okura, Asano, Fujita, and Shibusawa. There were also numbers of well-funded individual entrepreneurs of varying degrees of wealth.

The great capitalists were naturally concentrated in Tokyo and in the area of Kobe and Osaka, but the regional cities were home to lesser capitalists, still of substantial wealth, who dominated local industries. These individuals were, in terms of the currency of the time, millionaires or multimillionaires. They held stock in many companies and concurrently held directorships on the boards of several companies, showing up for board meetings, but not otherwise in the regular employ of the company. Moreover, large sums in directors' compensation were carved out of company profits, so they derived immense incomes from the companies.

Labor and farmers movements

Workers' pay, by comparison, was still extremely low. This was an age in which workers lived in cheap rental housing and wore coveralls. Class conflict was perceived as a genuine problem. This was the period in the Japanese prewar era in which workers and farmers movements were most active, as can be seen from figures 1.2 and 1.3.

The other day I happened to read Asano Tokiichiro's reminiscences on the Tsukiji Little Theater. Between 1929 and 1933, the repertoire of this playhouse almost entirely consisted of dramas of class struggle on the part of workers and poor farmers. Asano recalls that even when the scripts were slashed out of recognition by censors lines, gestures, and sound effects that hinted at struggle

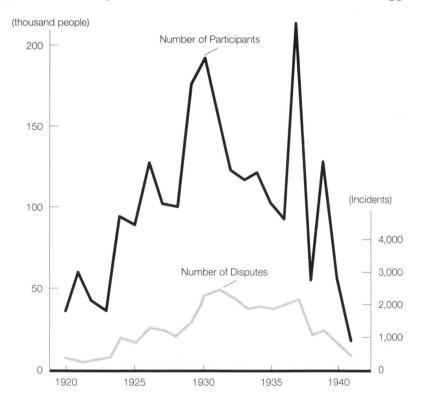

Fig. 1.2. Number of Labor Disputes and Number of Participants

Source: Nihon Rodo Undo Shiryo (Sources on the Japanese Labor Movement). The University of Tokyo Press. 1959. Vol 10.

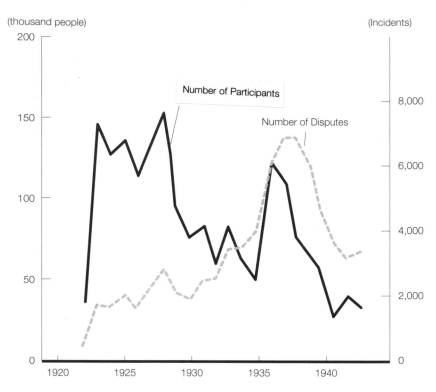

**Fig. 1.3. Number of Tenant Farmer Disputes and Number
of Participants**

Sources: Ministry of Agriculture and Forestry. *Kosaku Nenpo* (Annual Report on Sharecropping); *Nochi Nenpo* (Annual Report on Agricultural Land).

were sufficient to draw enthusiastic bursts of applause. One of the better-known works of proletarian theater of the time was a dramatization of Tokunaga Sunao's *Streets without Sun*. Drawing its material from a labor dispute at Kyodo Printing, *Streets without Sun* played to bursting houses that had to turn patrons away, including, it is reported, the author. The conflict between the fat boss, bedecked with gold watch chain, in his revolving chair and the oppressed workers came across as real to the playgoers. Today, when one reads the story, the characters—the militant female worker, the labor leader who appears to be a Communist Party member, the corpulent capitalist, the hypocritical bourgeois wife— remain stereotypical, yet vivid.

Out in the countryside, power was in the hands of the local landlords. Up until the years 1910 to 1919, landowners had exacted steep sharecropping fees from their tenants, but in many cases they had also served as leaders of their communities, playing public roles, taking the initiative in introducing new farm technologies, and in some instances providing private money for public facilities. Tobata Seiichi, a leading agricultural economist, in his important study of the development of Japanese agriculture, stresses the role of rural landlords as innovators for agricultural development. But by the 1920s, landlords were increasingly parasitical and did not take on these community roles. More and more were absentee landlords who lived in the cities and did nothing more than collect their sharecropping fees. The tenant farmers organized themselves, like industrial laborers, in farmers unions and clashed frequently and fiercely with the landlords. The class struggle flourished up until about the time of the Manchurian Incident in 1931, but withered away in the years between 1932 and 1935.

Zaibatsu and economic control

Another important economic fact was the zaibatsu that I briefly touched on earlier. Mitsui had been a major commercial concern since the latter part of the 1600s. Mitsubishi belonged to the Iwasaki family, originally country samurai from Tosa in Shikoku, who had built a vast fortune through their connections with the Meiji government. Sumitomo, like Mitsui, had been a merchant house in the Edo period and was primarily involved in copper production at its Besshi Copper Mine in Ehime Prefecture. Yasuda had come to the capital from Toyama Prefecture, on the Sea of Japan coast, begun a money changing operation, and eventually made a fortune as a lender. These four zaibatsu all had head office holding companies, the shareholders of which were restricted to family members. These concerns, especially Mitsui and Mitsubishi, had immense power to dominate.

Mitsui ruled the business world through three companies, the Mitsui Bank, Mitsui Trading, and Mitsui Mining. Mitsubishi profited from the four banking, mining, shipbuilding, and commercial operations that bore its name. The two zaibatsu also had a hand in a wide range of other activities, including insurance, trust banking, chemical industries, and paper manufacture.

Mitsui, in the form of Mitsui Bank and Mitsui Trading, had huge economic impact. The Mitsui Bank tended to the financial needs of many corporations and in return had a say in their operations. Mitsui Trading would hold the sales rights to those companies' products, or the right to supply their materials. The two together generated much business in this fashion. For this reason, the activities of the zaibatsu came in for a good deal of criticism. Lesser zaibatsu, such as Furukawa, Asano, Okura, Fujita, Shibusawa, and Kuhara, also had holding companies and expanded their activities from their core industries into new and diverse areas.

Spinning and yarn industries

One further comment is in order. The most important and powerful industry at the time was textiles. From the late 1800s through to the 1920s, Japan's biggest export item was raw silk. The silk manufacturing firms included such giants as Katakura and Gunze, but many were small businesses funded by local capital. Most of Japan's raw silk exports went to the United States, where they were used in women's stockings and other silk textiles.

Japan's second largest export was cotton textiles. During the late 1920s, it was cotton textiles rather than cotton thread that were being exported in large quantities, primarily to Asia and Africa. The most influential component of Japan's textile industry was cotton spinning. Based in the Kansai area, in and around Osaka and Kobe, were Kanebo, Toyobo, Dai Nippon Boseki, and Osaka Godobo. Based in Tokyo were Fuji Spinning and Nisshin Cotton Spinning. These major spinning companies had an organization called the Federation of Spinners, which had a powerful impact on industry.

One of these companies, Kanebo, had a famous president by the name of Muto Sanji. His strategy was to employ the best machinery and materials to make the best possible product and to treat the workers as well as possible. He took a conservative position on company financing, seeking to keep internal reserves high and to avoid borrowing or equity increases at all costs. For a long time, he maintained a dividend rate of 70 percent, even in times of recession. If one examines Kanebo's balance sheets from the period, one finds very few long- or short-term borrowings and little paid-in capital, the company's operations being financed for a long time by accumulated reserves.

Nisshin, another major spinning company, was long headed by an individual by the name of Miyajima Seijiro. Like Muto, he was known for his frugality. He long served as president of the Industrial Club of Japan, an organization that is located in a building constructed at the beginning of the 1920s in front of Tokyo Station. Miyajima lived well into the 1950s, and as long as he lived, he would not permit the club to have air conditioning on the grounds that it was an extravagance. No matter how hot the day, he always wore a suit and would sit with perfectly correct posture. The management style of the better companies of the time was one that held frugality and practicality in high regard, had a distaste for borrowed money, and tried to run the business without resorting to outside capital. It was old-fashioned, solid, and reliable, and it was typical of the spinning industry. I hope these brief vignettes will give you some idea of the atmosphere of the time.

Overall, the impact of the crash of 1920 and the subsequent recession was serious. The year was preceded by the World War I boom, in which almost every company enjoyed the benefits of prosperity. Companies aggressively bought up commodities and stocks. New companies were being formed and capital expansions planned. Then, in March 1920, the prices of stocks and commodities collapsed. Companies that had taken aggressive or speculative management positions (depending on one's view) were badly burnt. Many went under, and those that did not were gasping under the burden of their loans. The four big zaibatsu and the major spinning companies came through largely unscathed owing to their conservative management policies and so stayed ahead where other companies fell behind.

The late 1920s were a time of much economic debate, stimulated by the rise of the socialist movement following the Russian

Revolution and the rice riots of 1918. Capitalism came in for public criticism from a Marxist standpoint, and the debates critiquing capitalism attracted many young students. Commentator Takahashi Kamekichi, then in his 30s, often discussed what he perceived to be the impasse in capitalism, employing the phrase final-stage capitalism. Criticism of the social system gradually became more overt.

Agriculture and conventional industries

Bearing this climate in mind, let us look at the relationship between agriculture and traditional industries. At the end of the 1920s, half the population was farmers. The lives of these farmers were hard and miserable. During World War I, food shortages had boosted agricultural prices, and farms enjoyed a degree of prosperity. After the war, the farmers worked to boost their output, and after a few years of effort, farm products developed a surplus and prices fell. Something similar also happened after World War II. In the late 1920s, however, agricultural prices continued downward, and in conjunction with an overall deflationary trend, farm operations faced adversity.

Although farm incomes at the time were small, farms carried on average ¥800–¥900 in loans, and the interest rates were not low. It was hard enough to pay back the interest and principal on these loans. To compound matters, farm product prices were falling. Since farmers want to secure cash income, when prices fall they boost production and thus set off a trend in which prices spiral downward. During the food shortages after World War I, the government instituted plans to increase production of rice in the colonies of Korea and Taiwan. These projects finally began to reap success in the late 1920s, with the result that colonial rice began to compete with domestic rice, sending rice prices slumping further. Since rice output cannot be easily reduced, farm incomes dropped all the more. This economic climate sparked numerous disputes between tenant farmers and landlords. A dispute at Kizaki village in Niigata Prefecture broke all records for length.

What were the nonfarmers in the major cities and in the rural areas doing? The number of factories and company employees had of course increased, but many of those in nonfarming occupations were self-employed. If we go back and look at the figures for 1920 (fig. 1.1), the total number of people employed was 27,260,000. Of these, 3,900,000 were working in modern occupations, such as mining, factories, government offices, teaching, and merchant marine. Agriculture, forestry, and fisheries accounted for 15,110,000. If we deduct these people, along with those of unknown status from the total, we are left with 8,590,000 people. This population, which accounts for nearly one-third of the employed population, I refer to as those working in "conventional" industries. Some people have criticized my figures as too high. I will not attempt to defend them here, but they do seem fairly close to the mark, and so I will continue to use them. Although in nonagricultural occupations, these people were working outside the framework of modern industry and occupations. They outnumbered those in modern industry two to one.

What did these conventional industries consist of? In manufacturing there were 180,000 blacksmiths and tin platers; 70,000 people engaged in the making of buckets and barrels; 140,000 in furniture and cabinetmaking; 70,000 in tatami matting; 80,000 in sake, miso (fermented bean paste), and soy sauce; 60,000 in tailoring western-style clothes. Most of these were traditional occupations, but their numbers included tin plating and sewing of western clothes, imported industries that had become cottage industries. Some 3,470,000 people made their living in traditional industries in the secondary sector.

The population working in conventional industries in the tertiary sector totaled 5,130,000. Most of these were merchants, but there was a host of other occupations. In transportation, there were 300,000 rickshaw drivers, pullers of goods wagons, and drivers of bullock and horse carts and others associated with these occupations. Then there were the huge numbers of people in a wide variety of service industries, such as restaurants and hairdressing. These were found not only in the big cities but also in regional cities and rural villages. The conventional industries handled the production and distribution of the consumer goods and services of traditional Japanese life.

Occupations in modern industries included salaried workers in banks and corporate offices, workers in factories and mines, railroad workers, government officials, doctors, and school teachers. Altogether their number totaled about 3,900,000. In other words, Japan had become a capitalist society, with the big companies wielding immense power, but in terms of proportion of population, the impact of traditional society remained strong.

Urbanization

Nevertheless, changes were gradually taking place. Take urbanization, for example. When the Great Kanto Earthquake of September 1, 1923, destroyed Tokyo and Yokohama, the government of the time committed about ¥600 million in national budget funds to a five-year program of reconstruction. Regional development funds were also injected into the reconstruction effort. The scale of investment in reconstruction can be gauged by the fact that the total national budget at the time was in the region of ¥1.5 billion, and the gross national income something over ¥10 billion. Since individuals and companies also rebuilt homes and factories, post-quake reconstruction alone was sufficient to cause a spurt in investment in the urban areas.

Moreover, reconstruction provided an opportunity for modern urban development. Town planning was instituted. At the instigation of Goto Shinpei, mayor of Tokyo before the earthquake and later minister of Home Affairs in the Yamamoto Gonbei Cabinet, an urban development plan was drawn up in which two trunk roads were to be built on north–south and east–west axes. One was Showa Avenue, stretching north from Shinagawa Station through Shinbashi and Ueno to Senju. The other went west from Kameido, over the Ryogoku Bridge, passed in front of this building here in Jinbocho [where this lecture was presented] through Ichigaya to Shinjuku. A very similar project was undertaken in Yokohama.

Major cities that had not been damaged by the earthquake—Osaka, Kobe, Nagoya, Fukuoka, and Sapporo, for example—also invested sizable budgets in urban planning and began to build modern cities, constructing business centers and broad avenues suitable for motor vehicles. Urban transportation, water supply, and sewage systems were upgraded. At a time when if anything the central government's purse strings were being tightened, the proportion of spending by local, especially urban, governments rose sharply.

As the cities modernized, at least in terms of their external appearance, the impoverished rural dwellers flocked into the urban areas in search of a living. It has been said by some observers that in the old days people would return to the rural areas when times got hard and would come back to the cities when times improved. This picture, it appears, is far too simplistic. Having made the decision to leave the city, people could not simply go back to their villages if there was an economic setback. The reality was that in farm households that barely made ends meet, there was no place for an adult son or daughter who had returned unemployed. Once in the city, there was nothing for it but to make a living somehow. One could not afford to be choosy about jobs or demand extravagant wages.

When I was in elementary school, in the early 1930s, Tokyo was full of peddlers and open-air merchants. The streets that the streetcar traveled from Shinbashi to Kanda were lined with stalls, and the part near the downtown school that I attended bustled with vendors of candy and dumpling stew and paper-picture showmen, all aiming for children's few coins of pocket money. I have come to believe that these vendors represented the low end of the traditional industries and consisted of people who had come out from the countryside into Tokyo and were forced to make a living doing whatever they could.

Urbanization thus had its bright and dark sides. Just out of the city center there were slums in which dwelt housewives who took in piecework and day laborers who would not be able to eat at night if they did not go out and earn some money.

Heavy industries and rationalization
In the 1920s, a shift toward heavy industry and greater industrial productivity was progressing apace, although not in a fashion that was immediately obvious to the casual observer. On the surface,

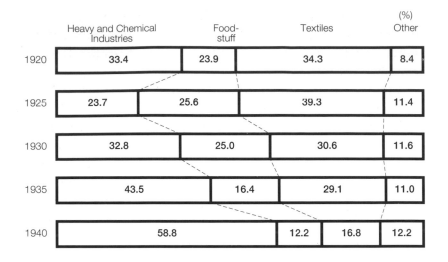

	Heavy and Chemical Industries	Food-stuff	Textiles	(%) Other
1920	33.4	23.9	34.3	8.4
1925	23.7	25.6	39.3	11.4
1930	32.8	25.0	30.6	11.6
1935	43.5	16.4	29.1	11.0
1940	58.8	12.2	16.8	12.2

Fig. 1.4. Growth of Heavy and Chemical Industries

Source: Calculated on the basis of data in Ministry of International Trade and Industry *Kogyo Tokei Gojunen Shi* (Fifty-year history of industrial statistics). International Trade and Industry Statistics Association, 1961.

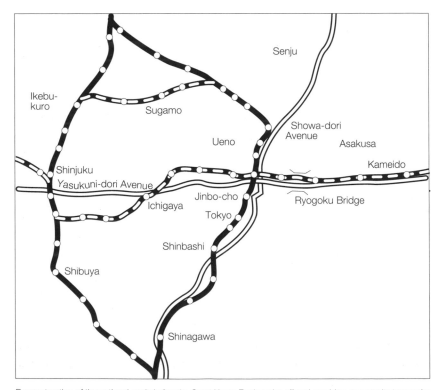

Reconstruction of the national capital after the Great Kanto Earthquake offered a golden opportunity to remake Tokyo into the business center of a newly capitalist country. The reconstruction land readjustments were implemented, and two new avenues crossing each other: 44-meter-wide Showa-dori Avenue and 36-meter-wide Yasukuni-dori Avenue were constructed.

the structure of Japanese industry did not appear to change a great deal, but it is worth noting that within the companies efforts to upgrade operations were becoming more sophisticated, laying the groundwork for the 1930s.

Up until World War I, Japan had imported many of its industrial goods from overseas. Steel, machinery, dyes, and chemicals were almost entirely import products. When these imports were cut off during the war, companies began to invest in the plant and equipment to produce them domestically. Many of these projects failed when the war ended before the plants could be completed and begin manufacturing anything, but a few projects survived and attempted to withstand competition from overseas products and to produce domestic alternatives. The resultant emergence of heavy industries is shown in figure 1.4.

The government, not unnaturally, provided support for these industries by raising tariffs and providing low-interest loans. However, the construction of heavy industry plants was a major undertaking. It was not easy, in the years immediately after World War I, for Japan to make something even as simple as an electric motor. The official history of Mitsubishi Electric recounts the following story. The company had started selling electric fans, but half of them were ultimately returned by customers, resulting in major losses for the company. The fans wouldn't work, or they would walk across the floor the complaints went. If something as simple as an electric fan was far beyond Japan's technological capabilities, how much more so the country's steel industry should have been. It went through a period of major difficulties.

The companies worked on their problems and, in the case of the electrical industry, strove to forge links with leading overseas companies. Toshiba embarked on a joint venture with General Electric, Mitsubishi with Westinghouse, and the newly created Fuji Electric with Siemens, handing over a portion of their stock in return for technology. The success of these joint ventures set the electrical machinery industry on the path to growth. Companies making machine tools and other industrial machinery and parts were too small to arrange joint ventures with overseas concerns; they apparently satisfied themselves with copying overseas products, or at least importing high-precision machine tools, in a frantic effort to raise their technology standards. Apart from the most sophisticated items, by the end of the 1920s Japan was able to build most ordinary machinery domestically.

I am not an expert in these matters, but take for example bicycles. The key to the domestic production of bicycles is whether one can domestically produce the ball bearings that govern the rotation of the bicycle wheels. Whether or not one can manufacture near-perfect steel balls determines whether or not the machine tool industry can be self-sustaining. If so, then the technology can be adapted to the manufacture of automobiles. Japan is reported to have become self-sufficient in ball bearings around about 1929, evidence of the gradual progress being made in the heavy industrial sector.

The 1920s were a time of productivity campaigns in the United States and Germany. This meant eliminating waste and raising workers' productivity. Many companies made efforts to streamline their operations in a time of recession out of fear that if they did not completely rationalize their operations they would not be able to stay alive in a competitive society.

Reticulation of electric power

One important accomplishment was the reticulation of electric power in the late 1920s. Electric light had entered Japan in the Meiji era. Between 1910 and 1919, hydroelectric power plants were operating in the mountain regions, and by the middle of that decade, high-voltage wires were carrying power long distances to major consumption centers in Tokyo, Yokohama, Osaka, and Kobe. High-voltage transmission technologies initiated rapid growth in electric power use in urban industries. Once primarily used for lighting, the use of electricity to drive motors grew dramatically as electricity charges fell.

Figure 1.5 shows the ratios of mechanization and electrification in factories. Mechanization refers to the use of motive power other than human labor and includes such things as steam engines and gas turbines. It can be seen that in 1914 small factories were almost entirely unmechanized; in other words, they depended pri-

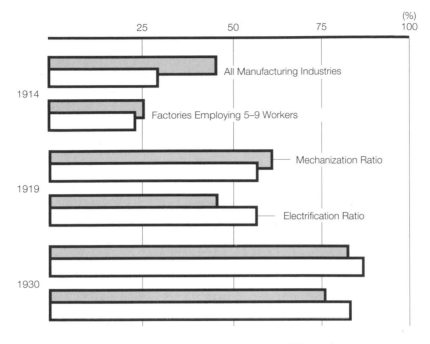

Fig. 1.5. Mechanization and Electrification of Factories

Source: Minami Ryoshin. *Doryoku Kakumei to Gijutsu Shinpo* (The Mechanization Revolution and Technological Progress). Toyo Keizai Shinpo Sha, 1976.

marily on human power. By 1930, however, three-fourths of the smallest factories had installed power-driven equipment.

The electrification ratio refers to the ratio of horsepower generated by electric motors to overall horsepower used. In 1914, the electrification ratio was very low, but in the period between 1919 and 1930, the ratio rose rapidly, with the smallest factories using electric motors for 84 percent of their power, signifying a raising of the technology standards in smaller companies. The efficiency of work that had once been conducted by hand was dramatically improved by the introduction of machinery.

In the textile weaving industry, for example, looms had been moved by the hands and feet of women workers. It was in this period that factories changed over to automatic looms, which only required the insertion of the thread. The introduction of such machinery varied from region to region, but by the end of the

1920s, many textile producing areas had mechanized, and those that had not went into decline.

The construction lumber industry, a typical conventional industry, introduced machine saws. Electrification transformed traditional industries, with the result that a growing number made the transition to modern small business.

Japanese labor relations and the dual structure

Major changes also took place in labor relations. In the textile industry, labor turnover was extremely high: its workforce chiefly consisted of young female workers, who, although untrained, would learn their jobs within six months, since the tasks were simple, but would leave after a few years. In the emergent heavy industries, however, skilled male workers were needed. In steel, for instance, skilled artisans could read the temperature of molten iron from its color and direct when it was to be poured into ingots. Such skilled laborers had to be treated well and retained by the company. Thus the percentage of workers in long-term employment rose sharply, as seen in figure 1.6. Companies began to take steps to keep their skilled workers within the company and to build a bulwark of sorts against the labor movement by providing a small increase in wages each year and by ensuring that younger workers were terminated first when job cuts had to be made. It was in this period, then, that the prototype of Japan's present-day wage structure, based on age and the number of years of service, became established.

In small businesses, there was a constant stream of workers coming and going. When looking to replace someone who had left, businesses would hire the new person at a lower wage if wages were generally going down. This would have the effect of pushing wages down further. Unlike the big companies, where the wages of long-standing employees did not go down much, small businesses employed young workers who were apt to change jobs. These workers' wages were deteriorating, so the wage gap between big corporations and small businesses began to spread. The dual structure of the economy—something I will talk about

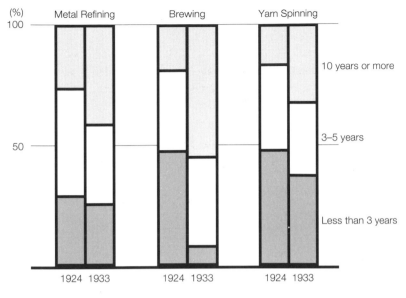

Fig. 1.6. Male Industrial Workers by Years of Employment

Source: Cabinet Statistics Bureau, *Rodo Tokei Jitchi Chosa* (On-location Survey of Labor Statistics).

when we get to the postwar period—had begun to emerge in this period.

I should also mention the political and social problems of the 1920s. After World War I, people around the world had had enough of war. The League of Nations was formed, and in 1928, the Kellogg-Briand Pact was signed in Paris. On the surface at least, the 1920s was a period in which a peaceful atmosphere prevailed. In 1921, President Harding of the United States called a conference in Washington, D.C., at which he proposed a bold program of naval disarmament. Japan, in line with its policy of cooperating with Great Britain and the United States and also because its fiscal situation did not permit the construction of warships, agreed to restrict its capital ships to 60 percent of that of those two countries. The army had to swallow two successive cuts in its divisions, returning large numbers of personnel to civilian life and attempting to use the freed-up funds to modernize its equipment. That Japan, which up until then had been expanding its armed forces, should agree to such disarmament is symbolic of the change that had taken place during that decade.

Disarmament and democracy

At the time, the labor movement was highly active, and many military personnel report how uncomfortable they felt wearing their uniforms in public. Navy officers would even report to work at the Navy Ministry in civilian suits and change into their uniforms at the office. Such was the pacifist atmosphere of the 1920s. However, a number of talented young officers, whose number included Nagata Tetsuzan and Tojo Hideki, had learned from the experience of World War I, especially that of Germany, that the war of the future would not just be fought on the battlefield, but would involve mobilizing the forces of the whole nation. If that was the case, they argued, then Japan should prepare for such mobilization. Industry and finance would have to be mobilized for war. If war came, there would be air raids, and ordinary citizens would suffer. Thus, the state should prepare for national mobilization in peacetime.

In 1918, therefore, the Armament Industry Mobilization Law was passed, and later, in 1927, an Office of Resources was established to study resources and prepare for mobilization of military goods. In an age of peace and democracy, there were advocates of national mobilization.

It was in 1925 that long-awaited general elections were realized, and males of 25 years and over were granted the vote with no income limits imposed. At the same time, the notorious Public Peace Maintenance Law was passed as a result of demands by the Privy Council and other conservative forces and fears of how the left wing movement in the Diet would act.

In other words, Japanese society in the late 1920s had two thrusts. At no time in Japan's modern history had liberal ideas and socialist ideas been so widely voiced and implemented in political and labor movements. At the same time, the right wing and forces of militarism were fiercely resisting, out of a growing sense of crisis, such developments and were mounting in strength. As in physics, the growing forces of the left were countered by increasing strength on the right. Social tensions steadily increased.

Impact of the Chinese revolution

The crucial issue that exacerbated those tensions was Chinese nationalism. From 1926 to 1928, the Kuomintang (Nationalist Party), based in Guangzhou (then known as Guangdong or Canton), together with the newly established Chinese Communist Party, was making a drive northward to strike down the northern warlords. Chinese nationalism, already high at the end of World War I, soared to new heights. This surge of nationalism collided with Japan's interests in China, especially its territorial leases in Guandong (Kwantung) Province and of the South Manchuria Railway, and upset the conservatives and the military.

Within Japan, recession, unemployment, and rural poverty created a dark atmosphere in which the left and right wings struggled for change. This unpleasant atmosphere became more and more part of the scene.

In 1922, Mussolini took power in Italy. Within Japan, interest in fascism seems to have been strong. Several versions of Mussolini's biography were published. Young politicians in the conservative parties became fascinated with fascism, and leading Kabuki actor Ichikawa Sadanji II is reported to have enjoyed great success in a play entitled *Mussolini*.

THE BANK PANIC

The early years of the Showa era, in other words, the late 1920s, were an interval of deflation around the world. In the period from the end of the nineteenth century until 1920, just after the end of World War I, prices had risen consistently. Now, in the period extending from 1920 to 1930, prices fell unremittingly, as can be seen from figure 1.7.

Why did prices fall? In every sense, there was an immense popular desire to return to the belle époque, directly prior to World War I. Around the world, politicians and businessmen shared this

Fig. 1.7. Wholesale Price Indices for Japan, Great Britain, and the United States (1929 = 100)

Source: Bank of Japan, *Meiji iko Honpo Shuyo Keizai Tokei* (Major Economic Statistics since the Meiji Period). 1966.

desire. From an economic perspective, this meant a return the gold standard.

Restoration of the gold standard

The gold standard works, at least in principle, as follows. The coinage used within the country is gold. Paper currency is convertible; if you take it into the central bank, it will convert it into gold coin. The central bank controls the money supply by means of credit policies that are in accord with its gold stocks (specie reserves). In addition, anyone can import or export gold freely.

If the import and export of gold are unregulated, the gold standard has the effect of stabilizing a country's exchange rate. In other words, if the exchange rate sags to some extent, then it is to one's advantage to export gold, even after taking into account the cost of shipping and insurance. If the exchange rate rises, gold is imported. Thus the exchange market has a stable center and rises and falls only within a very narrow band, so that countries' commodity prices begin to approach international prices. If domestic prices are higher than international prices, there is an import surplus and gold leaves the country, with the result that specie reserves become depleted. At this point the central bank tightens credit, and so eventually prices fall. If domestic prices are lower than international prices, an export surplus develops, gold flows into the country, the amount of currency in circulation increases, and prices rise. The advantage of the gold standard is that when the mechanism functions properly, countries' international payments balance, and their prices approach international prices. In principle, that was how it is supposed to work. The reality is a little more complex, since there is also importing and exporting of capital.

When World War I broke out, the protagonists—Great Britain, France, Germany, and the other countries of Europe—faced with the prospect of increased imports and dwindling gold reserves at a time when they were unable to export, banned the export of gold. Eventually the United States joined the war and also embargoed gold exports. Since Japan enjoyed huge export surpluses during World War I, it had no need to worry about an outflow of gold. However, Japan was the only participant that permitted gold exports, with the result that the exchange rate for Japanese yen rose. Since too high an exchange rate would hinder exports, Japan ultimately joined the gold embargo in 1917.

When the war was over, Japan did not immediately return to the gold standard. It is said by some that this was motivated by a desire to make an economic and commercial penetration in China, for which gold reserves might be needed. The United States, however, quickly returned to the gold standard at the old parity, which meant that the amount of gold that could be exchanged for one dollar was the same as before the war. The problem was that U.S. prices had doubled during the war, in other words, the amount of goods that could be bought for one dollar had halved, and the only way for this imbalance to be rectified was for prices to fall. In 1920 there was a major slump in which prices returned more or less to their prewar levels, and throughout the 1920s world prices followed the same downward trend.

After the 1920 crash, there was some discussion of what to do about the international currency system, but governments concluded that there was no option but to return to the gold standard. In 1924 and 1926 Germany and Great Britain, respectively, returned to the gold standard, and France and Italy followed suit shortly after. In France and Italy, however, inflation had been so great that the amount of gold equal to the value of the franc and lira had to be slashed: the rise in prices was recognized as a fact when these countries returned to the gold standard, and the gold embargo was lifted at new parity. Domestic prices in these two countries thus stabilized at higher levels than in prewar days, enabling them to avoid serious deflation. Great Britain and the other countries in the sterling bloc, however, lifted the embargo at prewar parity and were left struggling with deflation and recession.

In Japan, a return to the old parity seems to have been regarded as the right thing to do. Japan had been suffering a continuous deflationary trend, although the downward movement of Japanese prices was slower than that in the West, largely because the government supplied businesses with relief funds and boosted fiscal spending in an effort to buoy domestic demand in the face of recession. It is possible to take the view that the transition to heavy industry and the electrification of Japanese homes and industry made progress because of these measures, but it is not easy to judge the merits of the policies. It is clear that the lifting of the gold embargo was delayed as a result of such measures. It is also clear that the Japanese economy was in difficult straits.

Economic indicators for the period of World War I and its aftermath show that Japan enjoyed a huge export surplus during the war that lasted into 1919 (table 1.1). Yet, from 1920 on, and

Table 1.1 Trade and Specie Reserves in the 1920s and 1930s

	Exports	Imports	Difference	(million yen) Reserves at the End of Each Period
Total 1914–1919	12,065	9,190	2,875	2,045
Total 1920–1924	15,558	17,609	–2,051	1,413
Total 1925–1929	12,300	12,867	–567	1,343
Total 1930–1931	4,516	4,544	–28	557

Source: Okawa Kazushi et al. *Kokumin Shotoku* (National Income). In *Choki Keizai Tokei* (Long-term Economic Statistics). Toyo Keizai Inc., 1974.

throughout the 1920s, Japan suffered a chronic import surplus. Although the value of neither imports nor exports grew greatly, imports persistently outstripped exports. The import surplus occurred because Japan's domestic economy was not very large and because the country was still only weakly competitive in international markets. The upshot was that the reserves of specie and currency that Japan had acquired during the war peaked in 1920 and began to dwindle thereafter. To rebuild its foreign currency reserves, Japan would borrow a little from overseas, but its specie reserves continued to erode.

Faced with a weak economy and the slow growth of fiscal revenues and unable to boost imports at the beginning of the Showa era, the government was not in a position to aggressively expand spending. Nonetheless, the catastrophic earthquake in the Kanto region mandated spending for reconstruction. This was not an easy time for fiscal policy making.

In 1924, the year after the earthquake, Kato Takaaki, of the Kenseikai (Constitutional Association) became prime minister. After that the reins of government were alternated between the Kenseikai and the Seiyukai (Friends of Constitutional Government Party), the two major political parties of the time. The Seiyukai had consistently advocated an activist policy of spending for flood control and the construction of railroads, schools, harbors, roads and bridges to benefit rural areas and lever an expansion of their political power. The Kenseikai leaders, on the other hand, included among their number Wakatsuki Reijiro and Hamaguchi Osachi, former Ministry of Finance officials, who were more interested in balancing the domestic budget and the balance of international payments and were of the view that Japan should return to the gold standard. The activism of the Seiyukai contrasted with the fiscal restraint of the Kenseikai. When the Kenseikai came to power, there would be retrenchment. When the Seiyukai became the government, it would embark on new public investment projects, having no ideological objection to the government issuing bonds for such purposes. This competition between the two policies forms the backdrop for what follows.

Impact of the Great Kanto Earthquake

The Great Kanto Earthquake of September 1, 1923, killed over 91,000 people, mostly in Tokyo and Kanagawa prefectures. Another 13,000 were listed missing, and over 52,000 people were injured. Some 38,000 homes were burned to the ground. Altogether, some 69,000 houses were damaged, either wholly or partially collapsed or burned. The total number of people directly affected numbered in excess of 3.4 million. Reconstruction was plainly a matter of urgency.

The earthquake had the potential for major impact on the business community, over and above the direct damage it inflicted. Many of the companies, stores, and factories in the Tokyo and Yokohama areas had been burned down, with loss of equipment, merchandise, and materials. Many companies faced the danger of bankruptcy if they were unable to collect on the insurance that they had paid. To provide relief for the businesses in the earthquake region, the government acted with the following measures. First, a month-long moratorium was imposed on all collection of notes and other settlements in the affected area. Having bought some respite, the government took the following action. When the deadline for payment of a note issued or to be paid in the earthquake region came around, the note could be taken into a bank to be discounted. Then, when the bank presented the note to the Bank of Japan, the latter would rediscount the note, stamping it with the words Earthquake Bill. In the event that the Bank of Japan suffered a loss from these transactions, the government would guarantee it up to ¥100 million.

Let me explain briefly about what is involved in the discounting of notes. A note basically is a guarantee of payment within a certain time limit. If you take a note to the bank before it is due, the bank will convert it into cash, less the interest due on the remaining period, in a process known as discounting. Rediscounting occurs when the recipient bank presents the note to the Bank of Japan or some other institution, which converts it into cash, again less interest. Discounting and rediscounting are ordinarily straightforward matters when the payer's credit is good. But the earthquake shattered firms' creditworthiness, and there was the danger that a string of firms would be unable to make good on their notes when they came due. The government took the final responsibility, allowing the Bank of Japan to rediscount notes issued by people who were unable to repay on time, thus allowing the banks to issue credit without excessive concern. Many companies were saved by this procedure.

Shaky banks and corporations

I should note that many of the banks were on a shaky footing around about this time. At the end of 1924, there were about 1,700 ordinary banks in Japan, about 20 times as many as the 86 banks operating in 1984, 60 years later. Their number included big banks, with high credit ratings, but there were also many small institutions operating in a single village or region. Even in Tokyo, there were banks with a head office and no branches. Some small banks were well managed and financed, but not a few big banks were in financial difficulty, and the small banks were generally even worse off. Bank directors were at the time freely able to hold management positions in other industries, for example, manufacturing or commerce. It was by no means uncommon for local figures of power or renown to become bank directors and to use the bank's standing to gather up deposits which they would lend to their own businesses or those of others in their circle. Not infrequently, the bank would suffer when businesses went belly-up and the loans could not be recovered. Even though deposits and loans balanced on the books, the reality in many banks was that loans were impossible to recover, and so the banks themselves were in danger of failure.

This was also a time of recession, when companies were generally having difficulty making ends meet. In many cases it was hard enough for banks to recover their more ordinary loans. Companies, for their part, commonly went to great length to cook the books so that their assets and liabilities tables showed a profit even when the company was awash in red ink. Firms would fail to write off unrecoverable loans and accounts receivable and would appreciate the book value of securities or real estate in their possession, even when the reverse was the case, so that it would appear that the firm's assets had increased and that it was making a profit. There were many instances of this window dressing, complete with bogus dividends, for to report a loss would blemish the company's credit and cast doubt on the management skills of the directors.

The Bank of Taiwan and Suzuki Shoten

It was for reasons like this that Takada Shokai, then the second largest trading company after the Mitsui Trading Company, went bankrupt in 1925. But the most representative pattern was the relationship between Suzuki Shoten and the Bank of Taiwan, Taiwan's bank of issue. Based in Kobe, before World War I Suzuki Shoten had been a small trading company dealing in Taiwanese products. It had a famous manager by the name of Kaneko Naokichi, a dynamic individual who forged close relations with officials in Taiwan and expanded the business. Kaneko, foreseeing that when war broke out the price of everything would rise, speculated boldly in the marketplace and built up a colossal fortune. At one point, trading by Suzuki Shoten even outstripped that of the Mitsui Trading Company.

At the end of World War I, Suzuki Shoten was hammered by the slump owing to the huge inventories it had collected. The company regurgitated all its profits and started turning big losses. The company weathered repeated financial crises under Kaneko's leadership. Its biggest creditor was the Bank of Taiwan. It is unlikely that the Bank of Taiwan intended to lend as much as it ended up doing. However, if Suzuki Shoten had failed it would have been unable to recover its existing loans, so it continued to throw money at the company in the hopes of a reversal of its fortunes. The successive loans made to Suzuki Shoten climbed to gargantuan proportions.

The figures for April 1927—on the eve of the bank crash—contain a stunning fact. Loans to Suzuki Shoten stood at ¥396 million—almost ¥400 million. Since Japan's national budget at the time stood at ¥1.5 to ¥1.6 billion, Suzuki Shoten's loans ran to about one-quarter of the national budget. Its borrowings from the Bank of Taiwan came to a stunning ¥250 million. The Bank of Taiwan's total loans outstanding came to ¥720 million, of which ¥270 million was owed by either Suzuki Shoten or Suzuki Gomei, its holding company. By the time one adds Suzuki-affiliated manufacturing companies, the total owed by Suzuki was a staggering ¥350 million. In other words, about half the Bank of Taiwan's loans had been issued to Suzuki Shoten and its affiliates.

The existence of such rocky companies and institutions gave the Ministry of Finance food for thought. Just before the bank crash, the Banking Law was revised, the revisions going into effect in April 1927. The new provisions were tough. First, bank directors could no longer serve as officers of other companies. Second, banks had to have ¥1 million or more in capital. Third, banks with head offices in major cities had to be capitalized at ¥2 million or more. Fourth, institutions that did not meet these capital requirements had a five-year grace period in which to increase their capital or merge.

The Banking Law was rigorously applied, and by the end of 1932 banks numbers had fallen to 651 (including 538 private ordinary banks). At the end of 1937 the number had fallen to 461 (including 377 private banks), and at year-end 1942, the number was down to 226 (including 148 private banks). During World War II, a program of forced mergers was carried out, leaving one bank in each prefecture, so that by the end of 1945, there were 69 banks (including 61 private banks).

The beginnings of the bank panic

However, the Banking Law was too late to forestall the coming bank crash: serious problems had been lying hidden in all too many banks and businesses. When the crash occurred, Wakatsuki Reijiro of the Kenseikai was in power as prime minister, and Kataoka Naoharu was finance minister. It had been the view of the Kenseikai that Japan should follow the worldwide trend and revert to the gold standard, in which event it was predicted that gold would flow out of Japan, with the attendant danger of triggering recession. Worried that unsound banks might collapse under such circumstances and cause a scandal, Kataoka and the Ministry of Finance officials apparently thought that the best thing to do was to clean the industry up.

By March 1924, the value of earthquake notes rediscounted by the Bank of Japan had reached ¥430 million. Over the next 33 months, ¥230 million was repaid by the note issuers themselves, but as late as the end of 1926, ¥200 million was still outstanding. What had happened was that Suzuki Shoten, Kuhara Trading, Kokusai Kisen, and other companies had gone under, leaving the banks holding ¥200 million in earthquake notes. Of that sum, ¥100 million was linked to the Bank of Taiwan, with ¥72 million owed by Suzuki Shoten.

A legislative bill, the Earthquake Note Remedial Bill, was introduced in an attempt to clean up the mess. The bill proposed that the government would compensate the Bank of Japan for the ¥100 million loss, as originally promised, by issuing bonds. In other words, the government was prepared to acknowledge that ¥100 million was unrecoverable. The remaining ¥100 million would be covered for the time being by having the government lend ¥100 million in public bonds to the banks involved, notably the Bank of Taiwan. The issuers of the notes, starting with Suzuki Shoten, would be required to pay off this remaining ¥100 million in annual installments over a 10-year period. Since the bill proposed to rescue banking companies from their own bad management by paying out ¥100 million in government money, the bill was nothing if not problematic. The government reasoned that if it was to avoid a panic, it would have to spend at least that amount.

At the time, however, the opposition Seiyukai and the Kensei-kai were locked in fierce debate. When the bill was brought before the Diet, the Seiyukai challenged it, suggesting that it was a law to salvage politically well connected businesses, and demanded the release of the names of the banks holding earthquake notes and their issuers. Fearing a scandal, the government tried to conceal the names, but there were inevitable leaks. Questionable banks were swamped by depositors trying to withdraw their savings. Unable to pay out, some closed their doors. Runs on banks and bank closings had happened several times in the 1920s, but this was the biggest financial panic of all.

On March 14, 1927, the Watanabe Bank in Tokyo reported to the vice minister of finance that it was unable to make payments on deposits. Finance Minister Kataoka, having been handed a memo to that effect, referred to it in the Diet. The following day, the Watanabe Bank had found the money to continue business and attempted to open, but the newspapers had already printed Kataoka's remark. Reasoning that there was no point in continuing, the bank closed its doors. This was Act I of the bank panic, which was allegedly triggered by Kataoka's ill-advised remark. Whether it really was ill-advised is debatable, but nonetheless six banks went under on this occasion.

Cleaning up

The relationship between Suzuki Shoten and the Bank of Taiwan now became public knowledge. The trading company's debt could be written off, but the Bank of Taiwan, as the island's bank of issue, had to be salvaged. The Bank of Japan was supposed to fund a rescue, but the Bank of Japan wanted the government guarantee against losses written into law. Since the Diet was out of session, the government sought the approval of the Privy Council to obtain an emergency imperial order. The Privy Council refused to sanction an order on the grounds that this was not an emergency under the terms of the Constitution and that the correct procedure was to recall the Diet and pass a law. Wakatsuki and his cabinet resigned: the opposition Seiyukai had been plotting with powerful members of the Privy Council and had brought down the cabinet.

So Suzuki Shoten closed its doors, and there was a run on the Bank of Taiwan and a number of other banks. In the midst of the panic, Tanaka Giichi of the Seiyukai took office as prime minister. Tanaka had Takahashi Korekiyo, a veteran of public finance, become minister of finance for a spell and deal with the banking crisis.

For two days, banks voluntarily declared a holiday, long enough for the government to promulgate an imperial order prohibiting banks from paying out on large deposits. Having gained some breathing space, the Bank of Japan ran its presses nonstop to print currency to lend to the banks. The banks piled up the banknotes in bundles in full view on their countertops in an attempt to forestall a run, but the atmosphere of panic had already subsided. So rushed was the banknote issue, that the new ¥200 banknotes were printed only on one side.

One big banking institution that went under on this occasion was the Jugo Bank. A major institution founded in 1878 by a group of former daimyo (feudal lords) and court aristocrats and with ¥4.975 million in capital, the bank had served the Imperial Household Department. The president of the Jugo Bank was Matsukata Iwao, eldest son of Matsukata Masayoshi, elder statesman and former prime minister. The Kawasaki Shipyard in Kobe, headed by his second son, Matsukata Kojiro, was on the brink of bankruptcy. Another notable failure was the Omi Bank, established by merchants from the Omi region (now Shiga Prefecture) who lived in Osaka. With close connections to textile wholesalers, this was a major institution with ¥938,000 in capital. Altogether, 44 banks went under, taking with them ¥830 million in deposits. Since bank deposits nationwide totaled just over ¥9.1 billion, this meant that nearly 10 percent of all bank deposits were unrecoverable. After these banks went into receivership they were merged as the Showa Bank, which later merged with the Mitsui Bank.

There were many individual tragedies. Inaba Hidezo, an economic commentator, was a high school student in Kyoto at the time. He relates how three waitresses of his acquaintance who worked in traditional restaurants in the elegant Gion quarters lost all their savings and hanged themselves in despair, an event that inspired him to take up the study of economics.

THE SHOWA SLUMP

Prime Minister Tanaka Giichi and his cabinet had their hands full dealing with the cleanup after the bank crash. For the business community, the new government represented a fleeting glimmer of hope. The Seiyukai, which had traditionally taken an expansionist line on public investments, increased fiscal spending and delayed the return to the gold standard.

But relations with China were heading downhill. In June 1928, Komoto Daisaku, a colonel in the Japanese army in Guandong (Kwantung), blew up a train carrying Zhang Tsolin, the warlord who dominated Manchuria and Inner Mongolia. Zhang's death triggered new tensions with China. Komoto had intended to trigger a Chinese revolt that would provide a pretext for the Guandong Army to seize control of Manchuria and Inner Mongolia. That plan, however, failed. The plot, hatched by middle-ranked army staff officers, was a precursor to the later Manchurian Incident. Prime Minister Tanaka memorialized the emperor, asking to have Komoto and his coconspirators formally court martialed, but army opposition forced the government to settle for administrative penalties and suspension from duty. Having failed to win the confidence of the emperor, Tanaka and his cabinet resigned.

Thus, in July 1929 Hamaguchi Osachi of the opposition Minseito (Constitutional Democratic Party)—the Kenseikai having undergone a name change in the meantime—was appointed prime minister. In January of that year, the Minseito had announced a platform that included improving relations with China, success of the disarmament conference to be held in London the following year, economic retrenchment at home, and implementation of the long-pending return to the gold standard. The Hamaguchi cabinet thus brought these commitments into office.

Inoue Junnosuke was appointed minister of finance. Inoue carried with him a great deal of clout. He had been in the Bank of Japan, and for a period after 1919 had served as its governor. During the bank crash, he had been invited by Takahashi Korekiyo to serve in that capacity once again, for a one-year term. He had also been minister of finance in the cabinet of Prime Minister Yamamoto Gonbei after the great earthquake.

Up until this point, however, Inoue had had little taste for radical policy change and had preferred not to make waves in the business community. As governor of the Bank of Japan, he had attempted to assist companies and banks that were on the verge of going under, and in the period of the Tanaka cabinet he had been the advocate of circumspection whenever the issue of lifting the gold embargo came up. It was generally unexpected that this individual should become minister of finance in a Minseito cabinet and lift the gold embargo.

Yet Inoue may have had ambitions of his own. He may have wanted to succeed as a politician in his own right and to undertake this immense task himself. He may have reasoned that if the lifting of the gold embargo had to be carried out sometime, it had best be done by his own experienced hand. At any rate, the Minseito cabinet lifted the gold embargo under Inoue's supervision.

The operation demanded preparation. Since gold exports were banned, the exchange rate was determined by the supply and demand of foreign currency in the market under a floating-rate system not unlike that used today. The exchange rate was low, since Japan had had import surpluses for many years and was borrowing increasingly to cover its trade deficit. Back in the days of the gold standard, the rate was ¥100 = $49.85 (in other words, very roughly ¥1 = $0.50, or $1.00 = ¥2). After the great earthquake, the exchange rate had dropped to ¥100 = $38 for a time, but shortly before the embargo was lifted was back in the region of ¥100 = $44–$46. Thus, the yen was worth about 10 percent less than in the days of the gold standard. To lift the gold embargo at the old parity meant returning to a rate of $1.00 = ¥2. In present-day terms, this would mean an upward revaluation of the yen.

If the yen was revalued, it would become more difficult to export goods. Where $1.00 enabled one to buy ¥2.2 worth of goods, it would now be possible to buy only ¥2.0 worth. Japanese goods would become more expensive overseas, but conversely, from Japan's perspective, foreign goods would become cheaper, so imports would increase. The balance of international payments deficit would deteriorate, and gold would flow out of the country. This is all in conformity with economic theory.

To avoid these problems, domestic prices had to be ratcheted down. If the exchange rate was raised, as long as domestic prices were lowered by an even greater margin, exports would grow, imports would be restrained, and the gold standard could be maintained. To reduce prices, however, the domestic economy had to undergo drastic retrenchment. Without that preparatory step, there could be no return to the gold standard.

Retrenchment and the global depression

Inoue's gambit was first of all not to implement the budget for 1929 that had already been passed, but to have the new cabinet draw up a budget that would radically cut government spending. One result of these cuts was that all work on the present Diet building, then under construction, was halted.

His second step was to reduce the salaries of government officials. This was met with ferocious resistance from Kishi Nobusuke, then a young official in the Ministry of Commerce and Industry who would become prime minister in 1957, and others in the bureaucracy and had to be abandoned. One is struck by how little times have changed.

Inoue then moved to rein in credit, instructing the Bank of Japan to nudge interest rates upward so that it was less easy for funds to circulate in the marketplace. Finally, he embarked on a speech-making tour of the country, asserting that the economy lacked solid fundamentals and calling on the public to save, to cut consumption, and to use domestic products to rebuild the economy. So effective a speaker was Inoue that it is reported that one old woman in an audience threw him coins of votive offering as if he were a temple deity.

Thus, Inoue set about the task of readying the country for a return to the gold standard. His policy of retrenchment meant, quite bluntly, throwing the country into recession. Public spending was cut. Interest rates were raised. The public was called on to economize and save. The policy was designed to reduce domestic demand—to ensure that goods no longer sold.

At the same time, Inoue established lines of credit in New York and London to enable the government to borrow ¥100 million in funds if needed. Then he instructed the Yokohama Specie Bank (the forerunner of the present Bank of Tokyo, it specialized in exchange transactions) to buy up pound-denominated notes in London, thereby boosting specie reserves by about ¥300 million.

After all this preparation, in November 1929 he made the decision to lift the Ministry of Finance order banning gold exports. The embargo was lifted, as scheduled, on January 11, 1930, and Japan returned to the gold standard. However, just prior to this move, in October 1929, the financial panic had begun in America. Up to that point, America had enjoyed a stock market boom, so that everyone had their money in stocks. Little money was available for lending, and eventually there was not enough money to go round, with the result that the stock market crashed. This marked the beginning of the great global depression.

At this juncture the main gold standard country was no longer the United Kingdom, but the United States. The countries of Europe, whose economies had still not completely recovered from World War I, were operating on funds borrowed from the United States. While the United States stock market was booming, American funds were taken out of Europe, leaving the European countries short. Then came the slump. Because economies were declining everywhere at the same time, trade plummeted, bringing prices in tow.

Japan was already imposing policies of domestic retrenchment. Now the world economic climate was deteriorating, so that exports were no longer possible. It was clear that the economy could only go from bad to worse. Muto Sanji, then president of Kanebo, blasted the lifting of the gold embargo at a time when the world was thrust into depression. In a phrase that has since become famous, Muto decried Inoue's policy as being like "opening a window in the middle of a typhoon."

Lifting of the gold embargo at old parity

Nonetheless, academic economists and bank officials at the time generally favored the gold standard and strongly supported Finance Minister Inoue's position. Industries such as steel, machinery, chemicals, and paper pulp, which were not yet internationally competitive, were no doubt opposed, but they made no public statement for fear of getting on the wrong side of the government. The only major opponents of lifting the embargo were Muto and four journalists, Ishibashi Tanzan of the *Toyo Keizai Shimpo*, freelance writer Takahashi Kamekichi, Obama Toshie of the *Nihon Keizai Shinbun* (then known as the *Chugai Shogyo*), and Yamazaki Yasuzumi of the *Jiji Shimpo*. Muto had originally been an advocate of returning to the gold standard at the old parity, but he had been persuaded by Ishibashi to change his views. These individuals argued that it would be better to devalue the yen's gold parity to match current exchange rates and to reduce the amount of gold in a yen coin by 10 or 15 percent before lifting the embargo, thus avoiding any serious impact on the domestic economy. Lifting the embargo at old parity, they said, would throw the Japanese economy even deeper into difficulty.

Why did the government and Inoue insist on returning to the old parity? I believe that it had to do with the government's international prestige. Japan was one of the three great powers. It may have been that they felt it would be a national disgrace if Japan were to devalue the yen without a special reason for doing so.

Japanese prices, at their highest, had reached double their prewar level but had come down significantly and were now at a level that was slightly higher than before World War I. The conventional wisdom was that the difference was not enough to warrant a new parity. Those who advocated a new parity had learned from the bitter experience of the United Kingdom, discussed by Keynes in his essays, for example, "The Economic Consequences of Mr. Churchill." The United Kingdom had lifted the gold embargo under similar circumstances, setting off a recession in 1925–26 and major industrial strikes. Although calm consideration would have led to the conclusion that a new parity was the better course, the majority of commentators favored returning to the old parity.

There was another factor as well: numerous companies were only weakly competitive internationally. Many in banking circles favored an overhaul of business in which the less-competitive companies would be culled out, leaving the strong companies to rebuild Japanese exports.

Thus it was that the gold embargo was fated to be lifted at the old parity at a time of global economic panic. First there was the direct impact of lifting the embargo. Since it was known that the embargo would be lifted, speculators had converted their dollars to yen, anticipating that the yen would rise in value. When the embargo was lifted and the yen returned to its old official rate (¥100 = $49.85), they reconverted their yen into dollars for a profit. These transactions were an everyday kind of speculation and did not pose a moral issue. However, Japan did not have all that much specie, and if that were all to flow overseas, there was cause for concern down the line. Officials in the Bank of Japan and the Ministry of Finance were privately nervous about the outcome of the policy.

The crisis in agriculture

The moment the gold embargo was lifted, the impact of the global economic crash began to make itself felt. If you look at figure 1.8, you will see that prices, especially the prices of agricultural products, had fallen 15 percent between 1926 and 1929. Then they plunged another 30 percent. Within Japan there was recession. Prices of rice and other farm products slid steadily downward. At the same time, the price of raw silk fell owing to the American depression; the New York market crash being instantly reflected in lower cocoon prices in Japan. Economic setbacks at home and abroad assailed farming communities, throwing them into recession.

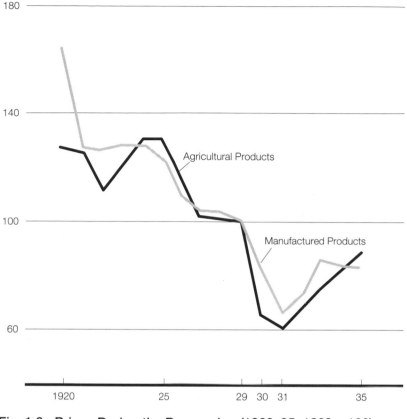

Fig. 1.8. Prices During the Depression (1920–35, 1929 = 100)

Source: Okawa Kazushi et al. *Bukka* (Prices). In *Choki Keizai Tokei* (Long-term Economic Statistics). Toyo Keizai Inc., 1976.

Figure 1.9 shows annual average household incomes. These were low enough as it was in 1929, at ¥1,326, but in 1931 had plummeted to ¥650, less than half their earlier level. In the rural villages, where the distress was especially severe, prices of agricultural products had been falling since the mid-1920s. Farmers want a steady cash income. If farm product prices fall, their sales, and hence their incomes, fall in proportion. What follows may seem like a contradiction, but when prices fell farmers were apt to increase their output in order to maintain their income. This was especially true of silk cocoons, which fell into a vicious spiral: the

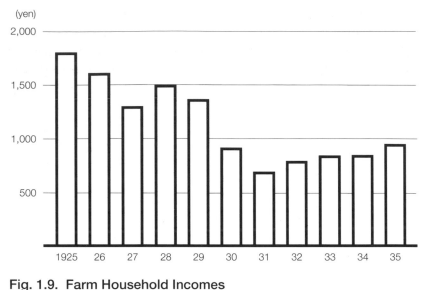

Fig. 1.9. Farm Household Incomes

Source: Ministry of Agriculture and Forestry, *Noka Keizai Chosa* (Farm Household Economic Survey).

more the price fell, the more would be produced, with the production surplus bringing a further drop in prices.

   With farmers' incomes falling like, farming ceased to be economically viable. Farmers became unable to pay their taxes or their light bills, let alone repay their loans. In Nagano Prefecture, farmers were living in darkness, their power supplies having been cut off because they could not pay their bills. Finance in farm communities was often supplied by mutual aid clubs, but since people could no longer pay their dues, the clubs would collapse. Lack of tax income meant that villages became unable to pay their elementary school teachers, whose wages would often arrive months late. It was not uncommon for the village mayor to call a school teacher into his office, inform the teacher that the village would borrow money to pay his salary from now on, and try to persuade the teacher to treat the unpaid portion as a donation to the village. Many farmers sold their daughters, an action that must be understood in the context of the dire poverty in the rural communities.

Trouble in manufacturing

It will be apparent that the recession was one in which prices fell without a corresponding drop in output. This was also true of manufacturing industries, which also suffered severe price drops. In the Dutch East Indies (now Indonesia), a surge of Japanese cotton products shut out British and Dutch products. In the end, the Japanese companies had won the price-cutting war, but it was not as if by doing so they made a profit or even improved their financial standing. Companies needed cash to keep operating, so they began exporting even if they couldn't break even.

Industries were being ravaged by the recession across the board. Kanebo, reputed to be the top company in Japan, was forced to cut wages, an action that triggered a major labor dispute. Other companies did likewise. The spinning industry had been regarded as a collection of Japan's soundest companies. Now, more and more spinners were reporting losses, and the industry was scrambling to raise its productivity and eliminate waste. Companies were seriously looking for ways to make the spinning machinery revolve a little faster so that they could reduce costs and boost production. One technique that was adopted was to raise the humidity significantly so that the thread would break less often. Sakurada Takeshi, onetime president of Nisshinbo, has told me that at no time was the yarn spinning business more difficult.

Since the industries that were strong were in such straits, the less-competitive heavy and chemical industries were even worse off, reporting losses across the board. Even a major company like Nippon Kokan conducted wave after wave of dismissals in an effort to minimize its personnel costs. I am told that because of successive losses, its directors went without remuneration.

Profits in the chemicals industry were slender. To illustrate how hard times were, the president of Nippon Soda, Nakano Tomonori, recounts how he picked up a newspaper extra in a train and learned that the government had abandoned the gold standard and banned gold exports. He recalls that he would have shouted *banzai* and jumped for joy if there had not been others present.

Characteristics of the Showa depression

Recession and efforts to trim operations continued hand in hand. Figure 1.10 compares gross national expenditures (GNE)—equivalent to the gross national product (GNP) in nominal and real values. Nominal GNE declined a whopping 18 percent, from ¥16.3 billion in 1929 to ¥13.3 billion in 1931. Real GNE, on the other hand, inched up from ¥13.9 billion to ¥14.2 billion in the same period (at 1934–36 prices). It is enough to make one wonder where the depression was. However, the price index (GNE deflator) used to compute real GNE dropped 20 percent during these two years. As I noted earlier, the main feature of this worldwide depression was that although the level of production of goods and services did not change, prices dropped. The reverse case, where production fell without any visible change in prices, can be found

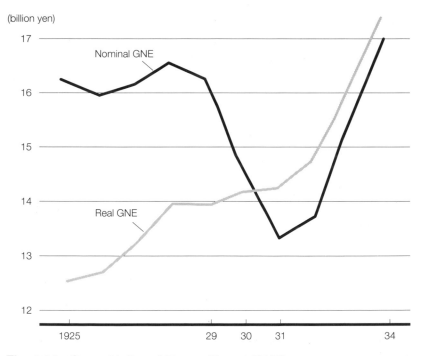

Fig. 1.10. Gross National Expenditures (GNE)

Source: Okawa Kazushi et al. *Kokumin Shotoku* (National Income). In *Choki Keizai Tokei* (Long-term Economic Statistics). Toyo Keizai Inc., 1974.

in the recession following the oil crisis of 1974–75. This I will talk about in a later lecture.

Industrial policy

The government did of course attempt to do something to assist industry. One of the things it did was to establish an Emergency Industry Rationalization Bureau in the Ministry of Commerce and Industry, the forerunner of the Ministry of International Trade and Industry. The bureau made all kinds of efforts to streamline industry, one of its jobs being to standardize the specifications for manufactured products, a precursor of the present Japan Industrial Standards.

In 1931 the Major Industries Control Law was passed, in a sense the first of the laws imposing economic controls in the period leading up to World War II. Article 1 of this law provided that when more than half the members of an industry formed a cartel, it had to be registered with the minister having jurisdiction over the industry. Article 2 allowed the minister to order businesses that were not members of the cartel to conform with cartel decisions if two-thirds of the members of the cartel so requested and if the minister deemed it necessary to protect reasonable profits in the industry and to ensure the sound development of the national economy.

This is what is known as a forced cartel. A cartel is an organization of companies acting in concert to determine price levels or to restrict production or machinery operating rates. Since membership is, in principle, voluntary, companies that do not find the cartel agreement in their interests are free to not join the cartel, to ignore the agreement, or to opt out of the cartel. For this reason, cartels have historically been said to be weak. The new law, however, mandated conformity with cartels and made their agreements legally enforceable: the government protected cartel activities to prevent companies from dragging each other under in the midst of a major depression.

There was also a provision in the form of Article 3 that permitted the government to order revisions in cartel agreements if in the event of an economic recovery it was found that the cartel was no longer in the interests of the national economy, a provision put in out of a concern for social equity. However, the government's overriding goal in expeditiously passing this law was to sustain industries that were in trouble by means of the forced cartels under Article 2.

Social turmoil

As the depression deepened, the rural villages saw a rise in disputes between sharecroppers and landlords and in left-wing activities. Right-wing activities calling for government relief before the farm communities were destroyed also gained momentum. Both left wing and right wing were active in rural areas at the same time.

Meanwhile, Japan signed the Treaty of London, which reduced the number of auxiliary warships, despite opposition from the Navy General Staff. This sparked allegations that the signing was an encroachment on the supreme command. Prime Minister Hamaguchi Osachi, who bore the full brunt of this onslaught, was attacked by right-wingers and shot. Seriously injured, he resigned the post, ceding it to Wakatsuki Reijiro, and died shortly thereafter. In February 1931, a plot was conceived by elements within the army to hold a military coup d'etat that would seat Minister of the Army Ugaki Kazushige in power in order to resolve Japan's problems in northern China. The plot failed, because Ugaki would not endorse it. Known as the March Incident, the plot unnerved those in politics.

The political and social situation was becoming increasingly unstable. The cities were full of people who were having difficulty making ends meet. Labor disputes were intensifying, and the right wing was getting restless.

The depression deepened around the world. The United States and Germany bottomed out much later than Japan, in 1932–33 and 1934, respectively. World trade began to shrink dramatically. Japanese exports slumped. Figure 1.11 gives nominal figures for the export and import of goods and services. Japan's exports plunged from ¥3.3 billion in 1929 to ¥2 billion in 1931. Wages dropped. Corporate profits plummeted. It was as if the economy had entered a cul-de-sac of recession, with no way out.

(billion yen)

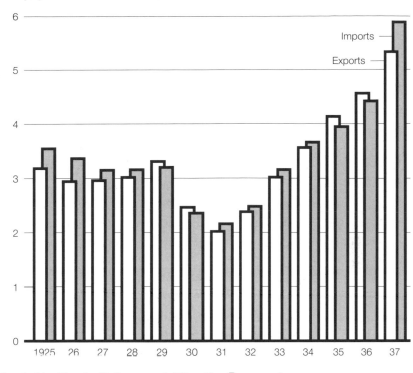

Fig. 1.11. Trade Before and After the Depression

Source: Okawa Kazushi et al. *Kokumin Shotoku* (National Income). In *Choki Keizai Tokei* (Long-term Economic Statistics). Toyo Keizai Inc., 1974.

Manchurian incident and anti-yen speculation

In September 1931 came two incidents that changed the path of history. On September 18, elements of the Japanese Guandong Army blew up the South Manchuria Railway at Liutiaohu, a little south of Mukden, present-day Shenyang. This act of sabotage was blamed on Chinese forces, and the Guandong Army occupied the walled city of Mukden and expanded its front of operations in what was the beginning of the Manchurian Incident. The government decided that it would not let matters develop any further, but the Guandong Army refused to obey central government orders, with the result that armed conflict spread throughout Manchuria.

As if things were not bad enough, on September 21 Great Britain went off the gold standard. To cut a long story short, Britain had lent gold to Germany, but in the summer of that year, the financial crisis in Austria and Germany had gotten out of hand, and British funds in Germany had been frozen. Observing this, French and Swiss investors started pulling out of Britain. The nation that fathered the gold standard now found itself stuck with unpleasant options and abandoned the gold standard. The sterling bloc followed suit.

Speculators anticipated that Japan would do so too in the near future. If Japan embargoed gold exports, the yen would lose value. If they sold yen for dollars now, when Japan went off the gold standard they stood to make a substantial amount of money by reconverting those dollars into yen. Anti-yen speculation became rife.

Over ¥700 million was converted into dollars, a huge sum for the time. The government denounced the perfidy of profit-taking at the expense of the nation's economic security. We now know that about half of this ¥700 million in transactions was conducted by foreign banks, who were conducting perfectly legal business. But the biggest target for the attacks was the Mitsui zaibatsu. True, the Mitsui zaibatsu had bought nearly ¥100 million worth of dollars at once. The Mitsui Bank, lacking any major investments in depression-wracked Japan, was taking funds to Great Britain, where interest rates were higher. In reality it was first buying dollars then converting those into sterling, which it was then investing in short-term Exchequer bonds.

Mitsui defended itself, claiming that it bought dollars because it had no choice. Because Great Britain went off the gold standard, Mitsui funds in that country were frozen, so it had to pay for its dollars. This did not become known until later. In the meantime Mitsui was denounced as a traitor for having bought dollars at the nation's expense. But Mitsui was only a scapegoat. The power of the Mitsui zaibatsu was so great that it had brought the resentment of the public, which now surfaced in this fashion. This incident spurred the zaibatsu to invest effort in social programs and other activities that were seen as socially constructive.

There was a rush to buy dollars. It was not just foreign banks that were involved. In 1943, the autobiography of a former Mitsui businessman Maeyama Hisakichi was published, in which he wrote openly of making a business of buying dollar-denominated Japanese bonds. I remember admiring his courage at publishing such an account in the middle of the Pacific War. But I digress.

Inoue Junnosuke, as minister of finance, instructed the Yokohama Specie Bank to keep up its sales of dollars to anyone that wanted to buy them, but at the same time he worked to dry up funds for dollar purchases by raising the interest rate. No matter what the reason, raising interest rates during a recession makes the recession worse.

In what later became known as the October Incident, Hashimoto Kingoro and other mid-ranked army officers plotted to overthrow the government, which still refused to permit an expansion of military activities in Manchuria. The officers attempted to mobilize troops to assassinate government officials and install a military regime but were thwarted when the plot was uncovered. The army covered up the incident, but word leaked out, raising the tension of domestic politics.

At this point, Prime Minister Wakatsuki wavered. Initially he appears to have agreed with the proposal of Adachi Kenzo, minister of Home Affairs, that the political situation could not be resolved by one party acting alone and that a coalition cabinet should be formed with the Seiyukai to resolve the political crisis. Inoue and Foreign Minister Shidehara Kijuro, however, adamantly opposed a coalition, claiming that it would not solve the country's problems and that the government should stay the course with its present policies. Wakatsuki eventually came round to this view. Adachi did not attend the cabinet meeting to show his uncooperative position but did not submit his resignation. Wakatsuki's cabinet, his second, fell apart and resigned en masse on December 10, 1931. It is rumored that Adachi's political campaigns were funded by speculation in dollars, but the facts of the matter are not known.

The Minseito cabinet that had lifted the gold embargo had now collapsed. Following normal constitutional procedures, the

Seiyukai formed a cabinet headed by Inukai Tsuyoshi, who immediately appointed in the capacity of minister of finance Takahashi
Korekiyo, an experienced politician who had already served once
as prime minister and who enjoyed the respect and trust of the
public. Takahashi promptly banned gold exports and terminated
the domestic convertibility of paper currency into gold. So the gold
standard, established in 1897, finally came to an end in 1931.
From this point on, Japan's currency would operate in a system
based not on gold, but on central bank management of the money
supply.

Lecture 2

GUNS AND BUTTER
(1932–1935)

The Central Ginza district, circa 1932.

1932	February–March	The Ketsumeidan Incident. Inoue Junnosuke (former minister of finance) and Dan Takuma are assassinated.
	March	Manchukuo is established, with Pu-Yi as chief executive (to become emperor in 1934).
	May	Prime Minister Inukai Tsuyoshi is assassinated in the May 15 Incident. The cabinet resigns, and Saito Makoto is appointed prime minister.
	August	A special session of the Diet approves a large budget containing an emergency rural relief program. During the year, the economy rapidly recovers as falling exchange rates push up exports and as fiscal stimulation measures take hold.
1933		Development of heavy industries becomes marked.
	May	Oji Paper Manufacturing merges with Karafuto Industries and Fuji Paper Manufacturing.
1934	January	Yawata Iron and Steel Works and five other iron and steel companies merge to form Nippon Seitetsu (Nippon Steel Co.).
	April	Okada Keisuke becomes prime minister.
1936	February	Former prime minister Saito and Minister of Finance Takahashi are assassinated in the February 26 Incident.
	March	Hirota Koki is appointed prime minister.
	November	Finance Minister Baba Eiichi, acceding to military demands, compiles a huge budget.
1937	January	Controls on fund transmissions and currency exchange are imposed after massive import surpluses appear at the end of 1936. The Hirota cabinet resigns, and Hayashi Senjuro becomes prime minister.
	June	Prince Konoe Fumimaro becomes prime minister and appoints his first cabinet. The army draws up the Five-Year Plan for Key Industries. Yoshino Shinji and Kaya Okinori publish their *Three Principles*.

Lecture 2

GUNS AND BUTTER
(1932–1937)

Today's lecture has been given its slightly odd title because I believe that the mid-1930s harbored two sets of possibilities for Japan. The period has a gloomy image as being the age of militarism, when Japan rearmed and the army became politically powerful. Yet it was also an age in which the economy recovered steadily under the fiscal policies of Takahashi Korekiyo and in which, as I shall relate, it appears that numerous industries advanced, national living standards improved somewhat, and the groundwork was laid for eventual postwar economic development. It was a period in which both guns and butter could coexist. In this lecture, I will consider why this state of affairs should have yielded to a wartime economy.

In September 1931, when the Manchurian Incident occurred, Japan became the object of much international criticism. Yet many Japanese undeniably hoped, for a brief period, that the Manchurian Incident would spark a train of events that would sweep away the depression. That it was not received as bad news by the Japanese public is an indication of how bleak the economy and society seemed up to that point and of how many people were seeking a way out of their hardships.

Society began to change under a storm of terrorism from the army and the right wing. The March Incident had been covered up, and the October coup d'etat plotted by mid-ranked officers had been called off, but the shock waves reverberated throughout political circles. The right wing, young navy officers, and students at the army academy would embark on a series of terrorist incidents.

Shortly after Inukai Tsuyoshi was appointed prime minister, the Ketsumeidan (Blood Oath League) Incident of February 1932 occurred, in which Inoue Junnosuke, former minister of finance, was shot with a pistol wielded by a member of this fanatic group whose members had committed themselves to assassinating one person each. In March, Baron Dan Takuma, the general director of the Mitsui zaibatsu, was shot and killed. Then, on May 15 of that year, navy officers, army officer trainees, and students at the Aikyo Juku, a private academy in Ibaraki Prefecture, attacked the prime minister's residence and succeeded in assassinating Prime Minister Inukai. Following that there was an unsuccessful attempt on the life of the lord keeper of the Privy Seal, Makino Nobuaki, and an attack on a power transformer in an attempt to leave Tokyo in the dark. In 1933 there was a further terrorist plot involving large segments of the armed forces. The plot failed, but the terrorism persisted, leaving a trail of political instability.

The cabinet collapsed upon Inukai's assassination, and it was concluded that cabinets composed of members of a political party with the chief of the party as a prime minister were no longer viable. The elder statesman Prince Saionji Kimmochi recommended to the emperor that Saito Makoto, a navy admiral and an experienced hand in international affairs, be appointed to succeed Inukai as prime minister. In 1934, Saito was followed as prime minister by Admiral Okada Keisuke, who commanded the political scene under the slogan of "National unity."

If I were to mention one other aspect of this period that gives some idea of the atmosphere, it would be the "recantations" of the communists. In 1933, Sano Manabu and Nabeyama Sadachika, two imprisoned communists, issued declarations renouncing the international communist movement and its rejection of nationalism. Their recantations triggered a spate of similar renunciations by communists. In the space of six months to a year after the Manchurian Incident, Japan had undergone a change from democracy to nationalism. European Fascism and Nazism had, of course, a strong impact on the change of public sentiment.

For all this, it is also true that the economy was making steady headway under skilled hands. Having set the scene, let us turn our attention to the economic process.

ECONOMIC RECOVERY UNDER TAKAHASHI KOREKIYO

Takahashi Korekiyo served as minister of finance under three successive prime ministers—Inukai, Saito, and Okada. When first appointed in 1931, he was 77 years old and by no means young, but he was healthy and enjoyed the confidence of the public and so took over the responsibilities of managing the economy. Since his younger days, his position had been protectionist rather than free-market oriented. Moreover, he was not concerned only with achieving fiscal balance, in the Seiyukai tradition, he was an activist when it came to public investment—to policies aimed at developing industry through the construction of railroads, roads, and port facilities.

Fiscal activism and Keynes' theory

Takahashi, like present-day politicians, sought to please regional voters by means of public investment and thereby to win votes for the party. But Takahashi had a consistent record of advocating public investment to promote industrial development. When Inoue Junnosuke, his predecessor, lifted the gold embargo, Takahashi wrote a short magazine article critical of Inoue's fiscal policies. The article anticipates some elements of Keynes' *General Theory of Employment, Interest, and Money*, published in 1936, so it is invariably cited in discussions of Takahashi.

Let me briefly review its main points. First, Takahashi observed that despite the calls for retrenchment in conjunction with the return to the gold standard, it is necessary to distinguish between the economy of the nation and the economy of the individual. For example, let us assume that a person has ¥50,000 in hand but only spends ¥30,000 and saves the remaining ¥20,000. From the viewpoint of that individual, his savings have increased and he is better off, but from the viewpoint of the national economy, domestic demand that should have been at ¥50,000 is down to ¥30,000. Since national output will decrease by that much, the nation is not better off. Conversely, spending money at geisha houses, while morally reprehensible, generates income for the cooks and the geisha and a host of other persons. The cooks and geisha then buy food and use public bathhouses, so that the money circulates as income for others. Spending even ¥2,000 may thus have an impact on the economy by a factor of 20 or 30. If our individual does not go to the geisha house and saves his ¥2,000 instead, the money stops there, and all that is left is the ¥2,000.

Thus, says Takahashi, when one considers the national economy, it is better for everyone if those who have the money use it. Inoue's policies had cut back government spending and put a stop to construction of the Diet Building. But then the construction companies, the laborers who worked for them, and the suppliers of building materials and everyone else involved lost income and jobs. Thus, if Inoue wanted to lift the gold embargo, he should do so after developing domestic industries and marine transportation, so as not to cause a balance of international payments deficit. The text, as I have just noted, anticipates Keynes' theory of the investment multiplier. The playful discussion of geisha houses was probably used in the interest of making the argument understandable to ordinary readers.

Takahashi's economic policies

Takahashi now brought this line of thinking to the post of minister of finance. I think we can safely identify three central elements of his policy. First, the government would not intervene in the fall of the exchange rate, which began as a result of reinstating the embargo on gold exports, but would wait until the rate had settled. If you look at figure 2.1, you will see that the exchange rate against the U.S. dollar averaged ¥2.05 in 1931, ¥3.56 in 1932, and ¥3.97 in 1933. With that the yen bottomed out and subsequently stabilized at about ¥3.5 to the dollar. Overall, its value fell from ¥2 to the dollar to ¥3.5, during which interval there was even a time when the yen fell as low as ¥5 to the dollar.

A falling exchange rate means that for other countries Japanese goods become cheaper. Lower prices mean more exports. For Japan, it means that foreign products become more expensive.

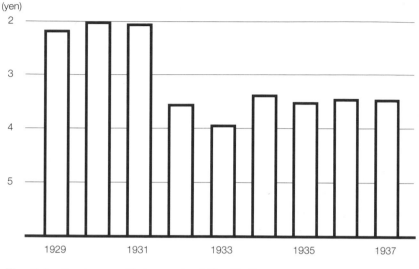

Fig. 2.1. **Exchange Rate against the Dollar**

Source: Bank of Japan, *Meiji iko Honpo Shuyo Keizai Tokei* (Major Economic Statistics since the Meiji Period). 1966.

Whereas it had been possible to buy one dollar's worth of foreign goods for ¥2, now it took ¥3.5 to buy the same amount of goods. In other words, the goods were more expensive. This makes conditions easier for import substitution industries. .

On the down side, the following can be said. If Japanese goods sell cheaply and foreign goods are expensive, it means that the terms of trade—the rate of exchange of Japanese and foreign products—are to Japan's disadvantage. To make this more comprehensible, assume that this pen that I am holding is an imported item and that it cost me $1. Assume also that this publication that I am holding is a Japanese product and costs ¥2. If the exchange rate is $1.00 = ¥2.00, then I can trade the book for the pen. If the exchange rate falls to, say, $1.00 = ¥4.00, then I need two books before I can do business. The cheap exchange rate leaves me at a disadvantage.

Even though the terms of trade are not advantageous, what Japanese firms ultimately want to earn is yen. If companies are able to export more and so bring in more yen, the domestic economy is stimulated and they are able to pull themselves out of the recession. A low exchange rate has its drawbacks, but it also has a stimulating effect on exporting industries inside the country.

The second pillar of Takahashi's economic program was low interest rates. The call rate—short-term interest rates for interbank loans—reflects most sensitively the surpluses and shortages of funds in the marketplace, as seen in figure 2.2. Inoue Junnosuke, as I noted earlier, finally raised interest rates, but before that he had ratcheted them down. When interest rates go down, business proprietors who borrow money find their lives easier.

Lower interest rates also push up the stock market. At risk of sounding like an introductory economics textbook, if we assume that the interest rate is in general at 6 percent and a company's stock dividends are also at 6 percent, then, if the company is financially sound and its credit standing is good, a stock with a face value of ¥100 will be worth ¥100 in the market. A balance is achieved. However, if the interest rate falls to 4 percent while the dividends remain at 6 percent, the interest rate on a deposit of

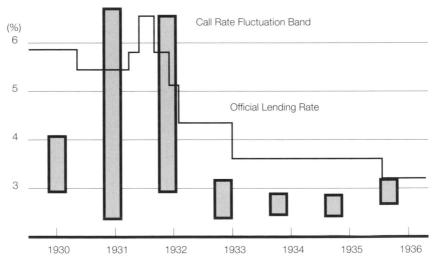

Fig. 2.2. Bank of Japan Official Lending Rate and Call Rate Annual Fluctuation Bands

Source: Bank of Japan, *Honpo Keizai Tokei* (Economic Statistics of Japan).

¥100 is ¥4, but the dividend on stock of the same face value is ¥6. This pushes the market price of stock up so that a new balance is reestablished at ¥150. When stock prices rise, not only do investors make money, it also becomes easier for companies to augment their equity capital. Stockholders are happy to approve share increases, since they obtain stock at below-market prices, and companies are able to round up the funds they need to finance an expansion.

From a fiscal standpoint, it is better that interest rates are low, since the government issues bonds to increase its spending, and higher interest rates mean higher bond interests.

The third feature of Takahashi's fiscal program was a major boost in fiscal spending in 1932 and 1933. Let us look at the numbers in figure 2.3. Under his predecessor's economic program, expenditures in the general account stood at ¥1.7 billion in 1929, but fell to ¥1.5 billion and ¥1.4 billion, respectively, in 1930 and 1931. Under Takahashi, the numbers rose to ¥1.9 billion in 1932 and then jumped to ¥2.2 billion in 1933, after which the numbers leveled off. Part of this increase was, of course, due to higher military spending largely in response to pressure from the army. In 1931, spending on the military had been ¥450 million, rising to ¥690 million in 1932, ¥870 million in 1933, and ¥940 million in 1934, before leveling off at something over ¥1 billion in 1935 and 1936.

The 1932 budget also contained an item that was not found in previous budgets. This was the Emergency Relief Program, under which the government undertook civil engineering projects in rural communities. Partly driven by the pressure of campaigns for rural relief, the program sought to undertake ¥800 million in public works over a three-year period with central and local government funding. At the same time, the government also engaged in what would now be termed fiscal investments, providing ¥800 million in low interest loans from the Ministry of Finance Deposit Bureau to rural communities to provide relief for farmers by taking over their debts.

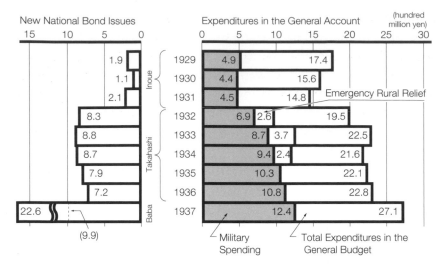

Fig. 2.3. Breakdown of National Budgets

Sources: Data in Toyo Keizai Shinpo Sha, *Showa Kokusei Soran* (Handbook of National Census in the Showa Era), 1980, and Ministry of Finance *Showa Zaisei Shi* (Fiscal History of the Show Era).
Notes: 1. Inoue Junnosuke was finance minister during the years 1929–1932; Takahashi Korekiyo held the post from 1932–1936; and Baba Eiichi served in 1937.
     2. Baba's initial bond flotation plans called for only ¥990 million.

Since the primary objective of these programs was less the construction projects themselves than the dispensing of cash to rural communities, it appears that the construction work had little impact. However, the programs did have the effect of improving liquidity in rural areas. Military spending and rural relief were thus the main driving forces behind the expansion of government expenditures.

Bank of Japan underwrites deficit-financing bonds

Takahashi's economic program featured lower exchange rates to promote exports, lower interest rates to improve liquidity, and expanded fiscal expenditures. The problem lay in the method used to raise the funds for the government to disburse. The government floated bonds underwritten by the Bank of Japan, a practice that is a contentious issue again today. Then, as now, ordinary financial institutions and securities companies underwrote government bonds as they were issued and sold them to investors. However, large issues of government bonds create the danger that the government will soak up all the funds that the banks were supposed to supply to the private sector, creating funding shortages in that sector. To get around this difficulty, the Bank of Japan would underwrite the bonds and hand the funds over to the government. When the government paid out those funds as expenditures, they would eventually find their way back into the banks in the form of deposits. The Bank of Japan would monitor deposits, and when there was leeway, would sell bonds to the banks, conducting what is known as a "selling operation." This would enable the government to float bonds without soaking up funds from the private sector.

This technique worked well enough at the outset, but once it succeeded it created the misconception that it was safe to float as many bonds as one wanted in this fashion in the event of war breaking out—as in fact was to happen. With no brake on fiscal spending, a round of inflation ensued. After World War II, the issue of bonds was initially banned under the Public Finance Law for this reason. Even today, the Bank of Japan is adamant that it should not underwrite government bonds.

For two or three years after 1932, however, the policy can be described as a success. As can be seen from figure 2.4, liquidity in the private sector improved, stock prices rose, and corporate performances took a sharp turn for the better.

Takahashi's closest adviser on such matters was Fukai Eigo, deputy governor of the Bank of Japan and later to become its governor. At the time of the Russo-Japanese War, when Takahashi, as deputy governor of the Bank of Japan, traveled to Britain and the United States to find buyers for Japanese bonds, Fukai accompanied him as his secretary. The two of them handled the task entirely on their own and were linked by a profound trust ever after. Fukai was well-read and knowledgeable about history and philosophy, but he was especially insightful on financial theory and had published a number of analyses of Japanese financial policy. His memoirs, spanning 70 years, were republished recently after being out of print for many years. This extremely interesting individual, with a scholarly bent, was Takahashi's confidant in financial matters.

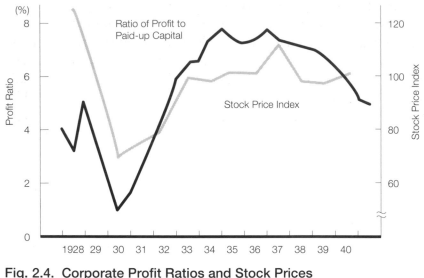

Fig. 2.4. Corporate Profit Ratios and Stock Prices

Sources: Mitsubishi Economic Research Institute, *Honpo Jigyo Seiseki Bunseki* (Analysis of Performance of Japanese Businesses); Fujino Shozaburo and Akiyama Ryoko, *Shoken Kakaku to Rishi Ritsu* (Stock Prices and Interest Rates), Hitotsubashi University Statistics Resource Center. 1977.
Note: Profit ratios are for the first and second halves of each fiscal year.

Need for spending cuts

Fukai appears to have already noticed the difference between full and non-full employment, as Keynes was later to define them. If government spending is boosted to stimulate the economy in an environment where there is a surplus of labor, equipment, and materials in the society, then the economy will recover steadily and approach a state of full employment. But once all labor and equipment is fully employed, further infusions of government spending boost demand, but cannot do much to raise production. All that happens is that prices rise. This, Keynes thought, was true inflation. Fukai, in my view, noticed the distinction, and in the autumn of 1935, after three years of economic stimulation had succeeded, Japan's economy had attained a state of more or less full employment.

The Ministry of Finance had long been wary of increasing the budget through bond issues. The budget leveled off in 1933, as I have already noted, and from about 1935 on, Fukai and

Takahashi both seem to have concluded that a lid needed to be kept on government spending. However, the military increasingly demanded more money. Takahashi resisted with everything he could muster, as a result of which government spending did not grow until 1936 and the growth of military spending was minimal. Takahashi was viewed as anathema by the military. His resistance to increasing the military budget was one of the reasons why he was assassinated in the February 26 Incident of 1936.

Changes in income distributions

As funds began to be fed to the rural regions and as government spending rose elsewhere, mostly owing to increased military spending, the private sector began to develop a degree of liquidity. At this point, the flow of incomes and funds within Japan underwent a significant change. In the 1920s, funds had accumulated in the hands of the big companies in the big cities and in the hands of wealthy individuals. Bank deposits were primarily concentrated in the big banks. Now large sums of money were flowing into the rural regions and rural communities. Institutions like Mitsui Bank, which had in the past done business through a very few branches and with a small number of big firms and wealthy individuals as their customer base, found their deposits were no longer growing as much in the past. Meanwhile, banks that owned a large number of rural branches—for example, the Yasuda Bank, the Daiichi Bank, and Sanwa Bank (created in a merger of the Sanjushi Bank, the Konoike Bank, and the Yamaguchi Bank in the Kansai region)—enjoyed conspicuous growth in deposits. The Mitsui Bank had for a long time led the nation's banks in terms of deposits, but by the end of 1933, Mitsui and Mitsubishi had fallen into fifth and sixth place, behind the Sanwa, Sumitomo, Daiichi, and Yasuda banks.

Figure 2.5 shows data on deposits by region: it will be seen that from the end of 1929 to the end of 1934, the proportion of deposits held in Tokyo and Osaka accounts dropped relatively, the value of deposits in the two big cities remaining roughly level, while that of other regions rose by some 15 percent. When we break the numbers down by type of institution, we find that bank

A. Deposits in Tokyo and Osaka as a Percentage of Total National Deposits

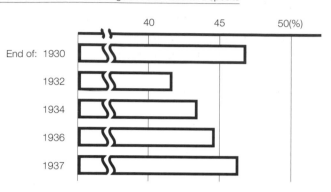

Source: Ministry of Finance, *Ginko Kyoku Nenpo* (Bank Bureau Annual Report).

B. Growth Rates for Deposits in Different Types of Financial Institutions

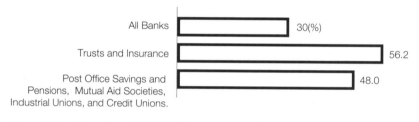

Source: Bank of Japan, *Honpo Keizai Tokei* (Economic Statistics of Japan).

Fig. 2.5. Changes in the Structure of Deposits

deposits grew little, that growth in deposits in insurance and trusts was highest, followed by deposits in institutions geared to ordinary people—post office savings and post office pension funds, mutual aid societies, industrial unions, and credit unions. The data may be interpreted as signifying a sudden shift in the flow of funds. The gap may have shrunk a little between the old wealthy and high paid salaried workers, on the one hand, and ordinary business proprietors and other white-collar workers, on the other. Small businessmen found themselves financially better off, and people in the rural areas were generating higher incomes. Otherwise, the changes in the flow of funds are inexplicable.

Amidst all this, the lifestyles of Japan's urban dwellers began to change. Western clothing became more fashionable. Western styles, especially in foodstuffs and clothing, became more wide-spread. I believe that people in the middle ranks of society were seeing a considerable improvement in their incomes and that, as the income gap shrank, lifestyles began to change.

Management of Manchukuo

Following on from the Manchurian Incident, the army decided to create a puppet state in northern China. In March 1932, it established Manchukuo, a state that was nominally independent, but in reality subservient to Japan's wishes, dragging Pu-Yi, the deposed last emperor of the Ching Dynasty, out of retirement in Tianjin and making him chief executive. Two years later, he was made emperor of Manchukuo. A centralized government was established in which the government ministers were all Chinese or Manchu, but the administrative vice ministers were all Japanese, controlling the key posts. The Fourth Section of the Guandong Army staff took command of domestic policy, ensuring that the army's wishes were reflected. The army effectively ran the politics of Manchukuo by what was known at the time as *naimen shido* (guidance from the inside.)

What kind of economic policies did Japan adopt in Manchukuo? Japan wanted to lay its hands on the key resources of the region—for example, iron ore, coal, oil shale, and farm produce, such as soybeans. It also wanted to start up heavy industries and even considered making automobiles. To these ends, the cabinet adopted an Economic Construction Program for Manchukuo in March 1933. Simply put, the program placed under state control coal, steel, automobiles, aluminum, oil, telephone and telegraph, and other key industries. For each of these industries, a company would be established that would unify production under a single roof according to production plans that conformed with government policy. Commerce and other areas were unregulated, but rice production, spinning, and other industries which might compete with segments of Japan's domestic industry generally came in for controls.

This was clearly an experiment in planned economics, a rejection of the flourishing capitalism and free-marketeering that prevailed in Japan at the time. With one company in each industry, key industries would be controlled by government policy. At the same time, there existed also a fierce hostility toward the zaibatsu. The army, in particular, bore them an animosity that led it to ban zaibatsu from doing business in Manchukuo.

Ever since the beginning of the Manchurian Incident, Mantetsu, the South Manchuria Railway Company, had cooperated with the Guandong Army. It had been the Mantetsu economic research unit that had drawn up the original economic plan, and it was Mantetsu that was to be the main agency for its implementation. For instance, when funds were brought into Manchukuo, the operation was carried out through Mantetsu, which would issue bonds in Japan. Funding for controlled companies in key industries was provided by having Manchukuo and Mantetsu put up 30 percent each in capital, and the ranks of management of the companies were filled with former Mantetsu employees.

The railroad company thus had the appearance of wielding immense power, and of controlling the Manchurian economy, but in reality, the company was beset by problems. Bond flotations within Japan did not go well, owing in part to resentment by zaibatsu-related industries. Moreover, Mantetsu's main line of business was railroad operations. It had some experience in coal mining, but when it came to making steel and launching automobile and chemical industries it was a rank amateur. The controlled companies did not succeed altogether as well as anticipated.

In addition, capable Japanese government officials from a variety of ministries and agencies transferred to the Manchukuo government, where they had effective power. As the Guandong Army officers were rotated, various people began to think that it was not a good idea for Mantetsu to have the country's economy under its thumb and that the company should concentrate on railroading and leave the development of Manchurian industries to skilled professionals. Manchukuo had initially been established with proclamations of harmony among the five ethnic groups (Han Chinese, Manchu, Mongol, Korean, and Japanese) and kinship being hailed as the road to national prosperity, but now

Japan's real colonial intent came to the fore. A rift developed between Mantetsu and the Guandong Army, resulting in a decline in the railroad company's clout with the government. This is one of the reasons that Mantetsu gradually came to actively support the Japanese invasion of mainland China.

In 1936, the Guandong Army invited leaders of newly emerging zaibatsu in Japan to Manchukuo to hear their views on Manchurian development. Eventually, a holding company by the name of Nissan was persuaded to transfer its head office to Manchukuo and to set up a holding company called Manchuria Heavy Industries Company. This company was partly capitalized by the Manchurian government and provided with guarantees of dividends and other special privileges, and it took over the construction of Manchukuo. The migration of Nissan to Manchuria took place in November 1937, by which point Japanese investment had risen to over ¥1.2 billion in Manchukuo. This climate, in which Manchuria's economic development was starting to take off, is an important reality of the time, and one that inspired many ambitious young Japanese to emigrate to the new state.

INDUSTRIAL DEVELOPMENT

I would now like to look at Japan's economic development in this period in a little more detail. As I discussed in my first lecture, heavy and chemical industries made substantial progress in Japan in the 1920s, and by the beginning of the 1930s these industries were at the threshold of a stretch of meteoric growth. If you look at the numbers in table 2.1, you will see that output in the textile industry, especially of cotton goods, climbed nearly 50 percent in the period between 1931 and 1936. It is clear that cotton textiles surged dramatically as an export industry.

Raw silk production, however, remained flat, even when the economy improved. This was partly due to the recession in the United States, but it was also a manifestation of the emergence of nylon, which started to oust as material for stockings and other products.

The biggest growth, however, was in heavy industries. Steel production grew significantly. Shipbuilding made steady progress.

Table 2.1 Trends in Industrial Production

	1931	1936	1940	1931–36	1936–41
				Rate of increase[c]	Rate of increase[c]
Coal (10,000 metric tons)	2,799	4,180	5,631	1.49	1.35
Cotton Textiles (million square meters)	2,375	3,499[a]	2,194	1.45	0.64
Artificial Textiles (million square meters)	273	775	528	2.84	0.68
Automotive (units)	504	8,892	37,772	17.64	4.25
Steel Vessels (1,000 gross tons)	101	247	307	2.45	1.24
Machine Tools (units)	2,100	16,227	58,088	7.73	3.58
Ammonium Sulfate (1,000 metric tons)	393	880	1,109	2.24	1.26
Pig Iron (1,000 metric tons)	917	2,007	3,512	2.19	1.75
Crude Copper (1,000 metric tons)	1,883	5,223	6,855	2.77	1.31
Plate Glass (1,000 cases)	2,319	3,810	4,282	1.64	1.12
Cement (tons)	3,430	6,116	6,085	1.78	0.99
Induction Motors (1,000 units)	60	166	185	2.77	1.11
Pulp (1,000 metric tons)	576	815	1,155	1.41	1.42
Freight Transportation					
National Railway (million tons/kilometer)	469	643	792	1.37	1.23
Sea Transport (million tons)	53	79	101[b]	1.49	1.28

Source: Economic Planning Agency, *Nihon no Keizai Tokei* (Japan's Economic Statistics) Shiseido, 1964.

[a] indicates figure for 1935.
[b] indicates figure for 1939.
[c] The numbers in the columns marked rate of increase are a measure of the change over the period, with the earliest year equal to 1.0.

Automobiles, the production of which had been near zero prior the 1930s, expanded, as did other industries, including machine tools; industrial machinery; motors, transformers, and other electrical machinery; ammonium sulfate, caustic soda, and other chemical products; cement; and plate glass.

Another standout was rayon production. Developed in the wake of World War I, production technology for rayon was perfected in the 1930s, and the ensuing export growth propelled Japan into the position as the world's foremost producer of rayon by 1936.

Recovery of conventional industries

Preexisting conventional industries also developed rapidly, their main source of new demand being exports, as can be seen from figure 1.11 in the previous lecture. The bulk of these industries were textile products and general merchandise. In the textile industry, for example, spinners slashed costs by thoroughgoing programs to raise productivity and moved into the export of fabrics of broad width. Regional cotton textile manufacturers contributed to export growth with active efforts to produce a diverse selection of cotton goods tailored to demands of their export markets. Take, for example, Nishiwaki in Hyogo Prefecture, a major textile producing area. The activities of the prefectural industrial testing office have recently been reported in a study by Abe Takeshi that shows how the head of the testing office investigated what goods were likely to sell in the Middle East, in Egypt, and so on and passed this information on to everyone in the industry, with the result that firms came up with a series of new products. An expansion of textile exports would have been impossible in the absence of such efforts.

Simultaneously, however, economic friction was arising as a result of competition with foreign products, as happened in Indonesia, as I mentioned in my previous lecture. In India, for instance, discriminatory tariffs were imposed on Japanese cotton goods. Japan responded by attempting to boycott Indian cotton. Friction also arose vis-à-vis Great Britain and the United States. The export boost provided by the drop in the yen's exchange value was the source of major international problems. In this respect, the situation was rather like that of the early 1980s.

Two major reasons also lay in the background to this growth of production and exports. One was that the cumulative technological experience and rationalization efforts since the 1920s had finally borne fruit, and new demand was being developed within Japan. The second was that as a result of lower exchange rates, the prices of imported products had risen, making it easier for companies to beat the competition.

The rayon industry, for example, had encountered numerous difficulties in its early days, but had by this time reached the point where it was producing a fairly decent product. Rayon had come to be used domestically as a substitute for silk and had established a reputation as an export that was highly valued in low-income regions overseas. In machinery, Japan became almost completely self-sufficient, except for special high-end items. This self-sufficiency formed the basis for the development of military supply industries.

Rise of new industries

It is important to remember that the 1930s were an age in which new industries also emerged. With the development of the electric power industry, electric smelting of aluminum became possible within Japan. Today, aluminum is widely used in all kinds of household articles, but originally the aim was to produce materials for aircraft.

Radio broadcasts began in Japan in the mid-1920s, and simple radio receivers began to make their way into homes. With this, a new industry emerged: the manufacture of vacuum tubes for use in radios. Large electric phonographs were initially a luxury item, and many companies, starting with Toshiba, entered this market. Production of records grew as phonographs became popular; names like Victor and Columbia dominated the field. It was around about this time that NEC came into being, with the development of wireless communications. Another new industry, one that we don't see much anymore, was the celluloid industry. Celluloid is highly dangerous because it flares up at the slightest touch of a lighted match, but at the time it was widely used in children's toys. Dai Nippon Celluloid, a Mitsui affiliate, was the major manufacturer.

The biggest new industries, and two fields that developed very rapidly, were automobiles, made by Toyota and Nissan, and airplanes, mostly for military use. Nakajima Aircraft and Mitsubishi Heavy Industries came onto the scene as the main aircraft manufacturers.

Accordingly, it is possible to make the following argument. The period of Takahashi's financial stewardship immediately after the Manchurian Incident in 1932 was by all standards one in which civilian demand was small. For this reason, fiscal spending was an important ingredient and, moreover, military spending occupied a major proportion of the budget, followed by rural relief programs. For this reason, the 1930s are commonly said to have been a period of economic development centered solely on military procurements. But a string of new industries such as those that I have just described was emerging and investing in plant and equipment. Although industries like steel and oil may in some sense be regarded as military industries, then, as now, there also existed the possibility for demand growth in areas unrelated to the military. Indeed, in the mid-1930s, over 80 percent of the demand for steel was for general civilian purposes, with civil engineering and machinery accounting for over half. Such examples suggest that at this time a wide spectrum of development possibilities remained.

I believe that conditions within the economy and within industry were being readied that might, if war had not broken out, have made possible a gradual transition to economic growth of the kind that characterized Japan's postwar era. This, as we all know, however, was not to be.

Development of industrial policies

The period was characterized by a variety of industrial policies. In 1932, a policy was introduced that provided subsidies to encourage the production of motor vehicles for army use. In 1933, a program was introduced to upgrade the merchant marine. The plan was for the government to subsidize construction of one high-speed cargo vessel powered by diesel engines in return for scrapping two obsolete vessels. With this, Japan's shipbuilding and maritime transportation industries made a quantum leap. Since the 1920s, the maritime corporation Osaka Shosen and the Mitsui Trading Company's Maritime Division had been building high-speed diesel vessels. Now, in the 1930s, the government promoted their construction through its program.

The steel industry saw the birth of Nippon Seitetsu (Nippon Steel Co.) in 1934. During the steel recession in the 1920s, there had been talk of merging the large number of financially troubled steel companies into a single huge trust, headed by the government-operated Yawata Iron and Steel Works, but the merger had been postponed owing to conflicting interests, to be finally made reality in the 1930s with the creation of Nippon Seitetsu. The major standout was Nippon Kokan, which, seeing a recovery on the horizon, refused to join the merger and thus became the only steel company other than Nippon Seitetsu to operate a blast furnace. The steel industry was thus largely reorganized under one roof, with Nippon Seitetsu in almost complete domination of the market. As demand recovered, steel production picked up, and the industry began to enjoy an era of prosperity.

Another event that took place in 1934 was the passage of the Oil Industry Law. Since the beginning of the 1920s, Japan had given up on trying to make do with its scant domestically produced oil and began building refineries on the Pacific coastline to convert crude oil into gasoline, kerosene, and heavy oil. This called for the importation of crude oil, and so joint ventures were set up with foreign oil companies. The main import sources were the United States, Sumatra, and Borneo. Oil being vital militarily for airplane fuel and for navy warships, the government passed the law, which, in return for special protection for the industry, sought to place oil under government control. The industry was granted tax, financing, and other benefits in return for a requirement that firms maintain a constant level of stockpiled oil. It is also true that the overseas-based companies strongly resisted the stockpiling requirement.

Following this, many other industries—mostly military supply industries—were placed under legislation governing their operations, for example, the Automobile Industry Law in 1936, the Artificial Oil Industry Law and the Steel Industry Law of 1937, and the Machine Tools Industry Law and the Aircraft Manufacturing Industry Law of 1938. These pieces of legislation, tailored to specific industries, placed the industries under government control, but also provided them with assistance. It is worth noting that this approach was resurrected after World War II, around about 1955, when a series of legislation was devised for the machinery and electrical equipment industries, the original model being the legislation of the 1930s.

In the case of automobiles, for example, there was almost no domestic car production. General Motors and Ford had come in with all the parts and were assembling cars in Japan from knockdown kits since 1920s. The Automobile Industry Law was written to assist Nissan and Toyota to compete with these foreign firms. Eventually Ford and GM would withdraw from Japan when World War II broke out.

For all the development that took place in Japan's heavy industries during this period, some areas such as automobiles remained weak. The materials used in domestic cars had a reputation for being poor. When military vehicles were driven harshly over rough, unpaved roads, domestic models would frequently break their drive shafts owing to poor-quality materials. Even the army's motor vehicle divisions were said to be delighted when they were supplied with Ford cars.

Nonetheless, although beset with a variety of difficulties, domestic heavy industries were beginning to approach self-sufficiency during this period.

Trusts and cartels

Let me give another example of a trust that is sometimes compared with Nippon Seitetsu. In 1933, the Mitsui subsidiary Oji Paper Manufacturing absorbed Fuji Paper and Karafuto Industries, its two major competitors in the earlier recession, creating a mammoth trust that monopolized 90 percent of Japan's domestic newsprint production. The new company then raised prices and gradually improved its financial position. Since the price increases were too obvious, of course, they became the target of criticism.

A further aspect of industrial development in this period was cartel activities, which increased during the 1930s. If you look at table 2.2, you will notice that the number of cartels jumps sharply in a range of industries. During the recovery from the recession, companies colluded on prices, sales volumes, marketing, production volumes, and equipment.

Cartel activities are, of course, accompanied by a great deal of waste. In order to hold production down, companies would agree to cut operations and would promise to seal 30 percent of their equipment so that it could not be used. If a company wanted to steal a march on its competitors by boosting production, it didn't

Table 2.2 Number of Cartels in Different Industries

	Pre WWI	1919–1926	1927–1929	After 1930[a]	Unknown	Total
Heavy Industries[b]	—	5	6	19	3	33
Chemicals	5	6	1	18	1	31
Textiles	1	1	3	6	—	11
Foodstuff	1	—	2	5	—	8
Total	7	12	12	48	4	83

Sources: Takahashi Kamekichi, *Nihon Keizai Tosei Ron* (Economic Controls in Japan), p 127; Ando Yoshio (ed.), *Kindai Nihon Keizai Shi Yoran* [Handbook of Modern Japanese Economic History], The University of Tokyo Press, 1975.

[a] Cartels still existing as of the end of 1932.
[b] Heavy industry data includes mining.

have the equipment to do so, since 30 percent of its equipment was off-limits. The solution was to write off 30 percent and invest in new plant and equipment anyway. All the company had to do was seal 30 percent of its total equipment. Nonetheless, even supposing there was the advantage of being able to place old equipment under seal and of using new, more efficient machinery, the cartel-imposed limits meant major losses in productivity. Waste of this kind is an inherent aspect of cartel activities, and such contradictions were a feature of Japan's industrial scene at this time.

The new zaibatsu

Another feature was the emergence of new zaibatsu. The best known of these was Nissan, built up by Aikawa Yoshisuke. The company's original lines of business were constructed around what is today Hitachi Mining and Hitachi Ltd., and until 1928 were under the management of Kuhara Fusanosuke, Aikawa's brother-in-law. When Aikawa took over, he established Nippon Sangyo (Nippon Industrial Company), abbreviated as Nissan. This he set up as a holding company and created a zaibatsu-like that controlled the subsidiary companies of Hitachi and Tobata Iron Works. What differentiated this organization from Mitsui and the other, old zaibatsu, was that the holding company, Nissan, was a public stock company and held a 20–30 percent controlling interest in the subsidiaries, the remainder being public stock.

Since, under Takahashi's finance policies, low interest rates pushed stock prices up and, moreover, Nissan was turning a high profit, the stocks of the new company soared. For example, a face value of ¥50 had a market value of ¥300. At that point, Aikawa sold new stock with a face value of ¥50 for a premium of ¥250 a share. There was no shortage of takers, as the stock was being floated at less than market price, and Nissan was able to pull in a premium of ¥200 a share. With the proceeds, Nissan bought up companies in financial difficulty at low share prices and sent in skilled management teams to turn the companies around.

In this manner, Nissan aggrandized itself. Under Aikawa, the company launched Nissan Motor Company and bought into the chemical and fishery industries, yielding high profits. Eventually, it would "emigrate" to Manchuria in the form of the Manchurian Heavy Industries Company, apparently because, under the revised tax code of 1937, the holding company and its subsidiaries became liable to dual taxation, which put a damper on profitability. Once in Manchuria, however, it came under the rigorous control of the military, as a result of which it was unable to attract foreign investors, and nothing went as Aikawa intended. The automobile industry project did not go as planned, ultimately resulting in his resignation. But for awhile, Aikawa seemed unstoppable.

Another noteworthy figure was Noguchi Shitagau, of Nippon Chisso (Nitrogen), known as Nitchitsu. The firm had succeeded in mass producing ammonium sulfate and later tried its hand at artificial petroleum. The company ran a large-scale hydroelectric power project in the northern part of Korea, with which it produced low-cost electricity, thereby reducing the costs of electrolysis of water for the mass production of ammonium sulfate. This made it Japan's top chemical firm. Noguchi's projects were ambitious, including the production of rayon at Asahi Chemical Industry's Nobeoka plant and the development of new industrial technologies.

Another newcomer was Mori Nobuteru of Showa Fertilizer, now Showa Denko. This company began manufacturing amonium sulfate by electrolysis using surplus electricity, employing a method developed by the Tokyo Industrial Testing Laboratory. The firm also began producing aluminum at Omachi.

Nakano Tomonori's Nippon Soda developed a wide range of chemical concerns around its core manufacture of caustic soda. Then there is Riken Industries, built up by Okochi Masatoshi, which developed industrial applications for the inventions developed in the Institute of Physical and Chemical Research (Riken). The company made everything from vitamins to a synthetic sake to piston rings. Another company was Nakajima Aircraft Company, founded by Nakajima Chikuhei, a former army captain, who produced airplanes domestically after leaving the army. This was another growth company that benefited from the backing of the army and the navy.

With the exception of Showa Fertilizer and Nakajima, the above companies share a number of features in common. They expanded into a diversity of fields and exhibited the capacity to develop in new, technology-oriented fields. The central figures, Aikawa, Noguchi, Nakano, and Okochi were all engineers. By the same token, with the exception of Nissan, their ability to capitalize their ventures was not as good as it might have been, but they had sufficient momentum to achieve rapid growth rates.

One conceivable reason for their success was the economic situation in the 1930s following the lifting of the gold embargo. Prior to the lifting of the embargo, money was tight, and these companies had little wherewithal to grow. They were completely at the mercy of the banks. But in the 1930s the financial crunch eased, and government lending institutions such as the Industrial Bank of Japan had more funds for lending, creating conditions in which the new zaibatsu could spurt ahead with the aid of these institutions. Noguchi Shitagau of Nippon Chisso, for example, had once relied on Mitsubishi Bank, but when he set out to generate hydroelectric power in northern Korea, he was able to induce the Korean governor general's office to transfer to him the water rights that Mitsubishi owned on the Heocheon Gang River. Mitsubishi, naturally, cut him off from new credit, but Noguchi was able to raise loans from the Bank of Korea and the Industrial Bank of Japan.

The new zaibatsu made their way into China and Korea under wartime conditions and were pummeled in the aftermath.

However, Nissan, Hitachi, Showa Denko, and many other companies recovered splendidly after the war. The descendants of Riken Industries and Nakajima are also performing admirably. The emergence of the new generation of zaibatsu is somewhat reminiscent of the way in which in later years Sony, Matsushita, Sanyo, Sharp, and more recently Pioneer would wield their technology to force their way to the forefront.

Mitsui, Mitsubishi, Sumitomo, Yasuda, and the other old zaibatsu had come in for criticism from society at the time of the lifting of the gold embargo and were to end up keeping a low profile for awhile. Mitsui, for example, established a fund for social programs to which it donated sums of money and opened up some of its stock to the public. The day when the zaibatsu ruled the roost was now past. When war broke out, Mitsui and Mitsubishi would, of course, become actively involved in the production of military supplies, but it would be somewhat inaccurate to suggest that the old zaibatsu regained their former position or were strengthened by war.

The reason I say this is that the old zaibatsu had conducted business independently, acting entirely in their own interests. In wartime, however, they had to follow government orders to build weapons and build aircraft. In addition, the old zaibatsu were characteristically financially conservative, funding their expansions out of their own profit reserves. When they had to establish large-scale heavy industries at the instigation of the state, they were not able to do so solely on the basis of their own funds. In that respect, then, they were no longer able to sustain their insular, conservative management practices, and the position of the old zaibatsu slipped relative to other industries.

A QUASI-WAR-TIME FOOTING

All this changed with the February 26 Incident, which left the army overwhelmingly in power. On February 26, 1936, some of the army corps stationed in Tokyo, led by young officers, attacked and assassinated public figures and occupied a section of Tokyo in the vicinity of the Diet Building for four days. Those assassinated were Saito Makoto, admiral, former prime minister, and then lord keeper of the Privy Seal; Minister of Finance Takahashi Korekiyo; and director general of Education in the Army Watanabe Jotaro. Wounded were Suzuki Kantaro, admiral and grand chamberlain. Attacked but not wounded were Admiral Okada Keisuke, the prime minister, and Makino Nobuaki, former lord keeper of the Privy Seal and senior statesman. All of these individuals shared with Saionji Kimmochi the goal of smooth relations with Britain and the United States. Takahashi's financial policies had won him general public support. They had the trust of the emperor, who on hearing of the revolt was infuriated and ordered that the rebellion be put down. The revolt was quelled and its leaders executed, but it changed the balance of political power, in that there were no longer any forces left to stand up to the army. The army, which one might have expected to have kept a lower profile, having allowed such a major rebellion to occur, interfered with Hirota Koki, who had been instructed to form a cabinet. It objected because candidates were liberals and demanded that the number of cabinet members drawn from the political parties be reduced. These demands, though hard to swallow, were all met.

Growing political clout of the military

The minister of finance in Hirota's new cabinet was Baba Eiichi. This hailed a major shift in fiscal policy. Baba, an ex-bureaucrat who had served as governor of the Nihon Kangyo Bank, was well informed on fiscal matters, but he was also shrewdly aware of the climate and appears to have concluded that it was unlikely that he could withstand the army's ultimatums. That being the case, he felt that he might as well accede to the military's demands and get on with the business of politics.

The army and navy sent large expansion plans to the Hirota cabinet, the army demanding a total of ¥3 billion in a six-year military expansion project, and the navy asking for ¥770 million for its third supplementation plan, which included funds for the super-battleships *Yamato* and *Musashi*. The budget for 1937, as compiled by Baba, jumped from Takahashi's ¥2.2 billion to ¥3.04 billion, with military spending rising over 40 percent, from ¥1 billion to just under ¥1.5 billion. These figures were finalized at the year's end, but it was clear directly after Baba came into office that the next budget would contain a large component of military expansion.

Tax increases had been repugnant to Takahashi, who had taken the position that taxes should be as low as possible to facilitate national economic development. Taxes were to be kept down, even if it meant floating bonds. Thus, Takahashi had kept a firm hand on the budget to keep fiscal spending down. Now, there was nothing for it but to raise taxes. Baba's strategy was to raise direct taxes, starting with corporate taxes. The business community objected violently.

It appeared that an increase in bond issues was also in store, rising to ¥1 billion. Since this meant a higher interest burden, Baba sought to reduce interest rates. Direct taxes and lower interest rates then became the hallmarks of his fiscal policy. The business community, seeing the prospect of expanded military procurements and inflation, was enthusiastic. Baba's new policy marked the turning point toward prosperity in the 1930s.

The Ishihara Concept

Baba swallowed the military's demands, in the background of which lay an army project called the Ishihara Concept. Ishihara Kanji was a fiercely individualistic character who, as a lieutenant colonel, had planned the Manchurian Incident and brought about the establishment of Manchukuo. In summer 1935, Ishihara returned to the headquarters, where he initially worked as head strategist and then as head of the War Directive Section. Finally he was promoted to full colonel and became chief of operations, where he controlled the nerve center of Japan's strategic planning. Thus, the central figure in army central planning from 1935 through 1937 was Ishihara.

As head strategist, Ishihara had been stunned by the clear numerical inferiority of Japanese forces on the Manchuria-U.S.S.R. border. There was no prospect of winning in a fight with the Soviet Union. Ishihara concluded that military readiness was inadequate, basically because Japanese industry was still too weak. He proposed that for a period of five years, Japan should avoid potential military conflicts with other countries and concentrate on developing heavy industries, especially weapons production.

Ishihara then set up a think tank, called the Japan-Manchuria Finance and Economic Research Group, under the general staff headquarters, which was headed by Miyazaki Masayoshi, a confrere from the establishment of Manchukuo. Under a veil of great secrecy, the group drew up plans for the large-scale expansion of heavy industries. This proposal was debated within the army and approval obtained.

In Manchuria, the proposal was immediately translated into the Five-Year Plan for Manchurian Industrial Development and implemented as policy in 1937. Within Japan, the proposal was presented to Prince Konoe Fumimaro (later to become prime minister), a select few politicians and senior army officers, and the leaders of the business community, including Mitsui and Mitsubishi, to be implemented as national policy. In view of the power wielded by the military, the political and business leaders could do little but assent.

After the fall of Hirota and his cabinet, a cabinet headed by General Hayashi Senjuro was put in office in February 1937 to implement the plan. It is safe to say that Hayashi's was a cabinet established by Ishihara. When the Hirota cabinet resigned, General Ugaki Kazushige, former minister of the army and former governor general of Korea, was appointed prime minister. However, Ishihara and his group blocked his attempt to appoint the minister of the army, ostensibly for the reason that no one was available who would serve under Ugaki, who had been implicated in the March Incident of 1931. The attempt to form a cabinet under Ugaki was aborted, and so Hayashi was asked to appoint a cabinet.

Under the Hayashi cabinet, Yuki Toyotaro, former chairman of the Industrial Bank of Japan, was appointed minister of finance. The budget was held to ¥2.8 billion, the tax increase was trimmed, and the budget passed. However, the Hayashi cabinet was short-lived. It dissolved the Diet and held a general election in which the government was soundly defeated.

Next, in June 1937, Konoe Fumimaro was instructed to form a cabinet, the mission of which included the implementation of the Ishihara Concept. In fact, the army drew up an Outline of the Five-Year Plan for Key Industries, based on the Ishihara Concept, which it formally presented to the cabinet. The main features of the Five-Year Plan are found in table 2.3. Kaya Okinori, minister of finance, and Yoshino Shinji, minister of commerce and industry, were directly charged with implementing the plan.

Yoshino and Kaya's Three Principles

Toward the end of Baba's tenure as minister of finance, around the end of 1936, Japan's balance of international payments suddenly plunged into an ever expanding deficit. I will give a breakdown of the factors contributing to the deficit in my next lecture. The trade account deficit had arisen because of a sharp increase in imports, since at that time, the large budget had triggered expectations that demand would grow and that inflation was inevitable. The deficit rapidly piled up, and the Yokohama Specie Bank found it difficult to adequately fund its transactions. Since the international environment deterred other countries from lending to Japan, the country had to meet its payments on its own. At the beginning of 1937, Japan had been forced into a position where the Bank of Japan had no option but to ship overseas precious specie reserves to settle its accounts.

Under ordinary circumstances, an import surplus would trigger a round of fiscal and financial belt tightening, which would bring prices down by dampening domestic demand, thus cutting imports and boosting exports and bringing the trade account back into balance. But if the government tightened the purse strings, it would be unable to embark on the Five-Year Plan advocated by the army. The Konoe cabinet was faced at its outset with the impossibility of retrenchment.

Shortly after the cabinet was installed, Minister of Finance Kaya and Minister of Commerce and Industry Yoshino put forward what have come to be known as the Yoshino-Kaya Three Principles, which called for expansion of production capacity, adjustment in the supply and demand for goods, and balance in

Table 2.3 Capacity Expansion Targets under the Five-Year Plan for Key Industries

	Production Targets			Current Capacity			Expansion Rate		
	Total	Japan	Manchuria	Total	Japan	Manchuria	Total	Japan	Manchuria
General Machinery[a] (thousand vehicles)	100	90	10	37	37	—	2.7	2.4	—
Machine Tools (thousands)	50	45	5	13	13	—	3.8	3.5	—
Steel Materials (10,000 metric tons)	1,300	900	400	485	440	45	2.7	2.0	8.9
Petroleum[b] (10,000 kiloliters)	565	325	240	36.4	21	15.4	15.6	15.5	15.6
Coal (10,000 metric tons)	11,000	7,200	3,800	5,556	4,200	1,356	2.0	1.7	2.8
Aluminum (1,000 metric tons)	100	70	30	21	21	—	4.8	3.3	—
Magnesium (1,000 metric tons)	9	6	3	0.5	0.5	—	18.0	12.0	—
Electric Power (10,000 kilowatts)	1,257	1,117	140	721	675	46	1.7	1.7	3.0
Ships (10,000 metric tons)	93	86	7	50	50	—	1.9	1.7	—

Source: Nakamura Takafusa, Nihon no Keizai Tosei (Economic Controls in Japan). Nihon Keizai Shimbun Sha. 1974.

Note: Not shown in this table is the expansion of weapons production, by a factor of 2.1. Aircraft and military vehicles were slated to increase by a factor of 10, to over 10,000 planes and 100,000 vehicles annually.
[a] The expansion of general machinery was approximately 180 percent.
[b] Figures for petroleum indicate the expansion of volatile oil production from domestic crude oil. Production capacity from imported sources was targeted to increase by a factor of just under 10, taking 1936 as a base.

the international accounts. Expansion of production capacity referred to the expansion of heavy industry production capacity touted in the army plan and was the top priority. However, since a continued deficit in the international payments would rapidly affect Japan's ability to settle its obligations, a balance had to be achieved at all costs. In this event, there was only one conclusion to be reached. Since a trade deficit was preordained as long as Japan retained a free-market economy, trade had to be brought under direct government control so that priority could be given to the importation of goods for the Five-Year Plan, the national policy, even at the expense of reducing imports relating to civilian consumption and peacetime industries. For this, an "adjustment in the supply and demand for goods," in other words, controls, were necessary. This was the real implication of the otherwise abstract three principles.

Soon after this, the Marco Polo Bridge Incident plunged Japan into protracted war in China. Even if war had not broken out, the decision that direct economic control might be needed was already enshrined in the three principles. The Japanese economy was now thrust into extraordinarily difficult straits.

THE CLAW MARKS OF WAR
(1937–1945)

Japanese wait for their food rations. The wartime controlled economy has begun to impact on the lives of Japan's people.

1937	July	The Marco Polo Bridge Incident leads to full-scale war between Japan and China
	September	A ¥2.5 billion special military budget is passed. Three economic control laws are enacted.
	October	The Cabinet Planning Board is established and begins drawing up materials mobilization plans.
1938	April	The National General Mobilization Law is promulgated. Electric power is placed under state management, marking the beginning of increasingly strong economic controls.
1939	January	Hiranuma Kiichiro becomes prime minister.
	September	Abe Nobuyuki is appointed prime minister. World War II breaks out in Europe.
1940	January	Yonai Mitsumasa is appointed prime minister and forms a cabinet.
	July	Konoe Fumimaro becomes prime minister for a second time.
	September	The new economic order proposal creates an uproar. Japan, Germany, and Italy sign the Tripartite Pact. Commodities are in short supply. Foreign currency reserves are exhausted.
1941	June	War breaks out between Germany and the Soviet Union.
	July	Japanese troops are stationed in southern Indochina, prompting the United States to embargo oil exports to Japan.
	October	Tojo Hideki becomes prime minister.
	December	Japan commences hostilities in the Pacific and in six months captures most of Southeast Asia and parts of the Pacific.
1942	June	Japan is defeated at Midway.
	August	The battle of Guadalcanal begins. The tide of war begins to turn against Japan.
1944	July	The Mariana Islands fall to U.S. forces.
	October	U.S. troops land in the Philippines.
1945		Bombing raids on the Japanese mainland intensify, reducing Japan's major cities to ashes.
	April	U.S. forces land in Okinawa.
	August	Atomic bombs are dropped on Hiroshima and Nagasaki. The Soviet Union enters the war against Japan. The war ends.

Lecture 3

THE CLAW MARKS OF WAR
(1937–1945)

Today I will be talking about the economy in the period from the War in China to the end of the Pacific War. This is a depressing period, but at the same time it was an important period that in a number of respects determined the direction that Japan would take after the war. For this reason, I will go into it in some detail.

War broke out between Japan and China on July 7, 1937, when Japanese troops clashed with Chinese at the Marco Polo Bridge on the outskirts of Beijing. From there, the war expanded unremittingly under the pressure of expansionists within the army who demanded that Japan should send troops to beat China into meeting its demands. That a small clash should precipitate such a major conflagration was in reality due to the fact that relations between Japan and China had already broken down irrevocably.

By way of background to the prehistory, as it were, of the Sino-Japanese War, I should say something briefly about Japan's economic maneuverings in northern China. Having established the state of Manchukuo, Japan was trying to develop its resources within the framework of a controlled economy, but it became clear that Manchuria was not able to supply enough of the commodities that Japan expected to be able to obtain. Plans by the Guandong Army and the South Manchuria Railway Company for moving into northern China, and the gross ambitions on the part of the army already stationed in that region melded in the summer of 1935 in the form of undisguised political and economic encroachment. Economically, Japan's goal was to acquire the five major resources from the region: first, coal, of which there were thought to be inexhaustible reserves; second, iron ore; third salt

87

for industrial use, made by evaporation under the sun along the northern China coast, but which Japan imported at the time from Africa; and fourth and fifth, cotton and wool.

Japan applied an assortment of political and military pressures to separate the northern regions from the control of the Nanjing government and to install a regime friendly to Japan. Relations with China were thus irreparably damaged, and the northern regions of China were a tinderbox ready to explode. Ishihara Kanji, as I noted in my last lecture, had not wanted a war for five years, but in the end he was pushed into it by the expansionists. Thus began eight years of war.

THE BEGINNING OF ECONOMIC CONTROLS

The outbreak of war in China came as a major shock to a domestic economy that was already in dire straits, and it was the signal for the government to impose direct controls. The idea that a capitalist free-market economy had reached a dead end and that economic controls and planning were the answer was widely held in Japan. The fact that only the Soviet economy, with its five-year economic plans, continued to thrive and develop despite the depression was taken to be evidence of the success of a planned economy, but criticism of capitalism and a support for controls and planning were not the exclusive province of socialists. Many in the military and the bureaucracy were also inclined to such ideas. The commanding officers at the general staff headquarters were of the view that economic planning was necessary to conduct war under a national mobilization. In Manchuria, Japanese bureaucrats were working to build a managed economy. From left and right alike, the free-market economy was under attack.

Japan was not Manchuria, and it should not have been easy to introduce controls and planning within Japan proper, since the business community could hardly have been expected to take the introduction of controls and planning lying down. Yet circumstances conspired to ensure that controls were introduced. The question is why were they introduced so quickly?

A ¥2.5 billion emergency military budget
With the commencement of hostilities in China, in September 1937 the army demanded ¥2.5 billion in emergency military spending, almost as much as the entire national budget for fiscal 1937, which ran to ¥2.8 billion. The international balance of payments had been in deficit ever since Finance Minister Baba expanded fiscal spending, and obviously imports were about to increase further. Balancing the international payments being one of the stated goals of Yoshino and Kaya's Three Principles, it called for extraordinary measures to hold a lid on imports, so the government embarked on a policy of economic controls and planning.

Economic controls
At an extraordinary session of the Diet in September 1937, the same session that passed the ¥2.5 billion military budget, three wartime control laws were hastily pushed through. These three laws—the Temporary Capital Adjustment Law, the Law Relating to Temporary Export and Import Commodities Measure, and the Law for the Application of the Armament Industry Mobilization Law— had a major impact on the economy thereafter.

Article 1 of the Law relating to Temporary Export and Import Commodities Measure specified that in the event that it is "particularly necessary that the government secure the functioning of the national economy in connection with the China crisis, it can designate goods by order and restrict or prohibit their export or import." Article 2 permitted the government to issue ordinances or notifications on matters pertaining to, and to restrict, the manufacture of products using such designated products as materials and to issue ordinances or notifications pertaining to necessary matters concerning their "distribution, transfer, utilization, and consumption."

To put it more simply, if the government decided that certain kinds of goods were nonessential, it could limit or ban their import, and under Article 2 the government could limit or ban the manufacture of products using those goods as raw materials. The cotton industry, Japan's largest at the time, used imported raw cotton. What this meant was that the government could now restrict the imports of raw cotton, and what is more, it could restrict or ban the manufacture of cotton goods for the domestic market. It could also restrict the distribution, transfer, use, and consumption of cotton. Before one year was out, manufacture of cotton goods for the domestic market was indeed barred. The government could prohibit or cap the production of rubber, iron, and other military-related goods for general sale. All this became possible with a simple ordinance or notification from the government ministries.

Since distribution and transfer were also subject to ordinance, it was now possible to impose price controls and quotas of raw materials for producers. The Diet, without any debate worthy of the name, had enacted a monstrous law that, though targeted primarily at export and import items, gave the government jurisdiction over almost all commodities.

The Temporary Capital Adjustment Law was chiefly concerned with long-term funds and required government permission for flotation and underwriting of loans and corporate bonds for new installation, expansion, and improvement of equipment. Government permission became necessary to establish new companies and to undertake equity increases, mergers, or changes in fields of business. The government thus became empowered to control the flow of funding for establishment of new businesses and for investments in plant and equipment. To implement these new regulations, industry was classified into three groups. Class I was essential industries, consisting of armaments suppliers or directly related industries, which were granted unconditional access to funds. Textiles and other industries of relatively low military priority were placed in Class III and were barred from further new funding. Class II consisted of industries of intermediate military significance, which were handled on a case-by-case basis against predetermined criteria.

The third piece of legislation was the Law for the Application of the Armament Industry Mobilization Law. The Armament Industry Mobilization Law had been passed in 1918 to enable the military to manage, utilize, and expropriate factories, mines, and other facilities in time of war. "Manage" meant quite literally that the central government would supervise and direct production, "utilize" meant make temporary use of facilities, and "expropriate" that the government would take everything, lock, stock, and barrel, for its use. This was a horrendous piece of legislation that directly abrogated the notions of ownership and management rights. Now that war had broken out in China, the army and navy insisted on application of the 1918 law, and the order went out for the government management of factories and businesses, the thought being that only the "management" provisions would be applied in the present conflict. As a result, every decent-sized factory was placed under the supervision of the ministers of the army and navy, and military personnel were brought in to supervise production. The army and navy vied to designate factories. A further law, the Emergency Shipping Management Law, allowed the government to commandeer vessels for military use.

The Cabinet Planning Board and Materials Mobilization Plans

These items of legislation empowered the government to impose sweeping, direct controls over the Japanese economy, and shortly these powers were to be invoked. In October, an office was established called the Cabinet Planning Board, which combined the Resource Bureau, established in 1927, and the Planning Agency, which had been established under the Okada cabinet and reorganized under the Hayashi cabinet. The Resource Bureau had been assigned the task of surveying resources and making plans under the Materials Mobilization Law. The Planning Agency, originally called the Cabinet Research Bureau, had been reorganized in spring 1937 and expanded to implement the Five-Year Plan for Key Industries. The role of the newly-created Cabinet Planning Board was that of general headquarters for economic planning in wartime, the most important of its activities being the drawing up of Materials Mobilization plans.

In order that you may understand the significance of these plans, I should first speak briefly about the basic nature of the Japanese economy. The Japanese economy, since the late Meiji period, I think, has been built on the processing trade. That basic nature has not changed today. Although Japanese factories turn out large varieties of manufactured goods, the country is dependent on imports for almost all its raw materials and fuel. Cotton, wool, iron, aluminum, oil, all conceivable raw materials are imported rather than produced domestically.

These imported raw materials are processed in factories and turned into products that are then exported. When this happens, the price of the exported goods is greater than that of imported raw material. Today, for example, iron is imported as ore and exported as automobiles. In the 1930s, raw cotton was imported, and cotton textiles were shipped abroad. In each case, the value of the manufactured export is greater than that of the imported raw material, and the difference in price enables Japan to import the products it needs. This is a very different economic structure from that of, say, the United States or the Soviet Union, which have abundant domestic resources of their own. If anything, it resembles that of Britain.

The advent of war, however, means that immense quantities of goods must be imported, but the imports are swallowed up by military needs and so there is little prospect of export growth to match. In the Russo-Japanese War of 1904–5, Japan and Britain were allied, so that Japan was able to float large bond issues on the British market, despite its huge import surplus. In 1937–38, however, the international climate was no longer one that permitted Japan to float bonds abroad; Japan would have to raise the money to fund the necessary imports on its own.

This is where the Materials Mobilization plans came in. First, it had to be decided how much Japan could import, for example, in fiscal 1938. Import capacity was determined by totaling estimates of how much Japan would be able to export during that year and how much money could be raised domestically and through bond issues abroad—in other words how much money could be raised to make external payments.

Table 3.1 shows the differences in the value of Japan's imports and exports. In 1937 exports stood at ¥3.1 billion and imports at ¥3.7 billion, representing a substantial import surplus. However, closer inspection reveals a big surplus in trade to the yen bloc, consisting of Manchukuo; Guandong Province, with which Japan

**Table 3.1 Japan's Trade Accounts before the Pacific War
(million yen)**

	Total Trade			Trade with the Yen Bloc (including Northern China, Manchukuo, Guandong)			Trade with Third Countries		
	Exports	Imports	Surplus	Exports	Imports	Surplus	Exports	Imports	Surplus or Deficit
									or Deficit
1936	2,693	2,764	–71	658	394	264	2,035	2,370	–335
1937	3,175	3,783	–608	791	437	354	2,384	3,346	–962
1938	2,690	2,663	27	1,166	564	602	1,524	2,099	–575
1939	3,576	2,918	658	1,747	683	1,064	1,829	2,235	–406
1940	3,656	3,453	203	1,867	756	1,111	1,789	2,697	–908
1941	2,651	2,899	–248	1,659	855	804	992	2,044	–1,052

Source: Ministry of International Trade and Industry data

could trade in yen; and northern China, into which Japan had made an economic penetration. The import surplus vis-à-vis third countries requiring transactions in dollars or pounds, however, was even larger, at almost ¥1 billion. It was thus not possible to achieve a trade balance if Japan was bringing in some ¥3.7 billion in imports.

The Materials Mobilization plans were drawn up on the assumption that Japan could import only within the bounds of the total raised by export efforts and by scraping domestically and overseas for funds. In other words, a ceiling was placed on imports. As is clear from the totals row at the bottom of table 3.2, the government planned ¥3.0 billion in imports in 1938; in other words, it was initially estimated that if ¥3.0 billion in foreign currency could be garnered from exports and so forth, then the country would be able to import that amount.

However, export numbers came in far below expectations. For one thing, 1938 was the year in which the United States, which had been recovering from the Great Depression, fell into a sharp economic slump, so Japanese exports also fell. Secondly, with the priority on armaments production, restrictions on the imports of raw cotton and other goods had triggered a slowdown in exports of cotton goods. Faced with the need to cut imports, the Japanese government revised its figures at the end of June of that year to ¥2.5 billion.

This set in motion a vicious cycle of flagging exports that required imports to be further curtailed. In order to ensure that military production was not impeded, ordinary consumer goods had to be cut back. Every commodity imaginable became subject to rationing, and confusion due to unfamiliarity with the new rules helped produce sudden, serious shortages.

The import capacity figures shown in table 3.2 fell to ¥2.4 billion in fiscal 1939. There was a slight uptick in fiscal 1940 to ¥2.6 billion, the increase that year being due first to price rises under inflationary pressure and second to the outbreak of World War II, which prompted a spurt in military goods imports, with the Bank of Japan digging into its specie reserves in anticipation of imports eventually being cut off. In 1941 imports nosedived. It was clear that if Japan—having founded its economy on the processing trade—was to reduce imports, an overall production expansion was out of the question. Precious supplies of imported raw materials were being directed to military uses, with the result that raw materials for consumer goods and exports continued their precipitous downslide. The crux of the Japanese economy in this period was how much foreign currency could be raised to pay for imports. Foreign currency remained Japan's biggest bottleneck right up to the start of the Pacific War.

Table 3.2 Import Capacity under Materials Mobilization Plans (major items; million yen)

	1938	1938 (revised)	Jan.–Mar. 1939	FY 1939	FY 1940	Third Quarter, FY 1940	Fourth Quarter, FY 1940	First Quarter, FY 1941	FY 1941
Iron and Steel	557.1	442.3	390.4	497.2	469.1	259.6	270.4	133.2	54.2
Nonferrous Metals	293.9	300.4	351.6	347.9	284.4	187.2	256.4	203.6	98.9
Textiles and Paper	853.9	586.7	536.6	497.5	770.1	422.8	432.8	427.2	345.9[b]
Fuel	524.8	417.0	312.0	282.5	229.2	204.0	351.2	301.6	112.3
Foodstuff	43.9	34.3	22.3	23.9	142.4	46.0	8.0	55.6	33.3
Total[c]	3,056.9	2,554.3	2,230.3	2,395.0	2,629.0	1,614.0	1,846.4	1,600.0	787.6

Source: Nakamura Takafusa and Hara Akira (eds.), *Gendaishi Shiryo: Kokka Sodoin: (1) Keizai* (Materials in Modern History: National mobilization 1: The economy) Misuzu Shobo. 1969. p 67.
[a] In the case of January–March and quarterly plans, the annual rate was derived by multiplying by 4. All figures are computed from original tallies, and rounded.
[b] Includes leather, rubber, and lumber.
[c] The total includes, in addition to the items listed above, chemicals, fertilizer, machinery, and other commodities.

The National Mobilization Law

Next, the National Mobilization Law was passed. This legislation was drawn up by the Cabinet Planning Board under the direction of the army. Article 1 defined "national mobilization" as "controlled management of personnel and material resources in order that the forces of the nation can be utilized with maximum effectiveness to achieve the goals of national defense in wartime (including here and hereinafter crises and incidents analogous to war)." The part in parentheses permitted the law to be invoked in connection with the China crisis.

Article 2 of the law defined "mobilization commodities," and Article 3 listed "mobilization tasks," which included the production of goods, transportation, communications, finance, education and training, experimental research, and police. There then followed a series of provisions stating that mobilization could be carried out as necessary by means of a single order from the government. Article 4 provided for conscription, and Article 5 for ordering the cooperation of the public and corporations in mobilization tasks. Article 6 permitted the government to issue orders concerning deployment, hiring, dismissal, wages, and other working conditions, and Article 7 to issue orders concerning labor disputes, including the right to terminate or prohibit labor actions. Article 8 provided for orders concerning the production, repair, distribution, transfer, disposal, use, and consumption of goods. Article 9 allowed the government to restrict or ban imports or exports and conversely to order companies to import or export.

Article 11 was to create problems later. This article empowered the government to restrict or ban the establishment of corporations, increases of equity capital, mergers, changes in purpose of business, flotation of corporate bonds, and second and subsequent paying in of shares. It also allowed the government to issue orders concerning management decisions, such as the disposal of profits, and the manner in which financial institutions deployed their funds. Article 13 reiterated the content of the earlier Armament Industry Mobilization Law, allowing the government to manage, utilize, or expropriate factories and places of business covered under mobilization tasks, and extended these powers to include land and buildings. Under Article 16, the government was empowered to restrict, ban, or order the new construction, expansion, and improvement of production and transportation facilities. Article 17 provided for the establishment of cartels, while Article 18 empowered the government to order the establishment of compulsory cartels. Article 19 permitted the government to issue orders concerning prices, transportation fees, storage fees, insurance premiums, rental fees, and processing fees. In addition, it was also able to restrict the press.

This was a heavy-duty piece of legislation that in effect enabled the government to do anything it wanted by means of a single order from the emperor, a government ministry, or other government office. When the bill was submitted to the Diet, the political parties protested that it was equivalent to Nazi Germany's Enabling Act and that if passed there would be no need for a Diet. In the end, however, the law was enacted, under pressure from the army.

Following the enactment of this National Mobilization Law, a series of related orders, imperial orders, and ministry orders were issued, prescribing controls on personnel resources—for example hiring restrictions—national conscription, conscription of merchant sailors, and reporting by the public of useful skills. Orders were promulgated for the control of goods, everyday necessities, and prices.

A series of orders were issued to impose controls on corporate financing. These included the Companies' Profits, Dividends, and Accommodations Order, the Order for Control of Corporate Finance and Accounting, and the Bank Funds Utilization Order. The Temporary Capital Adjustment Law had targeted only long-term financing. Under the National Mobilization Law, even short-term bank loans for operating funds were brought under government control. When at the end of 1938 the army attempted to invoke Article 11 to order banks to lend funds to firms and to restrict stock dividends, the minister of finance in the first Konoe cabinet, Ikeda Shigeaki, formerly of Mitsui, represented the consensus of the business community and clashed head on with the army. The Bank Funds Utilization Order represented a compromise between the army and the Ministry of Finance.

State management of electric power

I would like to make one other comment in this connection. Around this time, the electric power industry was brought under state control. From the early 1920s on, electric utility companies had competed fiercely to expand, with the result that many ended up in financial difficulty and were unable to repay their obligations. The big banks therefore took the power companies by the scruff of the neck and forced them into a cartel known as the Denryoku Renmei (Electric Power Federation). In reality, the power companies were managed by representatives of the banks, who went in as advisors. Okumura Kiwao of the Ministry of Posts and Telegraphs then drew up a proposal to the effect that in order to cap excessive competition and eliminate waste, the entire country's electric power industry had to be controlled. A single company, Nippon Hassoden, the Japan Electric Power Generation and Transmission Company, would be set up to operate the generating facilities, hydroelectric power stations, thermal power stations, and long-distance transmission lines that were owned by the power companies. The power companies would be reduced to local power distribution. The industry cried foul, but the climate of wartime controls ensured that this legislation passed too, except for thermal power stations.

Later, in 1941, the power companies were all liquidated, and regional power distribution companies were set up. After World War II, Nippon Hassoden was dissolved, and the distribution companies became nine regional power companies, owning both generating and transmission equipment, such as Tokyo Electric and Kansai Electric. Japan's present electric power utilities are thus the descendants of the regional power distribution companies of this period.

Stronger controls and tighter foreign exchange

In this manner, state control of industry rapidly progressed. The base for production activities was import capacity, but when this was controlled, exports didn't do well, so imports would be cut. This would rebound in the form of further export stagnation, resulting in shortages of goods. If inflation in northern China progressed, anything could be exported to China for a profit, since the Japanese yen and the currency in northern China had the same value, but this didn't bring in foreign currency, so Japan couldn't boost imports. Now Japan had to control exports to China. As the state of the economy deteriorated, the controls were strengthened, in a vicious cycle.

The army and navy received huge emergency military budgets. Some 60 percent of these budgets was directed not to the pursuit of the war in China, but to build military stockpiles against the coming war in the Pacific. Figure 3.1 shows the ballooning of military spending from ¥2.9 billion in 1937 to ¥4 billion, ¥5 billion, and ¥6 billion, respectively, over the subsequent three years. Production in armaments industries could not keep pace, with the result that there was a jump in the number of small-business subcontractors. The low technological levels of these small firms generated a good deal of waste, and it is reported that many of the machine tools that were produced were of such poor quality as to be useless.

Since military supplies were first in line for the limited imports, everyday consumer items fell into short supply, especially cotton manufactures, woolen textiles, and rubber tires. There was downward pressure on the standard of living, and substitutes became routine, cotton being replaced by staple fiber, and cowskin leather shoes by cheaper pigskin or sharkskin. Eventually these substitutes, too, would become unavailable. Consumer goods manufacturers and merchants found their businesses idle and were unable to make ends meet. A sharp division emerged within the domestic economy between the prosperous military supply industries and the languishing civilian industries.

Government controls continued to expand in scope. Let us consider the mechanism involved. When supplies of goods fell short, their prices naturally went up. This created the fear of inflation, so the government would set an official price to cap prices. Merchants and dealers would take countersteps. Since the official

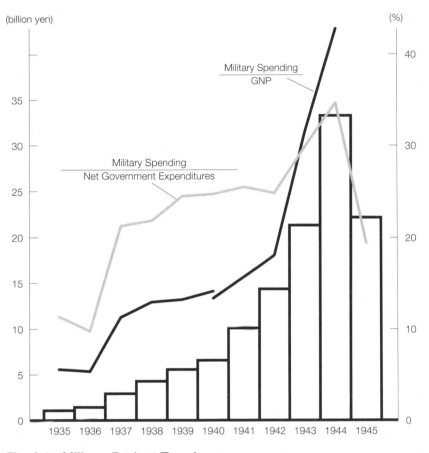

Fig. 3.1. Military Budget Trends

Sources: Ando Yoshio (ed.), *Kindai Nihon Keizai Shi Yoran* (Handbook of Modern Japanese Economic History), The University of Tokyo Press, 1975. GNP figures are estimates by Ohkawa Kazushi up to 1940, after which Economic Planning Agency figures are used. For this reason, two GNP ratios are given for 1940.

price was routinely less than the market price, the merchants squirreled away their merchandise and sold it by the back door on the black market. Producers stopped making products, as they could not break even at the official price, and they started looking around for other products that did not yet have an official price tag. For example, let us assume that white shirts had an official price, but striped shirts did not. Naturally, manufacturers would make nothing but striped shirts. But then there weren't any white shirts available, so the government would be forced to set an official price for striped shirts.

In fact, the government had originally intended to limit official prices only to major items, but the mechanism I have just described compelled it to extend price caps to merchandise of every kind. As the scope of official prices expanded, black market dealings flourished. An economic police was established to clamp down on the black market, and big and small merchants alike were arrested for illegal transactions.

In autumn 1939, two decisive events took place. First, World War II broke out when the German army invaded Poland and that country was split between Germany and the Soviet Union. Britain and France declared war on Germany, and the only major countries not embroiled in the war were the United States and the Soviet Union. Domestically and internationally, shortages became rife. The most basic commodities became hard to obtain, even when people had the money to buy them.

To deal with this situation, the government issued an imperial order, generally known as the September 18 Price and Wage Freeze Order, which capped the prices of all commodities and wages at their levels on September 18, 1939. The idea was that the government would freeze wages and prices in order to buy time to establish comprehensive schedules of wages and prices. The official price schedule was drawn up the following year, setting official prices for 40,000 items in the capital area and 430,000 items in the regions. Official rates were also set for wages and government salaries so as to prevent wage and salary increases from pushing up costs and eventually product prices. Age-based seniority was officially incorporated into pay-scale calculations at this time and became the practice throughout the entire country.

As I will discuss in a later lecture, price control legislation was once again introduced following the 1973 oil crisis. Shiina Etsusaburo, then vice president of the Liberal Democratic Party, who had been in the Ministry of Industry and Commerce during the war, is said to have remarked that if price controls began it would be necessary to set a price on everything right down to plant pots. I am entirely in agreement with Mr. Shiina here. If the government attempts to set prices that should be determined by supply and demand in the marketplace, there will inevitably be distortions. In the socialist countries, this is an issue that is constantly debated. The liberalization that has taken place in Hungary and more recently in China is a manifestation of the efforts to do away with these distortions.

Effects on living standards

The second event occurred in autumn 1939. Western Japan was visited by drought, as a result of which power shortages occurred and the rice harvest in western Japan and in Korea was poor. Although the rice harvest was not seriously below par, the public believed otherwise, and there was near panic. At one point toward the end of the year, there was only half a day's supply stock of rice in the rice shops in Tokyo, and the government feared riots. The government was forced to buy rice from Thailand and French Indochina, now Vietnam, by the use of several expedient financial devices.

By this time shortages of imported sugar, candy made from that sugar, and other everyday items began to be severely felt. There were even shortages of matches. It is said that in Nagoya, the ration was five matches per person per day.

In the end, everyday necessities—including rice, sugar, miso (fermented bean paste), and soy sauce—became rationed, and ration coupons were issued to the public. In 1941, the Foodstuff Control Special Account was set up, under which the government bought up all the rice produced and distributed it, the rationed rice being mixed with foreign rice. Extravagance was anathema: production of high-quality silk kimono, lacquerware, and handicrafts was banned, and the public was ordered to turn over valuables made of gold or silver. In the streets, outrageous incidents occurred in which patrols slashed the sleeves of women's kimono with scissors. Men wore staple fiber uniform-like suits and women baggy trousers (*monpe*).

The new economic order

One contentious issue at this point centered on why armaments production did not grow as much as the government had anticipated. The dominant view was that this pointed to the need for further socialization of industry and government planning. Rooted in critiques of the capitalist system, the argument went along the following lines. Companies operate with the goal of generating a profit. The reason that armaments output does not improve is that companies still think first in terms of profit, despite the national crisis. The nature of the corporation has to be changed so that the goal of its activities is production rather than profit.

Ryu Shintaro, a journalist for the *Asahi Shimbun* newspaper and later its editor-in-chief for a period after the war, expressed this line of thinking in a book entitled *Nihon Keizai no Saihensei* (Reorganization of the Japanese economy), which promptly became a best-seller. To summarize his argument briefly, Japanese economy, he claimed, was in a cycle of shrinking output owing to constraints on imports and growing military demand. The way in which firms operated on the basis of the profit principle had to be fundamentally changed and all obstacles to production capacity eliminated. It was the responsibility of corporate leaders to open their books for inspection and to permit government control of their profits and to raise output. The free-market economy aspects of capitalism had to be eliminated by controlling companies' financial affairs and profits and by turning companies into organizations motivated by production rather than profit. Ryu proposed that the reformed corporations take part in regional and industrial cartels, which would take responsibility for implementing economic controls. Since the cartels would not need to consider individual members' profits, controls would have their objectives undiluted by other concerns. Japan should switch from external controls, imposed from above, to internal controls, imposed from below.

At about this time, there was an organization called the Showa Kenkyukai (Showa Research Society), headed by Goto Ryunosuke, which served as a policy think tank for Konoe Fumimaro. Ryu was a core member of this group's economic division. The Showa Kenkyukai formulated for Prince Konoe a Draft Proposal for the Reorganization of the Japanese Economy, instantiating Ryu's ideas. This document took the position that, once priority is given to production, companies had no responsibility to their shareholders other than to provide a certain level of dividends. Ownership and management of corporate capital needed to be separated. The company's primary obligation was to produce for the nation. Managers would be given the status of government officials and would undertake to boost production on the basis of commands from above. The proposal, grossly naive in thinking that corporate managers would change their spots so easily, manifests the principle ideas of socialization and the introduction of planning in industry.

Just at this time, in 1940, Konoe was appointed prime minister for a second term. Konoe proposed a new national polity and created the *Taisei Yokusankai* (The Imperial Rule Assistance Association), which incorporated reformist groups and political parties. After enjoying a brief burst of national popularity, the movement petered out, but not before the Cabinet Planning Board created an uproar by coming up with plans for a new economic structure based on the Showa Kenkyukai's proposal. The board's version tended to emphasize control from the outside and from above rather than from the inside and from below, as in the Showa Kenkyukai's earlier draft, but it put forward explicitly the notion of a shift in underlying principles, from a profit-based to an output-based economy.

The business community rose in a storm of protest when news of this proposal leaked out. The authors of the proposal, Akinaga Tsukizo (former army officer), Mori Hideoto and Sakomizu Hisatsune (both former Ministry of Finance officials), and other Cabinet Planning Board officials were attacked as reds and communists. In what came to be known as the Cabinet Planning Board Incident, Wada Hiroo, Inaba Hidezo, and Katsumata Seiichi, who had been studying Marxist economics within the board, were arrested on charges of violating the Public Peace Maintenance Law. The minister of Commerce and Industry, Kobayashi Ichizo, a former businessman, fired Kishi Nobusuke, the administrative undersecretary of the ministry.

The upshot of all this was a compromise between the Cabinet Planning Board and army groups and the business community. A Framework for the Establishment of a New Economic Order was drawn up in which all references to a shift from a profit-based to an output-based economy were eliminated, but forced cartels known as control associations (*toseikai*) were to be set up to impose economic controls on individual industries in conformity with government policies.

Conscription of labor and reorganization of industry

By this time, labor shortages had begun to arise in the armaments industries. Over a million young males who had formed the core workforce in agriculture and other industries had been conscripted into the army. At the same time, expanding military supply factories wanted all the workers they could get. Labor shortages naturally followed. So a National Conscription Ordinance was issued in 1939 under the provisions of the National Mobilization Law, the scope of this ordinance being expanded as time went by. Since the need to secure food supplies prevented the government from drafting people from rural areas who were engaged in the agricultural production, young workers in commerce, services, textiles, and other nonmilitary industries found themselves hauled of to work at military supply plants at the drop of a draft slip.

Reorganization of small businesses was a serious issue. In wartime, many small businesses fell into the category of non-essential industries. Many who had for generations made their livelihoods in these trades no longer had anything to sell under the government controls and were hard pressed to make a living. The Ministry of Commerce and Industry came up with the idea of closing down most of these operations and mobilizing their labor in military industries. Not unsurprisingly, this proposal came in for heated opposition from the Chambers of Commerce and Industry—largely representing small businesses—and other business organizations.

The Framework for the Establishment of a New Economic Order contained the following statement. "Small businesses will be fostered and supported, but in the event that maintaining them is difficult, they should voluntarily be reorganized and merged, and assistance will be provided to ensure a smooth transfer of operations." The phrase "will be fostered and supported" had been inserted at the insistence of the business community, but the government of the time had no intention of doing anything of the kind, but wanted instead to reorganize and merge them and transfer their labor to military industries. The wording of the proviso reflected the government's true intent. Large and small reorganization programs were subsequently carried out, with the result that people in small and petty businesses, mostly traditional trades, lost their family businesses and were forced to wield hammers and other unfamiliar tools. The estimates of the working population during the war period, shown in figure 3.2, indicate the extent of the drop in employment in commerce and service industries.

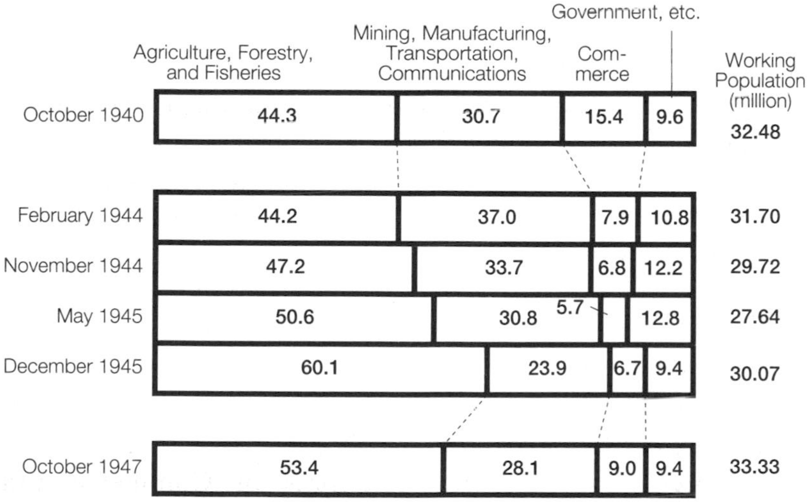

	Agriculture, Forestry, and Fisheries	Mining, Manufacturing, Transportation, Communications	Commerce	Government, etc.	Working Population (million)
October 1940	44.3	30.7	15.4	9.6	32.48
February 1944	44.2	37.0	7.9	10.8	31.70
November 1944	47.2	33.7	6.8	12.2	29.72
May 1945	50.6	30.8	5.7	12.8	27.64
December 1945	60.1	23.9	6.7	9.4	30.07
October 1947	53.4	28.1	9.0	9.4	33.33

Fig. 3.2. Wartime Working Population 1940–1947

Sources: Figures for 1940 are national census data; the remainder are estimates by the author and Arai Genbu.

THE PACIFIC WAR

When war broke out with China, the army had confidently antic-ipated that the Chinese would immediately give up. However, the army found itself barely maintaining a front that stretched across an immense geographical area under tenacious Chinese resistance. It had established the North China Development Corporation and the Central China Promotion Corporation and had inaugurated plans that attempted to develop coal, iron ore, salt, and other resources and bring them to Japan for use in munitions plants, but there was no prospect of bringing the war to a resolution. Given these conditions, why, one may ask, did Japan become embroiled in a war with the United States, Great Britain, and Holland?

Economic relations with the United States deteriorate

I believe that from an economic perspective, we can sum up the reasons as follows. First, Japan naturally took the position that the reason China would not give up was that it was supported by Great Britain and the United States, so it applied pressure on the United States, and especially Great Britain, in occupied China. When it blockaded British lease territory in Tianjin during its occupation of China, relations with these two countries, which had already deteriorated, went even further downhill. In July 1939, during negotiations with Britain over the blockade of the leasehold territory, the United States announced that it was abro-gating the Japan-U.S. Treaty of Commerce and Navigation.

Abrogation was a momentous step. The treaty had contained provisions granting Japan favored nation status. In other words, the most advantageous conditions of those granted to any other country in a treaty applied to Japan; moreover, the United States was prohibited from restricting trade with Japan. At the outbreak of hostilities in China, Japan had not declared war with that coun-try because under this treaty Japan was able to import strategic materials freely from the United States. If it had declared war, the provisions of the Neutrality Act, which prohibited U.S. exports of military goods to countries engaged in war, would apply. Not declaring war thus made it easier to obtain raw materials and fuel.

Now, however, the United States had revoked the treaty. Once the six-month grace period was up, the treaty would cease to exist, and the United States would be free to restrict or prohibit exports to Japan. Then, in August, Germany and the Soviet Union concluded their Non-Aggression Treaty, and in September World War II broke out. Japan broke off negotiations for an alliance with Germany and Italy and sought to improve relations with the United States, but the negotiations did not go well. The United States had lost all faith in Japan.

Once the treaty expired, the United States began to use export restrictions as a weapon against Japan, starting with a ban on exports of machine tools. The most important resources for which Japan depended on the United States—gasoline, crude oil, and scrap iron—were kept back for the time being as a potential trump card.

In May 1940, German troops rolled across Europe, forced France to surrender, and planned for an invasion of Britain. In Japan, Germany's total victory was thought to be a matter of time, and so the situation in East Asia was seen as having suddenly changed. As a result of the surrender of France and of the Dutch government taking refuge in London, French Indochina (Vietnam and Cambodia) and the Dutch East Indies (Indonesia) suddenly lost their overlords. Britain, too, it seemed might crumple under a German invasion. These countries' colonies in Southeast Asia were rich in resources: French Indochina offered rice and coal; British Malaya rubber, iron ore, and tin; the Dutch East Indies the oil that Japan desperately needed. Within the army the opinion was voiced that Japan should act now to bring these lands within its control and obtain these resources before Germany or the United States could do so.

The army overthrew the cautious Yonai cabinet, and in July 1940 installed Konoe as prime minister for a second time. On July 27, the Imperial Headquarters and Government Liaison Council adopted a highly dangerous new policy—the Outline of Dealing with the Situation Accompanying Changes in the World Situation. If the war in China ended, an occupation of Southeast Asia would be considered. If it was not brought to a conclusion, an opportu-

nity would be sought for an attack on Southeast Asia. Ties with
Germany and Italy were to be strengthened, even at risk of war
with Great Britain and the United States.

Estimates of national strength in 1941

In September 1940, Japan occupied the northern portion of
French Indochina (around Hanoi and Haiphong) and signed the
Axis Agreement with Germany and Italy. Relations with Great
Britain and the United States promptly took a definitive turn for
the worse. Prime Minister Konoe and his foreign minister,
Matsuoka Yosuke, had taken the step of signing the Tripartite
Alliance because they had thought that they would be able to
bring Germany, Italy, and also the Soviet Union over to their side
to pressure the United States into a compromise that would end
the war in China and allow Japan to build the Greater East Asia
Co-Prosperity Sphere. However, beginning in fall 1940, relations
between Germany and the Soviet Union cooled, and four-power
cooperation became an impossibility. In April 1941, Foreign
Minister Matsuoka visited Europe and concluded the Japan-
U.S.S.R Neutrality Pact, but during his absence talks between
Japan and the United States began, arranged by segments of the
army and private citizens with the aim of negotiating with the
United States a solution to the war in China. However, while these
negotiations were protracted, relations between Germany and the
Soviets collapsed, and in June 1941, German troops invaded the
Soviet Union. With that, the plan that had originally motivated the
signing of the Tripartite Alliance fell through.

The army, navy, and government debated whether to attack
the Soviet Union or to advance southward. It was concluded that
the U.S.S.R. should be attacked just as it was ready to fall and that
for the time being, bases would be sought in southern French
Indochina. The decision to station troops in southern Indochina
was reached in July. In stinging retaliation for this move, the
United States embargoed all oil exports to Japan and froze all
Japanese assets in the United States, which meant that all Japanese
funds in that country became unusable. For practical purposes,
this was the economic equivalent of breaking off diplomatic rela-

tions. At this point, the army and navy inclined to the view that Japan should expeditiously open war on the United States.

The United States was Japan's largest oil supplier at the time. Japan's stocks as of October 1941 were 8.4 million kiloliters.* That was all the oil stocks Japan had up its sleeve. If the army and navy were to wage war, 8.4 million kiloliters would only last two years. Since oil was needed even in peacetime, if the oil embargo were to continue for two years, the combined Japanese fleet would become a paper tiger, and planes would be unable to fly even if no war was fought. If Japan was to open hostilities with the United States, now was the time possible the army and navy strategists held.

At a meeting attended by the emperor on September 6, the decision was reached that unless some prospect of concluding negotiations was possible by early October, Japan would launch an attack on the United States. When early October came around without progress in negotiations, Prime Minister Konoe could not bring himself to open hostilities; he clashed with Tojo Hideki, minister of the army, who insisted on the September 6 decision being carried out, and was forced to resign from office.

Tojo became prime minister at the recommendation of Kido Koichi, the lord keeper of Privy Seal, who was the one person who might at a pinch have been able to hold the army at bay and avoid a war. At the instructions of the emperor, the September 6 decision was revoked, and the debate as to whether to make war or not carried on into the Imperial Headquarters and Government Liaison Council. At the meeting with the emperor at which the final decision was made, Lieutenant-General Suzuki Teiichi, director general of the Cabinet Planning Board, gave an explanation, which I will now outline.

If Japan were to declare war on Great Britain and the United states, the question was whether it would be able to maintain its wartime economy. First, assuming that Japan was able to occupy the resource-rich regions of Southeast Asia, it would be able to

*Today, despite much effort to economize on oil, Japan imports more than 200 million kiloliters of crude oil. 8.4 million kiloliters is equivalent to about two weeks' supply by present-day standards.

maintain supplies of materials at the level of the Materials Mobilization Plan for Fiscal 1941 only if it were able to secure at least three million tons of merchant shipping, that is, cargo vessels excluding those used by the army and navy in their operations.

Second, if war were to break out, shipping would be damaged. If damage were held to about 800,000 to 1,000,000 tons a year, with a domestic shipbuilding capacity of 600,000 tons it would be possible to hold the 3 million ton line. To this end it would unequivocally be necessary to secure 300,000 tons of steel for shipbuilding.

There would be enough rice, since this was obtainable from Thailand and French Indochina. If the Dutch East Indies fell to Japan, large quantities of nickel, tin, bauxite for making aluminum, rubber latex, and other valuable commodities would become available.

On the matter of oil, an advance into Southeast Asia would likely yield 850,000 kiloliters in the first year, 2.6 million kiloliters in the second year, and 5.3 million kiloliters in the third year. Adding in the present stocks of 840,000 kiloliters, stocks would be projected to fall to a bare minimum by the end of the second year, but in the third year the supply situation would improve, giving Japan a little leeway, Suzuki contended.

Thus, it was the judgment of the Cabinet Planning Board that despite the perils, a wartime economy was sustainable. On the other hand, if Japan did not make war, the outlook was as follows. Apart from materials available within the yen bloc, those materials for which Japan was dependent on the U.S. and U.K. blocs would become difficult to obtain. The biggest snag was liquid fuel, namely oil. Even if Japan were to put an effort into constructing artificial petroleum industries—coal liquefaction—it would not be able to cover the needed quantities, hindering military readiness and production expansions. Meanwhile, the United States would be free to boost its military readiness, with the ensuing gap widening until Japan was unable to wage war. The assessment from the economic side was that if Japan was to go to war, now was the time.

That assessment was, needless to say, over optimistic. In fact, one might say that it was a positive assessment intended to bring war about. Setting aside issues of military strategy, the most overly optimistic issue from an economic viewpoint was the issue of shipping. It was predicted that Japan would be able to make up losses of 800,000–1,000,000 tons a year, but in reality losses far outstripped this figure, as we will see later.

The Pacific War begins

The Tojo cabinet decided that it would attempt to conclude negotiations by the end of November and that if it did not succeed in doing so, Japan would go to war. The Japanese government made a provisional offer that traded a withdrawal from southern Indochina in return for a lifting of the oil embargo, but finally a note from Secretary of State Cordell Hull came, dated November 26, that denied even the existence of Manchukuo as a state. Japan decided for war. On sending Japan the Hull note, the United States clearly abandoned all further attempt at peaceful resolution. I believe that the Hull note, in which the United States declared that it recognized none of Japan's actions since the creation of Manchukuo, was the strongest possible expression of the United State's position and that the United States had decided to go to war and was simply waiting for Japan to make the first strike.

Be that as it may, on December 8,* 1941, hostilities commenced. The war progressed far more advantageously than Japan had originally anticipated, and within six months, Japan had occupied, to the west, Burma, Thailand, Malaya, Singapore, the Philippines and Borneo, as well as the Celebes, Java and Sumatra in the Dutch East Indies. To the east, Japan had not only landed in parts of New Guinea, but even occupied the Solomon Islands southeast of New Gunea. In China, it gained control over the lease territories in Shanghai and Hong Kong. The so-called Greater East Asia Co-Prosperity Sphere appeared to become a reality overnight.

Looking at government documents from this period one is taken aback at how many chickens were being counted before

---

*December 7 in the United States owing to the international date line.

they were hatched. The Greater East Asia Construction Council was set up and discussed issues like how many resources would be available in 5 and 10 years time and how many supervisors would need to be posted to regions from Japan, as the leader of the Co-Prosperity Sphere. Everyone was swept up with the euphoria of victory, and no one was paying attention to the efforts needed to pursue the war. The Materials Mobilization Plan for 1942 shows no sign of an effort to scale up production in order to pursue the Pacific War, but reeks of attempting to make do with an extension of previous plans

The euphonious mood lasted only six months. The Japanese navy's fighting capacity was decisively broken at the Battle of Midway in June 1942, at which it lost four of its key aircraft carriers. With the Battle of Midway, the balance of Japanese and American naval forces turned, and Japan was forced into a defensive posture for the rest of the war.

Limited transportation capacity

Meanwhile, the Materials Mobilization plans underwent a change. Foreign currency constraints on import capacity were no longer a problem. Japan had occupied resource-supplying regions and was now able to obtain goods using Japanese yen or military scrip denominated in local currencies. Foreign currency was no longer needed.

Japan began a rush into Southeast Asia. Big companies moved into the occupied territories to begin resource development. Oil drilling equipment, technicians, and workers were brought from the oil fields in Niigata and Akita to Sumatra, where they were set to the task of restarting oil production. In Malaya, the Philippines, and elsewhere, Japanese mining companies began ore extraction at the command of the military. No attempt was made to set up control companies or engage in planning, existing companies being assigned to development in an effort to obtain oil, nickel ore, copper ore, bauxite, chrome ore, and manganese ore. Mitsui Mining was in charge of 3 mining operations, Mitsubishi Mining and Nippon Mining 7 operations each, and Ishihara Industries 11 operations. In addition, a good many textile companies and commercial trading companies worked to develop raw cotton sources in a variety of localities throughout Southeast Asia. Some yarn spinning companies moved equipment into the region and set up local production. Nippon Chisso and Nippon Soda engaged in hydroelectric development and attempted to start up aluminum refining and chemicals industries.

Now that it had access to the resources of Southeast Asia, Japan's problem was transportation. Unless it could ship the materials to Japan, they were no use for armaments production. As director general of the Cabinet Planning Board explained, the biggest question was how much civilian transportation capacity Japan would be able to secure. Once the war had begun, the army and navy refused to return the vessels they had conscripted for their tactical operations, so not unnaturally there weren't enough ships to go round. When tankers were needed to transport Palenbang crude oil from Sumatra, all the large tankers had been conscripted by the navy for its operations, so that it was impossible to ship adequate supplies of crude oil to Japan proper. I have heard from Okada Kikusaburo, director of strategic readiness in the Ministry of the Army at the time, that the excess crude oil was being dumped into a local river.

Thus, even in 1942, when the war was otherwise largely going well, transportation was not. Eventually, however, an even more serious problem was the absolute shortage of vessels. Table 3.3 shows Japan's merchant fleet numbers. Japan's oceangoing merchant fleet totaled 6.38 million tons at the beginning of the war. The construction figures show that Japan built 40,000 tons in the

Table 3.3 Depletion of Merchant Marine (in thousand tons)

		New Ships Built	Losses During the Year	Fleet at Year-End
December	1941	44	52	6,376
	1942	662	1,096	5,942
	1943	1,067	2,066	4,944
	1944	1,735	4,115	2,564
August	1945	465	1,502	1,527

Source: Ando Yoshio (ed.), *Kindai Nihon Keizai Shi Yoran* (Handbook of Modern Japanese Economic History), The University of Tokyo Press, Second edition, 1979.

month of December 1941, 660,000 tons in 1942, 1,070,000 tons in 1943, and 1,740,000 tons in 1944. Although these figures far surpass the annual 600,000 tons estimated at the outset of the war, they were outstripped by losses from bombings and submarine attacks. In 1943, Japan lost 2,070,000 tons, and in 1944, 4,110,000 tons, so that finally, at the end of the war, it retained only 1,500,000 tons, or less than one-fourth of its prewar fleet, and much of this was damaged and unusable. This, in my view, was the biggest economic miscalculation of the Pacific War.

The war turned against Japan in the latter half of 1942. In the battle for possession of Guadalcanal, in the Solomon Islands, the Japanese army and navy sent in their best ships in an all-out effort to relieve the Japanese forces stationed there, but these were sunk en masse. Here for the first time, the situation of the war foundered. Further battles for the Solomon Islands and New Guinea ensued in 1943, but by now American submarines had entered the sea-lanes to Southeast Asia and even the seas around Japan, resulting in ever increasing losses of vessels.

In 1944, the naval base for the combined fleet on the Truk Islands was badly damaged in a major air raid, and in June 1944 American forces landed in Saipan in the Marianas. Not only did the navy suffer irreparable setbacks, it was now possible for the United States to build airfields in Saipan from which to launch B29 bomber attacks on the Japanese mainland. Patrols could now attack the Japanese mainland and Taiwan, and from the latter half of 1944 on, the navigation routes between Japan and the southern occupied territories were effectively cut off. The war turned increasingly against Japan. Japan, for its part, drew up new Materials Mobilization plans, prioritizing the use of airplanes and ships, but it was already too late.

Estimates of national strength in August 1944

After the loss of the Marianas and the closing of the southern shipping routes, the Tojo cabinet resigned, and Koiso Kuniaki became prime minister. Officials from the Munitions Ministry, which in the meantime had absorbed the Cabinet Planning Board, submitted a report to the Supreme War Council, which stated in part.

Since the outbreak of the Great East Asian War, the material strength of our nation has declined with each successive year owing to depletion of reserves and supply sources. Damage to shipping, chiefly from enemy submarines, has been far greater that anticipated just prior to the war and has far outstripped the volume of vessels built. Not only has the number of ships in our possession rapidly dwindled, but the successive conscription of vessels for A- and B- (army and navy) use has cut sharply into C- (merchant) use shipping capacity. Thus, although we have met growing military demand at the sacrifice of the civilian sector and under the present situation are able in general to secure supplies of major foodstuffs, the situation is one in which other industries have been forced to reduce or shut down operations across the board, and even in munitions production, which constitutes our highest priority, there has undeniably been a declining trend since the peak at the beginning of fiscal 1944. The momentum is such that it will be increasingly difficult to maintain the national standard of living at present levels. In other words, at the end of fiscal 1944, in the fourth year of the war, we recognize that our national resilience has been lost.

The authors bluntly acknowledged that Japan had boosted its munitions production at the expense of the rest of national life, but that after peaking at the beginning of 1944, munitions output was heading consistently downward. By the end of the year, everything had taken a downturn. In 1945, not only would shipments of resources from Southeast Asia for all practical purposes cease, but lack of liquid fuels would likely deal a fatal blow to the transportation and production sectors. Aluminum production would decline. Munitions Ministry documents from summer 1944 reveal that confidence in Japan's ability to pursue the war had already been lost. A classic example of the shortages that followed the loss of the supply routes to Southeast Asia was the mobilization of school children to dig up pine tree roots to make pine root oil, a gasoline substitute.

American scholar Jerome Cohen, in his volume *Japan's Economy in War and Reconstruction*, writes that Japan was defeated twice, once with the closure of the shipping lanes and the second time by the air raids. Japan, in reality, held on for a year after it knew that the war was lost.

The Greater East Asia Co-Prosperity Sphere

What of the Greater East Asia Co-Prosperity Sphere? At the beginning of the war, it was known that Japan would not be able to sustain the living standards of the local peoples. One document written just before the war was quite explicit that "in the interim, it will be necessary to adopt an exploitative policy." During the Sino-Japanese War, there had been a major flood in northern China, resulting in food shortages. Nonetheless, the local army prioritized the transportation of coal and cut the number of trains supplying food. Riots broke out in Chinese cities, and inflation soared dangerously, forcing the Japanese government in 1940 to send shipments of flour and cotton goods to stabilize the local economies. Even exploiters had to stabilize local economies. But when the Pacific War came, it was no longer possible to supply the local peoples with their necessities of life. Local self-sufficiency was the rule, and even if there were real shortages, Japan lacked the spare resources to make up the gap. All it could do was issue military scrip.

The local currencies were printed in Japan and issued as military scrip. Since there was nothing to back these currency issues, inflation was inevitable. The further a region was from Japan, the harder it was to ensure the supply of goods and the worse inflation was. By any yardstick, inflation in Burma and neighboring regions reached incredible heights. Taking 1941 prices as a standard, by August 1945, prices in Burma had risen by a factor of 1,800, those in Sumatra by a factor of 33, Java by a factor of 30, Borneo by a factor of 40, Tianjin by a factor of 32, and Shinjing (present-day Changchun) in Manchukuo by a factor of 2.1. Within Japan the inflation rate rose by a factor of 1.35 when calculated on the basis of official prices, but since there was also the black market to take into account, that figure is too low. I estimate an inflation factor of about three-fold. At any rate, Japan sparked inflation in the occupied territories and made off with local goods.

Compulsory military production

Within Japan, a major overhaul of civilian industries, starting with the textile industry and small businesses, was undertaken in 1943. Nearly all firms in these civilian categories were closed down, and the bulk of the textile industry's plant and equipment was converted into scrap metal for steel production. Factories were converted to munitions production. Firms and whole industries were closed down, and their employees conscripted into munitions industries. Unbelievable as it may sound, bridge railings and streetcar tracks were removed to meet steel shortages.

The Munitions Ministry was established in November 1943. This was an amalgam of the Cabinet Planning Board and the munitions-related departments of the Ministry of Commerce and Industry, the remaining civilian departments being combined with the Ministry of Agriculture and Forestry to form the Ministry of Agriculture and Commerce. These reforms were directly linked with the munitions company system. In a nutshell, the Munitions Company Law allowed the Munitions Ministry to designate companies as especially important to the production of military goods and to assign to the president and other company representatives the status of government officials as had been envisaged in the earlier new economic order and to order production blitzes. The ideas that had been bandied around since the new economic order proposal finally found their realization. Throughout the war, 600 companies were designated under the law.

The Munitions Ministry's greatest priority was aircraft production. Without planes the war could not be fought, so it set a production target of 55,000 planes for fiscal 1944. This figure was quite unrealistic, and something in the region of 40,000 planes was closer to the ministry's real expectations. Aircraft plants expanded on a large scale in the midst of war, mobilizing much equipment and personnel in an attempt to meet the blueprint, but by summer 1944 exhaustion began to set in.

The shipbuilding industry was faced with having to make up for sunk vessels and with then increasing the fleet. An avalanche of shipbuilding plans ensued. The idea was that a certain number of vessels were to be used to convey iron ore from Southeast Asia

and coal from northern China exclusively for use in shipbuilding
and that the ships built would then be further used to carry
resources to increase shipbuilding output. But the colossal losses
and the closing of the shipping routes to Southeast Asia sent production tumbling.

In 1944, every available person was mobilized. Labor shortages were rife, since by this time four to five million people had
been drafted into the armed forces. Not only were men targeted,
women's volunteer corps were established and were put to work
in the factories, at least for a brief period. Almost all middle and
upper school classes were canceled and the students sent to work
in factories. My younger sister, then at what would be the first
year of middle school, recollects having almost no classes and
instead being taken to work in factories.

The results of these extreme efforts at munitions production
can be summed up as follows. Although airplane production was
the greatest priority, there was a major imbalance between production of engines and aircraft fuselages as table 3.4 shows.
Engines were built in large numbers, but only 26,000 fuselages
were constructed. In the case of naval craft, large vessels could no
longer be built toward the end of the war, and besides these
weren't much use anyway, so only small vessels were being constructed. Thus, the number of vessels increased overall, but the
number of tons peaked in 1944. Production of rifles, gunpowder,
and other munitions did not increase to any significant extent.

Table 3.4 Trends in Production of Military Supplies

	1941	1942	1943	1944	1945
Aircraft (units)	6,174	10,185	20,028	26,507	5,823
Engines (units)	13,022	18,498	35,368	40,274	6,509
Warships (vessels)	48	59	77	248	101
Warships (tons)	200,860	230,724	145,760	408,118	98,240
Rifles (thousands)	729	440	630	827	209
Gunpowder and Explosives (metric tons)	52,342	67,461	71,574	81,324	21,279
Total (Index of Real Value, 1937 = 100)	474	659	923	1,406	447

Source: Okazaki Bunkun (ed.), *Kihon Kokuryoku Dotai Soran* (Handbook of Basic National Strength). Institute of Research on National Economy. 1953.

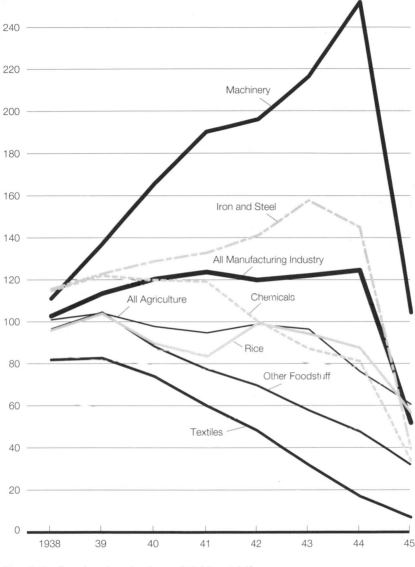

Fig. 3.3. Production Indices (1937 = 100)

Sources: Data for all agriculture and rice are from Ministry of Agriculture, Forestry and Fisheries sources; others are based on Ministry of International Trade and Industry indices.

When the government called for the final defense of the mainland, even military personnel didn't have guns or bayonets.

The production indices in figure 3.3 show that, among the manufacturing industries, steel and machinery—the latter including weapons—were directly involved in munitions production and that those industries alone saw continuous increases in output up to 1944, but that agricultural output slumped dramatically in 1944. Rice production went into decline in 1944, and in 1945, partly owing to poor weather, there was a rice crop failure that reduced output to 60 percent of a normal year.

In the case of other industrial goods, output of foodstuffs, textiles, paper pulp, and chemicals all fell sharply at the beginning of the 1940s. It was only in the final stages that munitions production fell as shipments stopped coming in from Southeast Asia, but before that general industrial production had already collapsed. Compared even with Nazi Germany, which took care not to let production of consumer goods decline until about 1943, Japan's prioritizing of munitions production was extreme from the start and ignored the everyday needs of its own people and those in the territories it occupied.

Living standards deteriorate

Life in Japan had become grim. Everyday items were in desperately short supply and there was nothing to eat, so everyone working in the military plants would take leave to go out into the countryside to buy food. The trains were crowded with people shouldering backpacks. Since rations were inadequate for survival, black market dealing continued relentlessly. It was in violation of

Table 3.5 Availability of Everyday Commodities

	1941	July 1945		1937	July 1945
Rice	11.74 million kg	9.42 million kg	Cotton textile goods	100	2%
Meat	100	20%	Woolen textile goods	100	1%
Fish	100	30%	Workman's light boots (jika tabi)	100	10%
Condiments	100	50% or less	Soap	100	4%
			Paper	100	8%

Source: Ohara Institute for Social Research, *Taiheiyo Senso Ka no Kokumin Seikatsu* (National Life during the Pacific War).

the rationing laws to go out and buy food in the rural areas, but everyone did so quite openly. The material quality of life declined precipitously and unstoppably.

Table 3.5 shows the availability of everyday commodities in July 1945. Starting with foodstuffs, using 1941, when supplies were already tight, as a base at 100, meat had fallen to 20 percent, fish to 30 percent, and condiments to less than 50 percent. If one compares other goods with the figures for 1937, woven cotton goods had been reduced to 2 percent of the 1937 numbers, woolen goods to 1 percent, light workman's boots to 10 percent, soap to 4 percent, and paper to 8 percent. Under these conditions, the national living standard was clearly unsustainable.

In 1944, a fourth-year student at Takasaki Commercial School (a first-year high school student in today's terms) who had been mobilized to work in Nakajima Aircraft's Koizumi plant, near Kumagaya, and was living in the plant hostel, described the scene at the plant cafeteria as follows.*

When there was a larger helping [of food] it would be a "lucky day," when we were out of luck it would be a "bad day." The rice of course was not the white rice that we eat today. At first, the rice was mixed with dried sweet potato, soybeans, dried noodles, or sorghum, but over time, the difference between the amounts gradually decreased, and eventually it was reversed, so that the main portion consisted of sweet potato, soybeans, dried noodles, sorghum, or maize, with only a tiny amount of rice mixed in. On top of that, the quantity was unimaginably small. Once breakfast was over, we started thinking about lunch, and once we had finished lunch, we were immediately ready for dinner.... [the plumper members of the group] were especially tragic. When the meal was over, they would look unhappy and suggest that it would be better if lunch and dinner were served at the same time.

Here is an excerpt from his diary of July 1:
Today was the first day that I have been allowed to go home in a fair while. I got the food staff to make me a packed lunch and left the

*Nagai Kenji, *Jurokusai no Taiheiyo Senso* (The Pacific War in the eyes of a sixteen year old). Shudan Keisei.

hostel at about four, getting to Takasaki at 7:30. My family was surprised to see the lunch, which consisted of a small quantity of brownish rice that left about half the box empty and deep-fried dried carrots.

This was typical of the life of the school children drafted to work "behind the lines." The writer relates other episodes, of how, unable to stand the hunger, he and a group of others went AWOL from the hostel and returned to Takasaki, where they found themselves in trouble, and of how he made iron tongs and frying pans in an unsuccessful attempt to trade them with farmers for sweet potatoes and rice cakes. Superficially humorous, the anecdotes have a bitter edge. By 1945, the author had left the factory, and in the diary of a friend from Tomioka Middle School, the focus had shifted from hunger to air raids and the death of friends. The diary lets us glimpse the collapse of production:

> The amount of time lost taking refuge from the bombing has increased sharply, and combined with the gaps in the work from absentees and lack of materials, we can't work even if we want to.

A last-ditch defense of the mainland

By now the air raids were intensifying. By the end of 1944, the U.S. forces had completed their bases on Saipan and the other islands of the Marianas and were sending out reconnaissance missions. Eventually the bombing began. In 1945, first the big cities, starting with Tokyo and Osaka, were hit, and then the smaller cities, resulting in the complete collapse of national life.

A few years ago, Matsutani Makoto, who began work as secretary to the minister of the army in 1944 and was secretary to Prime Minister Suzuki at the end of the war, published a volume entitled *The True Story of the End of the Great Asian War.* * I was struck by one of his observations. At the beginning of 1945, the army screamed for a final defense of the homeland, drafted civilians to dig trenches and dugouts along the coast, and was

*Matsutani Makoto, *Dai Toa Senso Shushu no Shinso*. Fuyo Shobo.

considering mobilizing the entire civilian population into volunteer corps for national defense. But the section chiefs in the general staff headquarters in the Ministry of the Army had already in their own hearts given up hope of winning. The section workers beneath them were still eagerly pursuing the war and could not be restrained. This was how things stood at the beginning of 1945.

At a time when the army was calling for a final defense of the homeland to be carried out with bamboo spears, Ishibashi Tanzan of *Toyo Keizai Shimpo* (Eastern Economic Review) magazine remained coolheaded. The magazine had maintained itself as a voice of rationalism right up to the beginning of the war, and although critical of the government made it through to the end of the war without being banned. In June 1945, Ishibashi wrote that he was in complete agreement with Prime Minister Suzuki Kantaro when the latter commented that the battle for Okinawa was an air battle and that it was meaningless to make bamboo spears for the final defense of the mainland. Okinawa should be regarded as the final battle, Ishibashi argued. Although he appeared to be supporting the government of the time, Ishibashi was in fact saying that if Japan lost Okinawa, it would be better to give up. I am surprised the essay didn't get banned; it says a lot for Ishibashi's composure and courage.

In July 1945, the Allies issued the Potsdam Declaration. Before that, peace negotiations had, at the order of the emperor, begun through the Soviet Union, but they didn't go well. The army made the prime minister declare that he would "ignore" the Potsdam Declaration. This was taken as a rebuff on Japan's part, setting off the train of events that led to the dropping of the atom bombs, the Soviet Union's entry into the war, and the final defeat of Japan. For a year, Japan had fought a war in which there was absolutely no prospect of victory. It took a year for the army to abandon hope. The time it took to convince the ardent militarists to give up was paid for in hideous, irreparable losses.

THE FOUNDATIONS OF THE POSTWAR ECONOMY

Finally, let me draw some conclusions about the impact of the war. First, we can say that this horrible war left immense damage. Some

Table 3.6 Destruction of National Wealth (billion yen)

	Total Damage	Estimated Value of Undamaged State	National Wealth Remaining at War's End	Percentage of Damage	National Wealth in 1935, Calculated at Value as of War's End
Gross Value of National Assets	64.3	253.1	188.9	25	186.7
Buildings and other Structures	22.2	90.4	68.2	25	76.8
Industrial Machinery	8.0	23.3	15.4	34	8.5
Ships	7.4	9.1	1.8	82	3.1
Electricity and Gas Supply Facilities and Equipment	1.6	14.9	13.3	11	9.0
Furniture and Household Effects	9.6	46.4	36.9	21	39.3
Production Goods	7.9	33.0	25.1	24	23.5

Source: Economic Stabilization Board, *Taiheiyo Senso ni Yoru Wagakuni no Higai Sogo Hokokusho* (Comprehensive Report on Damage to Our Country in the Pacific War).1949.

2,120,000 had died in battle, and 300,000 had died in air raids. Although there is no way of obtaining exact figures, by the time civilian deaths overseas and missing persons are added to the tally, over 3,000,000 Japanese were victims of the war.

Physical damage from the air raids was immense, mostly to buildings and other structures, machinery, and shipping. It can be estimated that about one-fourth of Japan's physical assets, as calculated at their wartime peak, were lost. What remained was at about the level that prevailed in 1935, so everything that had been built up at such great cost in effort during the war had in effect been reduced to ashes. The destruction of cities and factories was particularly heavy.

Production capacity and skilled workers

However, the economic process during the war became the direct starting point for the postwar economy. The war bequeathed postwar Japan a number of things, one of which was production capacity. The need to produce armaments during the war and the output-boosting plans and so on that were demanded by the military had compelled heavy industries and chemical industries to increase their plant and equipment. Much of this remained at the end of the war. To cite one example, steel production capacity had stood at 3 million tons in 1937 and at the wartime peak had risen to 6.6 million tons. At the end of the war, 5.6 million tons in capacity remained. Copper refining, lead, and aluminum saw major capacity expansions, even after subtracting war damage. Machine tool production capacity had risen from 22,000 machines in 1937 to over 60,000 at the wartime peak, with a capacity of 54,000 remaining at the end of the war.

The one industry that suffered a severe setback was textiles. Yarn spinning capacity was down to one-fifth prewar levels, rayon plant to 17 percent, and staple fiber to about one-third. Only about one-third of textile weaving looms and other equipment remained. Most of the losses were due less to the air raids than to corporate reorganization and the scrapping of equipment.

The fact that the plant and equipment of heavy and chemical industries survived the war, as did their technical specialists and laborers, provided the necessary conditions for the postwar economic recovery that was centered on these industries. This, I believe, to be an important legacy.

Institutional continuity into the postwar era

Another legacy relates to the organizational structure of industry. In the fields of machinery, aircraft, and automobiles, firms had developed the practice of contracting work. Most of those doing the contracting were, of course, big firms, which would do the final assembly, while the subcontracting factories would make the raw materials and components. After the war, subcontracting remained the practice, the automobile industry being the stereotypical example. Nowadays the term subcontractor is in disrepute, and some people prefer to use the phrase "cooperating plants," but it was during the war that the practice became institutionalized. Before the war, firms had avoided contracting their work out since there were no guarantees of quality, but during the war this ceased to be a consideration, and the practice stuck.

When the munitions company system was established in the fall of 1943, a program of designated financial institutions was set up so that the munitions companies did not need to worry about financing. Financial institutions and large companies were linked one-on-one, and specific banks looked after the financial needs of the companies. In the old zaibatsu, Mitsui subsidiaries would be served by the Mitsui Bank, and Mitsubishi subsidiaries by the Mitsubishi Bank. Now, institutions like the Fuji Bank and the Daiichi Kangyo Bank, which had not hitherto had much connection with industry, possessed their own groups of companies, which they had established relations with during the war. The corporate groupings centered on banks were also a product of this time.

Japan is internationally famous for its "administrative guidance," in which government offices had the power, directly and indirectly, to instruct businesses on various issues. The prototype of this system developed during the wartime period. It was also during the war that the Bank of Japan began to exert strong control over private-sector banking. The fact that the banks had little funding capacity after the war helped ensure that the Bank of Japan remained firmly in control.

Postwar labor unions were organized in enterprise-based units. During the war the older, trade-based labor unions were disbanded and replaced by Industrial Patriotic Associations set up within each company to promote cooperation between labor and management. When labor unions were reestablished again after the war, management representatives withdrew from the Industrial Patriotic Associations, which were reconstituted as labor unions. Health insurance and pension systems were expanded and improved during the war, forming the basis of the present-day social security system: precisely because it was wartime, it was important to protect workers' health and ensure that they could work secure from accidental injury or illness. These social insurance systems, in fact, constituted a cornerstone of postwar economic development.

Separation of ownership and management

Finally, I would like to mention that the old-fashioned capitalism that I referred to at the beginning of this seminar series was gradually dismantled during the course of the war. I mentioned earlier the business community's vehement opposition to proposals to separate ownership from management when the new economic order was proposed, but as a result of the war, something close to separation of ownership and management was achieved. To meet the huge military demand, companies had continued to expand. But even the biggest capitalists could not cover the costs out of their own pockets. They had to increase equity, bringing in funds from ordinary stockholders and borrowing from financial institutions.

In the case of the Mitsui zaibatsu for example, the percentage of investments by the Mitsui Honsha (main company) and Mitsui family members in direct subsidiaries had fallen from 91 percent of the total in 1928 to 67 percent in 1946, shortly after the war ended. In the case of Mitsubishi, the percentage dropped from 78 percent to 33 percent in the same period. Moreover, at the end of the war, paid- up capital and internal reserves accounted for only one-fourth of the gross utilized capital of Mitsui subsidiaries, while bonds, loans, and other external capital accounted for the remaining three-fourths.*

Since the self capitalization ratios of Mitsui and Mitsubishi had declined, so too did they decline in other companies. The ratio of stock owned by large stockholders had fallen, and the status of stockholding directors was eroded. Employees who had worked their way to the top now stood in the front line of management. The decline of the capitalists and the growing power of employee managers was a sign that the nature of capitalism had begun to undergo a major change as a result of the external forces of war.

Reduction of sharecropping fees

The strong relationship that existed between landowner and tenant farmers before the war also changed under the impact of wartime controls. Up until the war, landowners had had a large representation in the Diet, with the result that any law that contained elements to the disadvantage of landowners—for example, legislation that would have provided sharecroppers with subsidies to set up their own farms—was invariably gutted in the Diet.

*Shibagaki Kazuo. *Mitsui, Mitsubishi no Hyakunen* (A Century of Mitsui and Mitsubishi), Chuo Koron Sha, 1968.

During the war, however, the Ministry of Agriculture and Fisheries introduced controls over rice and the foodstuff control system, under which the government bought up all the harvested rice for redistribution. These institutions are still in place. But at the same time, the bureaucrats in the Ministry of Agriculture and Fisheries got their heads together and came up with ways to solidify the status of the farmers and downgrade the status of the landlords. The rice was delivered directly to the government, whether the producer was a sharecropper or a self-sustaining farmer. The tenant then paid the landlord an amount corresponding to the sharecropping fee. With this, the old payment in kind was replaced by cash. In addition, the direct producer, the farmer, also received separate cash production incentives.

The government purchase price for rice was ¥55 for one *koku*—about 150 kilograms, a price that was established in 1941. Initially, the production incentive was set at ¥5, so for the landlord the price was ¥55, but for the farmer it was in effect ¥60. The landlords may have decided that ¥5 was not worth arguing about, but subsequently the rice price was capped, and the the production incentive alone was raised. In the end, in 1945, the rice price was still ¥55, but the production incentive had been jacked up to ¥245. Thus, for the direct producer, the rice price was effectively ¥300 per one *koku*, but for the landlord it was still set at ¥55. In addition, land rental costs had in effect been slashed. This was a spectacular feat on the part of the Ministry of Agriculture and Forestry bureaucrats, and thus, thanks to wartime pricing and government controls over rice, a very real change was effected in agriculture that was to provide a foundation for subsequent postwar agricultural reforms.

Greater homogeneity of living standards

Because almost all everyday products were subjected to rationing, lifestyles throughout the country became more uniform. Women who had in prewar days worn Japanese kimono exclusively, had to wear western clothing during the war whether they wanted to or not. From the economic structure to the everyday lives of Japan's people, the war had changed everything.

Lecture 4

RECONSTRUCTION
(1945–1951)

Business booms at a stockbroker's office following this introduction of the $1.00 = ¥360 exchange rate by Joseph Dodge in 1949.

1945	September	The surrender document is signed. The *U.S. Initial Post Surrender Policy* for Japan is made public. Arrests of war criminals begin.
	November	Dissolution of the zaibatsu is ordered. Labor movements move into full swing.
	December	The Supreme Commander for the Allied Powers (SCAP) issues a directive on rural land reform.
1946	February	A revised draft of the constitution is adopted. Emergency financial measures are announced.
	July	War indemnity payments are suspended. The Japanese government adopts policies to assist corporate reorganization.
	December	The priority production system is launched.
1947	January	SCAP bans the general strike scheduled for February 1.
	July	July 7, official price lists are announced, setting prices at 65 times and wages at 28 times prewar averages. Production begins to revive.
		Fall, signs of change appear in American policy.
1948	June	The official price lists are revised.
	October	The United States National Security Council adopts a new policy on Japan.
1949	March	Joseph Dodge imposes his economic program and establishes an exchange rate of ¥360 = $1.00. Inflation is quenched, but the country is thrown into recession until mid-1950.
1950	June	War breaks out in Korea.
	July	Japan is ordered to set up a National Police Reserve. Special procurements and increased exports bring economic recovery.
1951	September	The San Francisco Peace Treaty is signed, ending war between Japan and the United States. The U.S.–Japan Security Treaty is signed and goes into effect in April 1952.

Lecture 4

RECONSTRUCTION (1945–1951)

CHANGES WROUGHT BY DEFEAT

Having been mobilized for war and having seen their cities and factories reduced to debris, the Japanese people faced Japan's sudden defeat with mixed emotions. They were numbed and weary, yet there was also a great sense of relief. Life was hard, the future uncertain, and no-one, of course, knew what policies the occupation forces might have in store. Governmental authority was nil, and society was in a state of disorder.

Government policies were in total disarray. Someone suggested that if military stores were going to be confiscated by the U.S. forces, it would be better to distribute them to the Japanese people. Some stores were dispensed and later found their way onto the black market. Extraordinary military budget funds that had been set aside were hastily disbursed after the surrender, fueling the soaring inflation.

By October 1945, voices of democracy began to make themselves heard. The labor union movement and the socialist movement began to rebuild their strength from wartime repression. Japanese society had embarked on a course of change. In the days directly after the war, Konoe Fumimaro was looked upon as a political leader around whom the nation could consolidate. But within a couple of months, the Americans began to raise questions about his wartime responsibilities, and the Japanese press took up the cause. He was designated a war criminal and died at his own hand a little over three months after the war ended.

In an earlier lecture I remarked how after the Manchurian Incident Japanese society lurched collectively to the right, as if it had suddenly seen the light. Now, it plunged in the opposite direction. In the space of a few months, a fit of national contrition was followed by public attacks on the old leadership and praise for democracy and the once-repressed socialists for their resistance. It would take a literary masterpiece to do justice to this national about-face.

On September 2, 1945, the surrender document was signed aboard the battleship *Missouri*, anchored in Tokyo Bay. Shortly thereafter, the occupation forces landed. It appears that the U.S. forces initially contemplated direct government and had readied military scrip denominated in yen for use as currency. At one point a directive even went out to the effect that this "B" occupation scrip should be used within Japan. The Japanese were concerned that if it were used, Bank of Japan notes and military scrip would end up in circulation side by side, making it impossible to control the money supply. After negotiations, the Americans eventually agreed to let the Bank of Japan supply the notes that the occupation forces needed and to refrain from using their occupation scrip.

The occupation forces permitted the Japanese government to continue to exist and adopted a policy of indirect administration, conveying their will and intentions through the Japanese authorities. Directives emanating from the U.S. forces (known to Japanese as Potsdam Directives) were to be carried out by the Japanese government immediately and without fail.

Thus began the American occupation of Japan. The occupation era lasted for six and a half years, from autumn 1945 until after the Treaty of San Francisco took effect in April 1952. It can be analyzed into two major periods and four sub-periods. The big dividing line was a watershed decision by the United States president in October 1948, presaged by gradual modifications in occupation policy in 1947–48. We can further identify an initial period of demilitarization and democratization in 1945–46, followed, in the latter part of 1947 through 1948, by an interval of policy drift, in which initial objectives had been achieved, but future directions had not yet been established. Then, in fall 1948, American policy abruptly and visibly changed: now Japan was to be resurrected and made an ally of the United States. The fourth and final stage came when the Korean War broke out in June 1950, prompting further policy changes that ultimately lead to the signing of the San Francisco Treaty in September 1951.

DEMOCRATIZATION

Long before World War II ended, the United States had been studying how it should deal with Japan when the war was over. The American government was split into those who sought to be hard on Japan and those who adopted a softer line. Their debates have been the subject of much academic research in recent years. Eventually, two key documents that struck a balance between the two factions were adopted. In September 1945, the first document, entitled *U.S. Initial Post Surrender Policy for Japan*, was transmitted to General MacArthur, supreme commander for the allied powers and released to the public. This was followed in November by a second document that elaborated on the content of the first, entitled *Basic Initial Post Surrender Directive to the Supreme Commander for the Allied Powers for the Occupation and Control of Japan*. These two documents represented the highest policy of the United States on Japan and were carried out remarkably faithfully.

The *Initial Policy*, the first of the two documents is the less complex of the two, and so I will summarize it here. Among the "ultimate objectives" of the occupation was to "ensure that Japan will not again become a menace to the United States or the peace and security of the world." In concrete terms, this meant demilitarization, starting with the dismantling of the Japanese armed forces: "The existing economic basis of Japanese military strength must be destroyed and not permitted to revive." Production of armaments was to be prohibited, and limitations were to be imposed on heavy industry and merchant shipping. In effect, Japan was to be limited to those industries that would enable it to maintain economic levels and living standards defined according to principles consistent with the Potsdam Declaration. Those principles were to lead to the adoption of a policy of reparations in kind through the transfer of industrial equipment and facilities.

Under the subheading of "Promotion of Democratic Forces," the *Initial Policy* takes a positive stance toward labor organizations, stating that "[e]ncouragement shall be given and favor shown to the development of organizations in labor, industry and agriculture, organized on a democratic basis." The supreme commander was instructed to purge business leaders in the interests of democratization, that is, "[t]o prohibit the retention in or selection for places of importance in the economic field of individuals who do not direct future Japanese economic effort solely toward peaceful ends." Another paragraph pointed toward the liquidation of the zaibatsu, stating that SCAP should "favor a program for the dissolution of the large industrial and banking combinations."

In a section titled "Resumption of Peaceful Economic Activity," the *Initial Policy* requires Japanese to make their own efforts to rebuild their nation. "The plight of Japan is the direct outcome of its own behavior, and the Allies will not undertake the burden of repairing the damage. It can be repaired only if the Japanese people renounce all military aims, and apply themselves diligently and with single purpose to the ways of peaceful living." The *Initial Policy* goes on to add that "Japan will be expected to provide goods and services to meet the needs of the occupying forces, to the extent that this can be done without causing...distress."

The Occupation Revolution
On the whole, the document took a harsh line that was later spelled out in greater detail in the *Basic Initial Directive*. The first order of business of the occupation forces was to implement these directives. How they set about that task is described in Theodore Cohen's *Nihon Senryo Kakumei* (The Occupation Revolution). Published in Japanese by TBS Britannica days before the author's death, this work has since appeared posthumously in English under the title *Remaking Japan*. Cohen was one those working on democratization for the occupation, and his work reveals fascinating insights into the internal workings of the occupation that could only be known to insiders.

Within SCAP, there were sections for Government, Economics and Science, and Natural Resources, each with its own divisions and branches, just like a Japanese government office. According to Cohen, the *Basic Initial Directive* was chopped up into its component paragraphs and subparagraphs, and each section, division, and branch assigned a portion to implement as its initial objective. The Japanese government had more work than they could handle, with new orders being issued almost every day. One day it would be purging of right-wingers from public office, the next day it would be reparations programs. Democratization and demilitarization directives followed one another in hot succession. From the end of 1945 to the beginning of 1946, the SCAP offices were working flat out to achieve their objectives.

The first goals of the SCAP policies and directives, disarmament and dismantling of the army, went without a hitch. The next objective was economic reform designed to strip Japan of its war potential. Armaments manufacturers were, of course, banned, as were any other industries that contributed to Japan's military effort. In practice, however, defining what constitutes materials for military use is not easy: steel, for example, is fundamental to arms production, but it has a broad range of peaceful uses. Here, SCAP hit upon a solution: it proposed that Japan pay reparations to the other countries of the region. An official by the name of Edwin W. Pauley visited Japan and Manchuria and produced at the close of 1945 an interim report, followed in November the following year by a final report. His proposals were harsh: the bulk of Japan's remaining production facilities was to be handed over as reparations in kind. In the final report, all equipment and facilities for military supplies, artificial rubber, aluminum, and magnesium were to be removed, along with a substantial part of Japan's plant for power generation and for making steel, machine tools, chemicals, heavy electrical machinery, and explosives; its communications equipment; and its railroad equipment and vehicles, shipbuilding facilities, and shipping. Anything left after reparations would by definition be for peaceful purposes.

There is some evidence that this was indeed the plan. On January 23, 1947, the Far Eastern Commission formally defined

Japan's peaceful needs as being the "standard of living prevailing in Japan in the period of 1930–34." Likewise, production levels were to be held to those of the same period. Harsher views were also voiced: one commission member argued that Japan's living standards should not be higher than those of the Asian countries that Japan had invaded. It is not surprising, then, that SCAP proposed reparations on a large scale. But the reparations proposals came as a major shock to Japanese industry. It is hard to commit to rebuilding if one might have one's equipment carted off at any moment. For nearly two years, Japanese industry was on tenterhooks.

Those business leaders who were seen as collaborators in Japan's war effort were forced from their positions, with the result that scarcely any of Japan's wartime business leaders remained in office. Deprived of its leadership, business and industry were thrust into deeper chaos, something that happened again with the dissolution of the zaibatsu.

The old militarism gave way to a vogue for democratic ideals. Communists who had been tried and imprisoned under the Peace Preservation Law were released from jail. The Communist Party resumed its activities, as did the Socialist Party. Labor activism flourished and occasionally got out of hand when union members subjected management to kangaroo courts known as People's Trials. The old was suddenly yielding to a burst of change. No one knew how far things would go.

The most important reform of all was that of the constitution. Following instructions from the Americans, a draft was initially prepared by Konoe Fumimaro in his capacity as adviser to the Lord Keeper of the Privy Seals, but upon his resignation, the Shidehara cabinet appointed Matsumoto Joji as minister of state without portfolio to come up with a proposal. It is now well known that Matsumoto's draft was too insipid, and so SCAP's Government Section put together a draft of its own, translated it into Japanese, and instructed the Japanese government to adopt it.

Dissolution of the zaibatsu

That was how things stood at the beginning of 1946. When we turn to the economic picture, three reforms merit attention. First is the dissolution of the zaibatsu. It was widely held by Americans that Japanese society had many holdovers from feudal days, that its living standards were being kept low by feudalistic oppression, that domestic markets were constrained by the low living standards, and that this was why Japan had turned to militaristic imperialism and invaded its neighbors. Much of this perception of Japan was based on E. Herbert Norman's book *Japan's Emergence as a Modern State*. In Norman's view, which was close to that of a Japanese academic Marxist group known as the *Koza* faction, the Japanese zaibatsu, being primarily family concerns in which a single family owned the stocks of the parent holding company, were a feudalistic organizations par excellence. Since they had immense power over a wide spectrum of business and industry, their dissolution was imperative if democratization was to succeed.

And so, the four great zaibatsu, Mitsui, Mitsubishi, Sumitomo, and Yasuda, along with seven others, were slated by SCAP to be dismantled and restructured. In the case of Mitsui, for example, the holding company held the stock of its subsidiaries, and therefore all important management decisions required the permission of the holding company, which also appointed all its officers. A Holding Companies Liquidation Commission was established to supervise the transfer of the stock held by the parent company to the subsidiaries, and the Mitsui holding company was dissolved. Mitsubishi, Sumitomo, Yasuda, and the other smaller zaibatsu also met with the same fate.

The zaibatsu, as I noted in an earlier lecture, were massive concerns that accounted for a huge proportion of Japan's corporate stock issues: in 1937 Mitsui possessed 9.5 percent, Mitsubishi 8.3 percent, Sumitomo 5.1 percent, and Yasuda 1.7 percent, for total of 24.6 percent of all Japanese stock, retained by just four companies. Since these numbers presumably include stock held by subsidiaries, not all of this stock was subject to transfer in the liquidation, and nor were all companies in which the zaibatsu held stock necessarily controlled by them. Nonetheless, the dissolution of the zaibatsu was a significant occasion. The members of zaibatsu families—even those who had not yet reached the age of majority—were purged from positions of corporate power and were banned from participating in the management of other large concerns.

In 1947, Mitsui Trading Company and Mitsubishi Trading Company were ordered to dissolve. Dissolution was total, even to the extent of banning more than 100 former employees of those companies from combining to form a new company. One scarcely exaggerates to suggest that these firms' dissolution reflected a goodly measure of hatred toward the zaibatsu.

The Anti-Monopoly Law and deconcentration

Hard on the heels of the dissolution of the zaibatsu, the Anti-Monopoly Law was enacted in April 1947, again at the instigation of the United States. One of the stiffest pieces of anti-trust legislation in the world, the Anti-Monopoly Law prohibited the formation of trusts, all cartel activities, joining of international cartels, cross-holding of directorships, and even stockholding by corporations. Later, in 1949, the bans on participation in international cartels and corporate stockholding were lifted, on the grounds that those provisions were obstacles to foreign investment in Japan.

The Anti-Monopoly Law was followed by the introduction of a policy designed to eliminate excessive concentration of economic power. The underlying theory—which had been much debated in the latter part of the New Deal period in the United States—was that in order to ensure free-market competition, it was necessary to ensure that no company held oligopolistic or monopolistic power. Now the United States presented the Japanese government with legislation that would translate this theory into reality. From an economic standpoint, if the activities of a single company affects prices and transaction volumes in a market, then that enterprise is of a monopolistic character. By this definition, many enterprises are monopolistic, and this meant that a large number of companies were to be slated for liquidation. The Law for the

Elimination of Excessive Concentration of Economic Power went into effect in December 1947, supplementing the already rigorous Anti-Monopoly Law with further provisions requiring the government to designate for structural reorganization companies it thought to hold monopolistic power.

In the end, however, the deconcentration did not get very far. As table 4.1 shows, ultimately only 17 companies were broken up under the law. The 11 corporations in the top part of the table were reorganized on receipt of the final directive, and the remaining 6 underwent reorganization upon being notified of their provisional designation. Initially, over 300 companies (banks and a few others were excluded) were designated for deconcentration and were on the verge of being fragmented. The small number of corporations actually affected in the end is due to an easing of the policy that came about with a change in American attitudes. This, I will discuss shortly.

In table 4.1, Daiken Industrial Company, which had a hand in many industrial fields, is today's Marubeni Corporation. Dai Nippon Breweries, the result of wartime mergers that left Kirin Brewery Co., Ltd. the only independent manufacturer, was broken up into Sapporo Breweries, Ltd. and Asahi Breweries, Ltd. Hitachi, Ltd., which had enjoyed a major expansion during the war years, was forced to spin off 19 of its numerous factories. Nippon Seitetsu (Nippon Steel Co.), which had been formed in the great steel merger of 1934, was carved into two companies, Yawata Seitetsu (Yawata Steel) and Fuji Seitetsu (Fuji Steel). Mitsubishi Heavy Industries, Ltd., about the same size as its present-day namesake, was split into three companies: a shipbuilding concern in Nagasaki, the plants in the vicinity of Nagoya, and the plants in the Kanto region around Tokyo. Oji Paper Company was sundered into three companies—Oji Paper Co., Ltd., Honshu Paper Co., Ltd., and Jujo Paper Co., Ltd.; this division has remained in force to this day. In this fashion, then, a series of measures were swiftly and zealously implemented to dissolve the zaibatsu and to eliminate monopolies and excessive concentration of economic power.

Table 4.1 Companies Receiving Final Designation under the Deconcentration Law

Company	Industry	Proposed Disposition	Date of Notification
Daiken Industrial	Cotton spinning	Separation of manufacturing and marketing divisions.	April 15, 1949
Dai Nippon Breweries	Foodstuff	Dissolution. Split into two independent companies.	January 7, 1949
Hitachi	Electrical machinery	Divestment of 19 factories.	March 18, 1949
Mitsubishi Heavy Industries	Heavy machinery	Dissolution. Split into three companies.	June 4, 1949
Nippon Kayaku	Explosives	Dissolution of holding company.	June 4, 1949
Nippon Seitetsu	Steel	Dissolution. Split into two companies.	December 17,1948
Oji Paper	Paper	Dissolution. Split into three companies.	January 7, 1950.
Seika Mining	Mining	Either divestment, with establishment of one new company, or dissolution to split into two companies.	August 3, 1949
Teikoku Oil	Petroleum extraction	Dissolution of holding company.	April 15, 1949
Toyo Seikan	Industrial machinery	Divestment, with establishment of one new company.	July 8, 1949
Tokyo-Shibaura Electric	Electrical machinery	Divestment of 27 factories and one research institute.	June 17, 1948
Mitsubishi Mining	Mining	Either divestment, with establishment of one new company, or dissolution to split into two companies.	July 30, 1949
Mitsui Mining	Mining	Either divestment, with establishment of one new company, or dissolution to split into two companies.	July 30, 1949
Imperial Textile	Flax spinning	Either divestment, with establishment of two new company, or dissolution to split into three companies.	July 19, 1949
Hokkaido Milk Farmers cooperative	Foodstuff	Dissolution. Split into three companies.	June 27, 1949
Shochiku	Entertainment	Dissolution of holding company.	July 30, 1949
Toho	Entertainment	Dissolution of holding company.	July 30, 1949

Source: *Keizai Dantai Rengokai Junen Shi* (Ten-year History of the Federation of Economic Organizations [Keidanren]).

Agricultural land reform

Then there is agricultural reform. The Ministry of Agriculture and Forests had long sought to raise tenant farmers' standard of living. In November 1945, the ministry seized the opportunity afforded by Japan's defeat to submit to a special session of the Diet an agricultural land reform bill that would have restricted landowners to about five hectares of farmland, with the rest to be sold off to the tenant farmers. While the bill was being debated, the United States issued a directive calling for tougher measures, and so, in mid-1946, a revised law was passed that incorporated the occupation agenda. Under the new law, resident landlords were permitted to own about one hectare, the remainder being sold to the tenants. In the case of absentee landlords, all landholdings had to be sold to the tenant farmers. This far-reaching legislation was to be implemented by the Japanese government itself.

The dramatic change in land-owning patterns that ensued can be seen from figure 4.1. In November 1946, nearly 46 percent of Japan's farmland was cultivated by tenant farmers, but by August 1950, the figure had plunged to 10 percent. In the Hokkaido, Kanto, and Hokuriku regions, where absentee landlords were common, and in the Chugoku and Shikoku regions, tenant farming fell to less than 10 percent. On the other hand, the percentage of tenant farmers remained relatively high in the Kinki region, where there had been many small landowners from the start. Nonetheless, not only were landowners compelled to sell their holdings, prices were set somewhat below market, and inflation pushed their real values even lower. Landowners were hard hit, and their tenants were released from their generations of hardship. The land reforms were to transform Japanese agriculture.

Democratization of labor

The third area of reform was the democratization of the labor movement. Figure 4.2 depicts the number of unions in Japan, together with estimated rates of union membership. The numbers are year-end figures. The surge in unionization was dramatic, even given the occupation directive. When one recalls that today just under 30 percent of Japanese workers are union members, the unionization rate of over 50 percent in 1948 and 1949 is quite stunning.

The Japanese government, following SCAP instructions, established an institutional foundation for industrial relations by passing three pieces of legislation: the Labor Union Law, the Labor

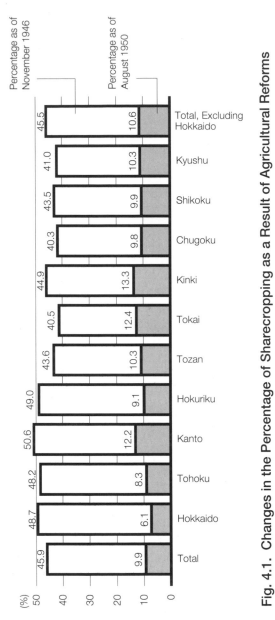

Fig. 4.1. Changes in the Percentage of Sharecropping as a Result of Agricultural Reforms

Source: Ando Yoshio et al., *Kindai Nihon Keizai Shi Yoran* (Handbook of Modern Japanese Economic History).

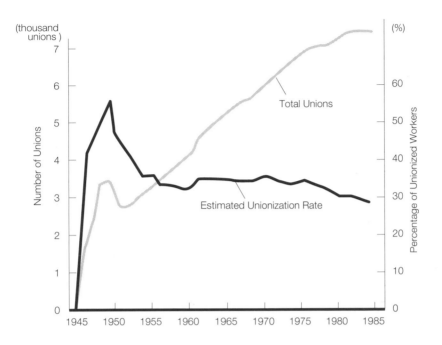

Fig. 4.2. Number of Unions and Estimated Union Membership Rate

Source: Ministry of Labor.

Standards Law, and the Labor Relations Adjustment Law. The Labor Relations committees, a system still in operation today, are rooted in this legislative framework.

With the formation of new unions, labor activity stepped up. Disputes became common and acrimonious. Figure 4.3 maps the number of labor disputes and the number of workdays lost per union member. The relatively low overall number of disputes is probably attributable to united front actions by umbrella organizations. The high number of workdays lost through strike actions and company lockouts, especially during the period from 1945 through 1955, may be taken as indicative of the intensity of the labor movement.

Labor disputes peaked in 1946–48, followed by a second wave in 1952–53 after Japan regained independence. One reason for the rapid surge in unionization was the base provided by the wartime Industrial Patriotic associations; their managements resigned, and

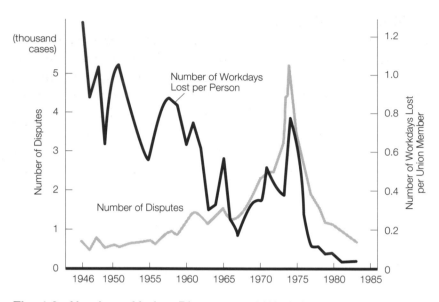

Fig. 4.3. Number of Labor Disputes and Workdays Lost per Union Member

Source: Ministry of Labor.

the names of the organizations changed, but the organizational framework remained intact. In the early postwar era, these unions joined the militant Congress of Industrial Labor Unions of Japan (Sanbetsu) or the Japanese Confederation of Labor (Sodomei) and were actively in keeping with the policies of the umbrella organizations. When Sanbetsu lost influence, the General Council of Trade Unions of Japan (Sohyo) assumed the mantle of militant leadership. Hence the high number of days lost in the early postwar period.

The fact that Japanese unions were formed on the basis of their members' employment in a specific business organization rather than in industries or trades was to have major consequences later on. In most countries, unions represent workers in specific industries or skills, and their organizational basis has nothing to do with individual corporations. In Japan, it is the company or the individual plant that forms the organizational basis for the union, a foundation on which Japanese industrial relations remain to this day.

Positive impact of democratization

In my view, these various steps toward democratization had a significant positive impact on Japan. The dissolution of the zaibatsu, and the divestments, carried out by fiat on the basis of a certain brand of economic vision, destroyed the hierarchy among companies and in one stroke established a new competitive environment in many industries. Economists sometimes talk of a Gulliver-like oligopoly. When Gulliver goes to the land of the little people, everyone there is in danger of being trampled to death by the giant figure. But once Gulliver left, the Lilliputians were in a position to compete with each other, on a small scale, but to compete nevertheless. In Japan, the intensity of that competition fueled the vitality for the postwar economy.

Agricultural reform, too, significantly changed the status of the small farmer, especially in northeastern Japan, where life was hardest. People who had once handed over much of their income in sharecropping fees became their own masters and were now able to put money in their own pockets. Life in rural villages improved. New technology was developed and introduced onto the farms; for example, insulated rice seed beds, insecticides, and herbicides. New fertilizers using ammonia and other chemicals were developed. Farmers, introducing these new technologies, pushed agricultural output to new heights. Moreover, as the farm economy improved, so, too, did consumption by farm households, creating new demand whose ripple effect penetrated other sectors.

Likewise in the case of the democratization of labor. Workers became able to band together to demand higher wages and better working conditions. They became able to demand wage increases in the face of soaring inflation. Management may have been hard put to deal with this new bargaining power, but it is also true it had the effect of raising income levels, boosting standards of living, and creating new markets for many industries.

Viewed through the medium-term lens of a 5- to 10-year period, the occupation's democratization policies thus brought about unanticipated social change. Admittedly, the policies triggered much friction at the outset, and in some cases the problems became protracted, as, for example, in the case of former landowners who later demanded compensation, claiming that they had been unfairly treated. But, in the balance, democratization had significant impact and transformed Japanese society along the lines of American democratic principles. As Cohen indicates, it was indeed a kind of revolution.

To this day, the debate rages as to the validity of a revolution imposed by a victor in war. Areas of society that I have not touched on—the family system, the education system, and the legal system—were also remodeled after the American system. Rather than be drawn into the ramifications of the occupation for these areas, I will confine myself to the economy and limit myself to the observation that the benefits of the reforms outweighed the drawbacks. It is also true that despite the democratic reforms that took place under the occupation, Japanese society continued to suffer from a variety of problems.

Practical realities of the occupation

The Allied forces, which meant for all practical purposes, the U.S. Army, set up its general headquarters in Tokyo and installed branch offices in different parts of the country. Its rule of Japan was indirect, and the Japanese government continued to exist, only the Army and Navy ministries having been eliminated. In 1947, the Interior Ministry was dismantled, and the police were divided into national and local police forces, but they continued in existence, and as did the offices of the Interior Ministry that handled local government affairs. The Japanese government continued to function. The occupation, for its part, fielded a Government Section and an Economic and Scientific Section, each with its own divisions and branches. Japan had, in effect, two governments, the Japanese government and SCAP.

SCAP's Economy and Science Section, moreover, had a Finance Division, an office corresponding to the Budget Bureau of Japan's Ministry of Finance. When the Japanese government drew up a budget, it had to be approved by the Finance Division before the budget could be submitted to the Diet. Japanese government agencies would submit budget applications to the Ministry of

Finance, but before that they had to gain American approval. Even SCAP projects that required a budget item were submitted to the Finance Division. The biggest problem was paying for the occupation forces. The army and the Finance Division would negotiate between themselves for what were called budget funds for the Termination of War Activities; once they had agreed on a sum, SCAP would instruct the Japanese government to include it as a budget item. This was a major burden on the impoverished Japanese government.

Thus it was, for example, that when education reforms ushered in the present system of six years of elementary school followed by three years of middle school, there was no budget to set up the new middle schools, since compulsory education in prewar days only covered the first six years. However, the matter was decided in discussions within SCAP, and the new middle school system was set up, even though there was no budget allocations.

Another reality of the occupation in 1947–48 is worth mentioning. Demilitarization and democratic reforms, as laid out in the two key SCAP documents, had run their course, and a new constitution was in place. SCAP's most urgent tasks were finished, but the occupation remained in place. At this point, individual SCAP officers started to get out of hand. For example, the rigorous deconcentration program was pushed through despite internal objections at the insistence of Edward C. Welsh, chief of anti-trust. As a result, the matter became an issue in Washington, and although the deconcentration law had passed, its requirements were greatly eased in practice. Seeing the opportunity presented by such loose cannons, Japanese government agencies would get in touch with SCAP sections to get their policies realized; even companies began to use SCAP to their ends. The occupation had become an institution, and the two sides were getting to know each other a little too well. The period 1947–48 marked the onset of a transition in SCAP policy. It was a time of disarray and scandals involving SCAP officials, such as politically motivated loans to Showa Denko.

THE HARD ROAD TO RECONSTRUCTION

How did the Japanese economy fare during the occupation period? Let us tally up the problems.

First, there were concerns about unemployment. About 7.2 million troops were to be demobilized. About 4 million workers in armaments factories would lose their jobs. Another 1.5 million Japanese overseas would be repatriated. It was said at the time that even if a few were to find work upon their return, 10 million Japanese might be unemployed.

The second problem was inflation. As I noted earlier in this lecture, in fall 1945, directly after the war ended, extraordinary military budget funds were released, boosting the amount of currency in circulation. Fears of inflation were intense, since money was being scattered where there were no goods to buy. For a brief period, some observers guessed that, since the extraordinary military budget funds would soon be exhausted, deflation, not inflation, would be the real concern. But from November on, prices, especially prices of everyday household goods, soared relentlessly.

The third major problem was the drop in coal production. Japan's main energy sources at the time were coal and hydroelectric power. Most of Japan's coal was mined by impressed labor: Chinese prisoners of war and Koreans. On Japan's defeat, these workers were repatriated. With no one to work the mines, coal output plummeted, stopping industry across the board.

At the end of the war, almost no production equipment remained operational. Japan's steel plants were at an almost total standstill, and plants producing ammonium sulfate, a vital agricultural fertilizer, were still operating at only 50 percent of capacity two years after the war. Nor was it just manufacturing that was affected. Without higher coal production, it would be necessary to cut back the operations of the railroads, Japan's transportation lifeline.

To make matters worse, there was a major crop failure in 1945. The rice harvest came in at six million metric tons, about two-thirds of a normal year. There was nothing to eat. An adult requires about 2,400 kilocalories a day, but the ration provided only about 1,000 kilocalories, and even with black market food, the average intake in 1946 was only about 1,900 kilocalories. Japan entreated the American forces to release or import food, but given the global food shortage, the occupation at first turned a deaf ear to the former enemies. In the end, some flour was imported, and in the major cities, surplus U.S. Army food was distributed. I remember being nonplused by cans of grapefruit juice being distributed instead of the hoped-for rice.

The capital levy

The question was how to rebuild the economy in the face of this mound of problems. There was no work for demobilized army and navy personnel or for those repatriated from abroad, production had stopped, food rations either came late or not at all. There was always the black market for people to fall back on, but prices kept on soaring. The Ministry of Finance came up with a policy to meet the crisis. A proposal was put forward by then Minister of Finance Shibusawa Keizo to impose a one-time capital levy on the principle that if the entire nation had been ready to sacrifice itself in war, then it could render a few assets to rebuild the government finances, now saddled with huge war debts. In order to impose the levy, assets would have to be assessed, and in the case of cash, this could only be achieved by getting it deposited into the banks in exchange for new banknotes. The idea then was to seize this opportunity to quench inflation: this could be done by forcing the public to deposit all cash in the bank and to limit withdrawals, thus slashing the currency in circulation. Each household would be permitted to withdraw up to ¥500 and no more each month for living expenses.

Known as the Emergency Financial Measures, the new policy served the dual duty of replenishing the government's coffers and holding down inflation while production restarted. In March 1946, the measures went into effect. All cash had to be deposited with financial institutions, new banknotes were issued, and limits on withdrawals were imposed. Since there was not time to print enough new banknotes, paper seals slightly smaller than a postage stamp were pasted in a corner of old bills as an interim substitute.

The Emergency Financial Measures, together with the establishment of official prices, marked the beginning of postwar economic policy. The government planned to hold down inflation and wait for output to recover, but reality proved to be rather more difficult.

Suspension of war indemnity payments

The government's thinking was along the following lines. Since the Japanese government survived from the wartime into the postwar era, it was obliged to meet commitments made during the war. The government had promised to indemnify future losses in order to extract sacrifices from citizens. For example, it had created a program of wartime insurance, so that if a person's house burned down in an air raid, an indemnity would be paid from the insurance fund. But with Japan's bigger cities reduced to ashes, insurance companies were unable to pay out, and unless the government covered their losses, the insurance companies would be wiped out. Moreover, after the great air raid on Tokyo, insurance payments were frozen in bank accounts and could not be withdrawn until a fixed period of time had elapsed. So this was another thing that the government had to deal with.

During the war, the government had ordered the impossible of armaments and military supply firms, demanding that they build factories for equipment for special forces, move factory operations underground to avoid air raids, or transfer plant and machinery to Manchuria and continue production there. These activities entailed substantial losses for the companies, which had been publicly promised compensation. So rather than imposing a capital levy and limiting access to bank accounts, the government really wanted to meet its wartime obligations and pay out the ¥106.5 billion in war indemnities. If it did so, companies would be able to repay their loans, and financial institutions would be able to repay their obligations to the Bank of Japan. Everyone would be able to restart, relieved of the burden of their old debts.

SCAP, however, gave thought to such scenario when it reviewed the capital levy proposal and ended up taking a hard line, calling on the Japanese government to end payments of its

¥76 billion in war indemnities in order to teach the Japanese people the lesson that war is unprofitable. Intense negotiations ensued. In July 1946, Ishibashi Tanzan, minister of finance in Yoshida Shigeru's newly appointed cabinet, received notice from SCAP that the government had to terminate its war indemnity program. Ishibashi must have wanted to tell SCAP that companies and banks would go broke, that the Japanese economy would never recover from such a violent blow. He remarked caustically that from an economist's perspective their position was unviable and that he would respond the following day in his capacity as minister of finance. This brought Ishibashi the ill favor of SCAP and later led to his being driven from power. In the end, war indemnities were terminated, except for a little over ¥18 billion. Banks and corporations were pushed to the verge of bankruptcy as companies became unable to receive compensation from the government and as banks became unable to recover their loans.

The government hastened to introduce two pieces of legislation, the Business Reconstruction and Adjustment Law and the Financial Institutions Reconstruction and Adjustment Law, which allowed firms to establish secondary companies to which they could transfer plant and equipment, raw materials, products, and cash needed for production activities so that these could carry on operations while the original companies were dissolved. Of the savings that had been frozen under the Emergency Financial Measures, everything above a certain amount was completely frozen, and that amount applied to cover the banks' losses, so that these monies were cut off, together with companies' capital, deposits, and receivables. This triggered a corporate reconstruction crisis that took until 1948–49 to resolve. Here we see the impact of the American policy of punishing Japan that remained in effect until summer 1946.

Ishibashi and the Priority Production System
Ishibashi's concept was original. Japan had a labor surplus and an equipment surplus. If funds were invested on a bold scale, production activities would pick up and the economy would recover. Since full employment did not exist, production should be stimu-

lated by investment, even at risk of price increases. Ishibashi strongly believed Keynes, who had argued in his *General Theory of Employment, Interest and Money* that price increases are not truly inflationary until full employment is achieved. Some objections to Ishibashi's proposal were raised on the grounds that since raw materials and resources were in short supply, funds would not be enough to boost production, and so there was a major danger of inflation. Ishibashi, however, stood his ground.

The upshot was the establishment of the Reconstruction Finance Bank, a government institution whose job was to provide funds for key industries. The Reconstruction Finance Bank floated bonds that were to be underwritten by the Bank of Japan. The likelihood that the amount of currency circulating would increase and that prices would rise was regarded as a necessary evil.

In an attempt to soften the blow to Japanese businesses incurred by terminating war indemnities, the Yoshida cabinet pleaded with the Americans to permit it to import key materials in order to lever a production recovery. A small quantity of heavy oil import was permitted. The idea was that this heavy oil would go to the steel industry. The steel would be used in coal mines to boost coal output, which would be sent to the steel mills. By initially focusing these two industries on boosting each other's output, it was sought to boost the production of both. In 1947, the government wanted to get coal output up to 30 million metric tons. Extra food rations were made available for mine workers, and the Reconstruction Finance Bank made coal mining its lending priority. With 30 million metric tons of coal, it would be possible to increase the amount directed to other industries, thus occasioning a general recovery in production.

This Priority Production System (*keisha seisan hoshiki*), as the concept became known, was the brainchild of a group of private advisers to the prime minister, whose number included Arisawa Hiromi, Okita Saburo, Inaba Hidezo, and Yoshino Toshihiko. The proposal was implemented by the government of Katayama Tetsu, the Socialist Party leader who became prime minister in June 1947, and the goal of 30 million metric tons was eventually attained.

The plan did not go entirely smoothly. Militant labor frequently struck the coal, electric power, and other key industries. On February 1, 1947, a politically motivated general strike was planned, affecting railroads, power stations, and even civil servants. In a crisis emblematic of the turbulence of the time, the strike was called off after SCAP finally issued a ban on strikes.

The Economic Stabilization Board

Beginning around 1947, American interest in spurring a Japanese recovery began to grow. The Economic Stabilization Board, established in 1946, was reorganized and expanded at SCAP's direction and began drawing up a comprehensive policy for economic recovery in consultation with SCAP's Economy and Science Section. In July 1947, the official prices of basic commodities vital across the entire spectrum of industry, including steel, coal, fertilizer, caustic soda, gas, and electric power, were anchored at relatively low rates. The prices for these basic materials and energy sources were then used as the basis for computing costs and thus determining the official prices of other products. The aim was to restore production while holding inflation at bay by maintaining an official price list.

The plan had two cornerstones. One was the prices of coal and other vital commodities, the so-called stabilization band items. The other was food production, with special attention to boosting the production of ammonium sulfate and other fertilizers crucial to boosting crop output. In computing the costs, the Economic Stabilization Board sought to keep prices on average to 65 times the prewar figures, but to hold wage costs to 28 times the prewar numbers, since labor productivity was now so low. Finance was made available from the Reconstruction Finance Bank to accommodate stabilization band industries like coal, steel, and fertilizer. In the event that official prices turned out to be set too low, a mechanism was set up to cover the gap between official prices and costs through government subsidies.

The plan, as just sketched, was less than successful. Incomes rose as workers across industry campaigned to boost their basic wages, and black market prices continued to soar. Industries were unable to break even under the official prices. The coal industry plunged into debt, and the government eventually had to band-aid the industry's debts with additional loans from the Reconstruction Finance Bank.

In June 1948, it was concluded that the official price system was not working, and the plan underwent revision. Prices were computed at 110 times prewar levels, and wages at 57 times. At first sight the policy looks like a string of failures, but in concept it was shrewd. Tolerating a degree of price increase in the interest of boosting production, it seems to have sought to get production up, so that a balance would be achieved between supply and demand with the result that price increases would slow and eventually stabilize. Production would be boosted and inflation kept to small increments. A joint product of the young SCAP economists and the bureaucrats of the Economic Stabilization Board, the plan was founded on the belief in the omnipotence of government to manage and direct the economy.

The young bureaucrats in SCAP were doubtless brimming with desire to take bold steps to democratize the economy and confidence in the efficacy of economic policy. They were often characterized as New Dealers, and, indeed, members of the generation that had rooted for Roosevelt's New Deal in the United States were now in charge of democratization and economic policy in Japan.

Reopening of trade

In July 1947, the window of trade began to open a crack. All trade was conducted by the government, and individual trading companies did not deal directly with their overseas counterparts. The government bought up goods within Japan for export and bought overseas goods which it then found buyers for in Japan. This was done through a special budget account, the Foreign Trade Fund, which recorded a substantial deficit. There was no exchange rate. To illustrate in a simple fashion how trade worked, let us suppose we were to import this book from America and that its price is $10. The Japanese government buys it and sells it in Japan for ¥1,000. The exchange rate would be established at ¥100 to the dollar after the fact. In the case of exports, the reverse would hold: the government would buy a product in Japan using yen and export it to America for dollars. After the transaction, it would find out that the rate was so many yen per dollar. Every transaction had a different rate.

In general, the government would buy goods in Japan at a relatively high price so that it would benefit the exporter and sell cheaply abroad. In the case of imports, it would buy at prevailing market prices and sell comparatively cheaply. With every transaction, the Foreign Trade Fund lost money, and the fund had to replenished by transfers from the general account. In effect, the government was subsidizing exporters and importers on every transaction. It also meant that the Japanese economy was isolated from the world economy. With no foreign exchange rate, there was no way of computing how low a company had to cut its costs in order to compete in international export markets.

At about this time, United States relations with the Soviet Union were deteriorating, and attitudes toward Japan were beginning to change. A new era of SCAP policy began to unfold.

THE DODGE LINE AND THE KOREAN WAR

SCAP's initial intent had been to punish Japan and to seek its demilitarization and democratization; if the Japanese wanted to rebuild their economy, that was their own business. But over time, it was no longer possible for the United States to remain uninvolved in Japan's reconstruction. This change in America's position was primarily due to the intensification of the Cold War. The State Department Policy Planning Staff was headed by George Kennan, a famous scholar of the Soviet Union and the author of many books on that nation. On his appointment at the beginning of 1947, Kennan first worked to promote the Marshall Plan for the recovery of Europe, and then, in summer of that year, he returned to Washington where he turned to analyzing the situation in Asia. With the prospect of a confrontation between the United States and the Soviet Union in Asia and civil war raging between the Nationalists and the Communists in China, he concluded that it would be in America's best interests to foster a Japanese recovery.

At the time, Undersecretary of the Army William Draper was in charge of the Army Department's Japan policy. Once a businessman, he had joined the government like many others during the war. He, too, had begun to think that American policy was going a little too far in its handling of Japan. Draper's change of mind was prompted by the following event.

A number of American companies had had business dealings with Japan before the war, for example, General Electric, which had had a tie-up with Toshiba, and Tidewater, which had invested in Mitsubishi Oil. These companies sent an attorney, James L. Kaufmann, to Japan to investigate the status of their assets. He arrived in Japan in the midst of the deconcentration program. American businessmen are generally supporters of the Republican Party and have typically been strongly and viscerally opposed to interventionist economic policies since the New Deal. Kaufmann reported back that socialist policies "far to the left of anything tolerated" in the United States were being implemented in Japan. Draper, on seeing his report, became greatly interested in what was going on and came to Japan to find out for himself. This was one of the reasons that the deconcentration program was never completed. The word went out from Washington that deconcentration was to be put on hold, and a Deconcentration Review Board, consisting of five businessmen, was sent to Japan to look into the matter. The deconcentration program was suspended, and divestments ended up being carried out on only a small scale.

There was also a strong body of opinion among Republicans, who were the majority in Congress, that the food and aid (Government and Relief in Occupied Areas) sent to a former enemy were a waste of American taxpayers' money and that Japan's economic reconstruction was a higher priority than democratic reforms. Thus, Kennan, acting on the basis of Cold War priorities, and Draper, recognizing the need to throttle back the excesses of democratization and eliminate aid to Japan, came to the same conclusion: occupation policy had to change and Japan had to be rebuilt fast.

One manifestation of this policy shift can be seen in war reparations. Table 4.2 shows changes in the value of proposed reparations under successive SCAP plans. The Pauley mission's final report called for ¥2.4 billion in reparations in 1939 prices. By 1946, the Department of the Army had concluded that this was too harsh and twice sent a committee of inquiry led by Clifford Strike to visit Japan to reassess the reparations program. The Strike Committee eventually revised the amount downward to ¥1.6 billion in its second report. In March and April 1948, however, Draper made his second visit to Japan, accompanied by Percy Johnston, who drew up yet another reparations plan, slashing the amount to ¥0.6 billion. Draper appears to have concluded at about this time that if substantial funds were available to Japan for recovery, after the fashion of the Marshall Plan, the United States could make use of Japan's newly regained economic strength and would be able to eliminate aid at an early date.

This prompted the coalition government headed by Ashida Hitoshi of the Democratic Party, which took office after the Katayama government fell in February 1948, to put forward a platform of economic recovery using American investment. This was a medium-term stabilization program that sought to eliminate shortages of consumer goods by importing with American funds and thereby stemming inflation in order to get production back on its feet. The budget for the program was trimmed in the Diet, with the result that it was never implemented on a large scale.

One program, however, that met with a great deal of success at the time was the Cotton Revolving Fund. Since the southern

Table 4.2 Changes in Reparations Proposals (at 1939 prices, million yen)

	Industrial Facilities	Military Facilities	Total
Pauley Mission Report (Final draft of November 1946)	990	1,476	2,466
Strike Mission Report (March 1948)	172	1,476	1,648
Johnston (Draper) Report (April 1948)	102	560	662

Source: *Ekonomisuto*, March 15, 1955, p. 72. Cited in Hayashi Yujiro and Miyazaki Isamu, *Nihon no Keizai Keikaku* (Japan Economic Planning), Toyo Keizai Inc., 1957, p. 38.

United States had a surplus of cotton, the U.S. government established this ¥105 million fund with the objective of having Japan import raw cotton, manufacture products for export, and thereby earn the money to import more cotton. The southern states would benefit from this arrangement, and the Japanese textile industry would recover, which it rapidly did.

NSC 13/2

George Kennan also visited Japan in spring 1948, at approximately the same time as Draper, met with MacArthur, and obtained the general's approval for his proposal. He returned to Washington and set about laying the groundwork for a policy change. The policy shift was clearly visible from Japan. Then, in October 1948, the United States National Security Council secretly adopted resolution NSC 13/2, the gist of which was that the occupation would continue on an interim basis, that Okinawa and other bases would be retained out of military necessity, but that SCAP powers would be transferred to Japan and the status of the Japanese government enhanced. In addition, constraints on economic recovery would be eliminated as much as possible and the process of recovery would be speeded up. In May 1949, the National Security Council adopted NSC 13/3, which abandoned all further attempt to seek war reparations.

The biggest motivation for this turn of events was the Cold War, but other factors also combined to bring about the change. The Republican Party was growing in political strength, and American businessmen with investments in Japan were concerned with protecting and enhancing those interests. There was also campaigning by pro-Japanese groups in the United States, led by former ambassador Joseph C. Grew, who was on friendly terms with Yoshida Shigeru, then prime minister, and his father-in-law Makino Nobuaki.

One of the earliest manifestations of the policy shift brought by NSC 13/2 came in the form of the nine-point U.S. Interim Directive on Economic Stabilization, issued by Washington in December 1948. At the same time, President Truman sent Joseph Dodge, chairman of the Bank of Detroit, to Japan in the character of minister, with instructions to carry out the new directive. The directive is a strange document, its nine principles of economic stabilization blending, in my view, two contradictory philosophies. It bears the hallmarks of the dirigisme of the SCAP New Dealers, the belief that with close control over the economy, and a skilled hand on the tiller, success would follow. At the same time, it places primary emphasis on rationalization on the basis of free-market principles, placing the responsibility in the hands of businesses and individuals.

Principles one through three related to fiscal balance and restrictions on credit.

(1) Achieving a true balance in the consolidated budget.
(2) Accelerating and strengthening the program of taxation.
(3) Assuring that credit extension is vigorously limited.

However, items four through three involved strengthening control:

(4) Establishing an effective program to achieve wage stability.
(5) Strengthening and if necessary expanding the coverage of existing price control programs.
(6) Improving the operation of foreign trade controls and tightening existing foreign exchange controls.
(7) Improving the effectiveness of the present allocation and rationing system, particularly to maximize exports.
(8) Increasing production of all essential indigenous raw materials and manufactured products.
(9) Improving efficiency of the food collection program.

It will be apparent that the first three principles are qualitatively quite different from the other six. The directive concludes by stating that implementation of the nine principles is a precondition for establishment of a single exchange rate. We may safely conclude that Dodge intended to implement the first three principles, eliminate economic controls and restore a free economy, and then make the leap to create a single exchange rate market.

The Dodge Line: free-market economics

Dodge had been selected to go to Japan because of the close trust that Draper held in him. A confirmed believer in free-market economics, he was self-educated and had worked his way to the top. He was of the philosophy that one's own efforts were the only way to succeed and that one should not rely on government or other people. On the subject of social security, he would write in his notebook: "There are those who want something out of the pockets of politicians, but they forget that what the politicians give them comes out of the taxes that they themselves paid." From the moment he arrived in Japan in February 1949, he worked methodically and thoroughly for about a month, assembling data from SCAP and the Japanese government and consulting with the staff of five or six individuals that he had brought with him.

In March, he held a press conference, at which he contended that Japan was living beyond its means. "Japan's economy is walking on stilts, one leg of which is built on external aid from the United States, the other on internal subsidies," Dodge declared. "...If you build your stilts high enough, you can break a leg or neck getting down. Now is the time to shorten the stilts." The metaphor was very much in keeping with Dodge's style.

Dodge followed by sending to the Japanese government a stiff new policy, with three main features. The first was a true balance of the general budget. The government accounts consist of the general account—comprising ordinary government income and expenditures—and a great number of special accounts. Today, the notion of fiscal balance normally refers to a balance of the general account, but Dodge's idea of balance involved the entire central government, including the special accounts. His plan was to plug all the holes through which funds flowed out of special accounts for trade, railroads, and the like and into private industry.

Second, Japan was to bring all subsidies to light and eliminate them. This meant not only price subsidies for coal but also the deficit in the Foreign Trade Fund, which was in effect an invisible subsidy to international trading companies. All these were to be consolidated into the budget and gradually reduced. Controls were to be removed and Japan returned to a free-market economy. Third, the Reconstruction Finance Bank was prohibited from issuing bonds and undertaking new loans, stiff medicine to halt the rising flow of credit. The bank was reduced to recovering old loans and ceased to function as a financial institution.

These three proposals were central to Dodge's program and diverged radically from the policies that had previously been in place. Dodge had come to Japan armed with the powerful backing of President Truman, so SCAP could not afford to resist, and the three principles became reality in the 1949 budget.

Once he had installed the new budget, Dodge established the exchange rate at ¥360 to the dollar, a rate that was to remain unchanged for 22 years. It seems safe to conclude that he established this rate as a yardstick of Japan's competitiveness, one that would bring the Japanese economy out of its international isolation. Dodge believed that ¥360 = $1 was a level at which 80 percent of Japan's export industries would somehow be able to compete in international markets.

The impact of Dodge's fiscal balance policy can be seen from the figures for the flow and absorption of funds between the government and private sectors. The outflow of treasury funds to the private sector stood at ¥32 billion in fiscal year 1946, ¥59 billion in fiscal 1947, and ¥21 billion in fiscal 1948. In fiscal 1949, the position was reversed: treasury intake exceeded outflows by ¥37.3 billion, with ¥58.3 billion in private-sector funds being absorbed by the government. These private funds were absorbed by the government, tightening the money supply. The Reconstruction Finance Bank figures tell a similar story. As depicted in table 4.3, the Reconstruction Finance Bank accounted for 70 percent of borrowings by the coal industry, 87 percent of those by the electric power industry, and 65 percent from the maritime shipping industry. That some 23 percent of all finance to industry was channeled through the Reconstruction Finance Bank attests to the importance of this institution and gives some measure of the shock when it was prevented from further new lending.

Table 4.3 Loans by the Reconstruction Finance Bank (as of end of March, 1949, in billions of yen)

	Loans Outstanding at all Financial Institutions (A)	Loans Outstanding at the Reconstruction Finance Bank (B)	$\frac{B}{A}$ (%)
Total	566.1	132.0	23.3
Loans to Coal Industry	67.3	47.5	70.6
Loans to Electric Power Industry	25.4	22.2	87.4
Loans to Marine Transportation Industry	20.6	13.4	65.0

Source: Nihon Kaihatsu Ginko Junen Shi (A Ten-Year History of the Japan Development Bank). 1976.

Table 4.4 Inflation Trends (average in 1934–36 = 1)

Year	Wholesale Prices	Rate of Increase in Wholesale Prices as a Multiple of the Previous Year	Consumer Prices	Rate of Increase in Consumer Prices as a Multiple of the Previous Year	Free and Black Market Prices as a Multiple of Official Prices	
					Production Goods	Consumer Goods
1945	3.5	1.51	—	—	—	—
1946	16.3	4.64	50.6	—	7.2	8.3
1947	48.2	2.96	109.1	2.16	5.3	5.1
1948	127.9	2.66	189.0	1.73	2.9	2.9
1949	208.8	1.63	236.9	1.25	1.7	1.8
1950	246.8	1.18	219.9	0.93	1.2	1.3
1951	342.5	1.39	255.5	1.16	1.1	1.1

Sources: Wholesale prices: Bank of Japan; Consumer prices: Prime Minister's Office, Statistics Bureau; Free and black market prices as a multiple of official prices: Bank of Japan.

One more thing must be said about Dodge's program. Table 4.4, Inflation Trends, shows the tremendous advance of inflation and the heights to which black markets rose. However, in figure 4.4 we see that the prices that had risen continuously until about mid-1948 had slowed visibly by the end of that year. Price indices for production materials on the black market and for consumer goods began to subside after peaking around the beginning of 1949. Prices had begun to settle before the Dodge Line was imposed.

The reasons for this slowdown in the inflationary trend are fairly obvious. Policies had been implemented that focused on pricing mechanisms, and industrial output had returned to about

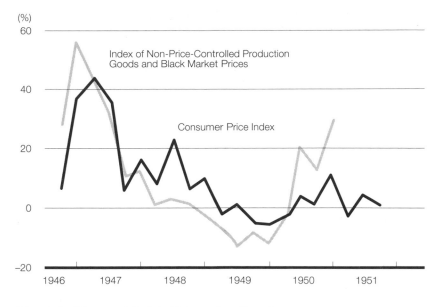

Fig. 4.4. Rise and Fall in Prices, by Quarter

Sources: See Table 4.4

60 percent of prewar levels around the end of 1948. Agricultural output was back to previous levels. Supplies of food and everyday goods were now adequate, even plentiful. On a personal note, I was living in Tokyo at the time, and I recollect that around spring 1948 I no longer had to go out into the countryside to buy food. As goods began to circulate, there was less need to buy from the black market, so the well-known phenomenon of black market prices leading other prices on an upward spiral evaporated, and the gap between black market and official prices began to close.

In the latter half of 1948, moreover, the government began to crack down on taxes. In the period from January through March 1949, the treasury accounts showed a big intake from the private sector, and since the private sector was already short of funds, Japan now found itself in a period of tight money supply. This can be seen from the numbers for Bank of Japan note issues in figure 4.5. The Dodge Line was announced in March 1949, and the budget implemented in April, so the truth is that inflation had begun to subside before Dodge's arrival. The Dodge Line, in my view,

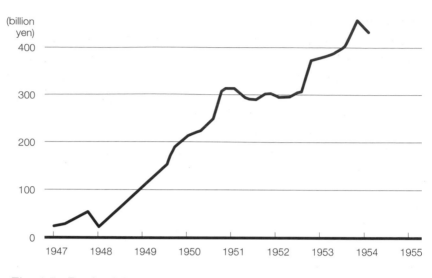

Fig. 4.5. Bank of Japan Note Issues

Source: Bank of Japan.

simply dealt the final blow. This does not mean that Dodge's policies represent effort wasted. Companies that had long bathed in the warm comfort of government controls awoke to his dash of cold water and learned that they would have to streamline their operations and cut costs if they were to return to a free-market economy and withstand international competition. It was in this lesson that we may perhaps discover the greatest significance of Dodge's program.

Under Dodge's program, companies were faced with a tight money supply. If no one acted business after business would fail. Both the Japanese government and SCAP were understandably worried about this prospect and came up with a policy package to ease the money supply by recycling the surplus funds back to the private sector. The primary conduit for recycling was Bank of Japan loans to commercial banks for relending to the private sector. The second route was Bank of Japan purchases of securities held by commercial banks—mostly public bonds—thereby increasing the banks' cash in hand for release to the private sector. By these two means, the credit squeeze was eased, but the resultant overloaning—banks having more on loan than on deposit—was to cause problems later on.

The Shoup Report

One other memorable event took place in 1949: the tax reforms introduced following a report of a team of tax experts headed by Dr. Carl Shoup. The committee came to Japan and wrote a set of recommendations advocating a philosophy of direct taxation and a system based on equitable burdens. As we will later see, although this tax system has undergone many modifications, the basic framework of direct taxation and progressive taxation of income continued until the 1980s. The recent growth of debate about the tax system, especially the persistent arguments in favor of increasing indirect taxes, may be taken as emblematic of an ongoing fundamental reassessment of the tax policies introduced in the Shoup committee recommendations.

In 1949, the Japanese National Railways, Nippon Telegraph and Telephone, and the tobacco monopoly were taken out from under direct government control and transformed into public corporations. In the transition, the Japanese National Railways dismissed 100,000 employees, sending labor unions into an uproar of protest and resulting in a series of mysterious cases of industrial sabotage and murder.

On the Asian continent, the period of 1948–1949 saw drastic changes. Chinese Communist forces pushed south, and the Nationalist regime moved to Taiwan, leaving the mainland unified in the hands of the Communists. Views of the situation in Asia changed overnight. In June 1950, the Korean War broke out. Cold War tensions that had been smoldering in one corner of Asia now burst into open flame. The global economy had been stagnating in recession since 1949, but with the outbreak of war, countries began buying up strategic goods, and prices began moving upward around the world. In table 4.4 and figure 4.4, you will notice the sharp upsurge in wholesale and retail prices beginning about mid-1950. Domestically, Japan had been in trouble with recession under Dodge's economic program; now suddenly business picked up. Importers abruptly found themselves frantically trying to meet the supply shortfalls in raw materials and other imported goods.

The Korean War

When war broke out on the Korean peninsula, the American Army in Japan went into action. Then the order went out that Japan should set up a National Police Reserve, possibly partly out of a concern for maintaining public order domestically, since just before war broke out, the occupation had ordered Japan Communist Party leaders purged from official posts and had banned publication of *Akahata* (Red Flag), the party organ.

In order for U.S. armed forces to go to Korea, they required large quantities of materiel. These, it was decided, would be procured in Japan. Since this was not part of the occupation costs, it was not paid out of the budget for Termination of War Activities, but came out of the U.S. miliary budget and, more to the point, was paid in U.S. dollars. As can be seen in table 4.5, these special procurements amounted to an influx of $300 million in the first and second years of the war and $500 million in the third, including repairs and other services.

As table 4.6, further shows, the Japanese economy changed rapidly during the Korean War period. In 1949, trade showed a

Table 4.5 Value of Special Procurement Orders (in thousand dollars)

	Goods	Services	Total
1st year	229,995	98,927	328,922
2nd year	235,851	79,767	315,618
3rd year	305,543	186,785	492,328
4th year	124,700	170,910	295,610
5th year	78,516	107,740	186,256
Five-Year Total	974,607	644,129	1,618,736

Source: Economic Planning Agency.

Table 4.6 Trade and Production at the Time of the Korean War

	1949	1950	1951	1952	1953	1954
Exports (million dollars)	510	820	1,355	1,273	1,275	1,629
Extraordinary Procurements (million dollars)	—	592		824	809	597
Imports (million dollars)	905	975	1,995	2,028	2,410	2,399
Industrial Production Index (1949 = 100)	100	123	169	181	221	240

Sources: Imports and exports: Ministry of Finance; Extraordinary procurements: Bank of Japan; Industrial production index (includes mining): Ministry of International Trade and Industry.

deficit of $400 million, with exports standing at $500 million and imports at $900 million. The thinking at the time was that there was little alternative to having the United States bail Japan out. However, the Korean War boosted exports to $800 million in 1950 and to $1.3 billion in 1951.

There was more. Extraordinary procurements income in table 4.6 includes dollars spent by troops and their families in Japan and surpasses even the value of special procurements shown in table 4.5. In 1951, for instance, the $1.3 billion in exports was matched by nearly $600 million in special procurement earnings for the two-year period 1950–1951. In 1952, special procurement earnings had risen to $800 million, compared with $1.2 billion in exports. This huge influx of dollars marked a major step in the development of the Japanese economy.

As I explained earlier, in my discussion of the wartime Material Mobilization plans, the Japanese economy is basically founded on processing trade. This means that the amount of raw materials and fuel that can be imported determines the output of the economy as a whole. When foreign exchange is in short supply, it is not possible to boost production by making an all-out effort (as in wartime) because the crucial raw materials are not available. During the Korean War period, imports of raw materials shot up right when plant and labor were in surplus, pushing output up 80 percent in the space of three years. Corporate profits soared, and the ensuing boom set the economic recovery on track, as can be seen in figure 4.6. The stars of this economic resurgence were cotton spinning, paper pulp, fertilizer, and other industries manufacturing materials for consumer goods that had been around since prewar days.

Extraordinary military procurements

One aspect of the special procurements is highly problematic. It relates to the nature of the military demand that propelled the boom. Table 4.7, ranks special procurement items by contract value. In the first year the principal items were trucks, cotton cloth, woollen cloth, and other daily necessities of army life. In the second year, motor vehicle parts and coal lead the roster, but by

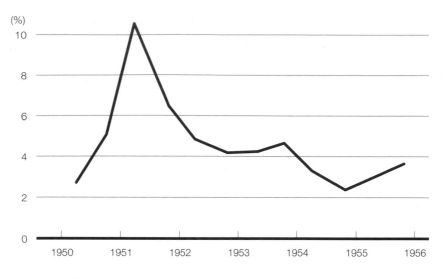

Fig. 4.6. Ratio of Profits to Gross Capital

Source: Mitsubishi Economic Research Institute, *Honpo Jigyo Seiseki Bunseki* (Analysis of Results of Japanese Business).

Table 4.7 Extraordinary Procurements Ranked by Contracted Value

Rank	1st year	2nd year	3rd year	4th year	5th year
1.	Trucks	Automobile parts	Weapons	Weapons	Weapons
2.	Cotton cloth	Coal	Coal	Coal	Coal
3.	Woollen cloth	Cotton cloth	Hemp sacks	Foodstuffs	Foodstuffs
4.	Construction materials	Drum cans	Barbed wire	Furniture	Furniture
5.	Hemp sacks	Hemp sacks	Cement	Dry cell batteries	Cement

Source: Economic Planning Agency.

the third year munitions show up in first place. In 1951, the United States was seriously considering fighting World War III with the Soviet Union. In such an event, Japan would necessarily become a base for American actions against the Soviets. We know from American documents that the United States was indeed thinking along those lines. In that case, an arms industry would be an important element in rearming Japan. It was planned to use Japan's arms industries to provide weapons for noncommunist

Southeast Asia, and some factories were already being used for repairs. Some Japanese industrialists began moving enthusiastically to revive the old armaments industries.

Japan's output of military supplies soared. Production of weapons had been banned at the direction of SCAP at the beginning of the occupation, but in 1952, just before the San Francisco Treaty went into effect, the Americans partly lifted the ban, and Japan resumed production of military supplies and weaponry. The United States laid in the groundwork before the treaty became effective. The Korean War era was an aberration, then, in that it represented the period in Japan's postwar economic history in which the potential for a revival of Japan's prewar armaments industry was its greatest.

That Japan did not slide down that slippery slope is attributable to the thaw in U.S.-Soviet relations. In March 1953, Stalin died, and the new Soviet leaders sought a thaw in relations with the United States. The United States responded in kind, and beginning in the mid-1950s, the two countries embarked on a period of peaceful coexistence, and Japanese armaments output declined accordingly. But the first two years of the Korean War marked the height of U.S.-Soviet tensions and provided the backdrop to the signing of the San Francisco Peace Treaty and the U.S.-Japan Security Treaty. Despite the efforts of Yoshida Shigeru, Japan was forced to recognize Taiwan over the Communist mainland.

Summing up
To sum up the occupation era: The process of postwar democratization and the subsequent economic recovery were marked by much turmoil. Japan advanced in a zigzag fashion, and sometimes marched in reverse, as talk of rearming surfaced. But overall, Japan emerged from the occupation era with higher living standards for the poorer segments of its society as a result of SCAP's vigorous democratization policies. Workers' and farmers' incomes had risen. The ranks of the wealthy had been thinned by the capital levy and inflation. True, there had been some who had made fortunes in the black market, but it is safe to say that on the balance progress had been made in the direction of greater economic

and social equality. Industry was no longer dominated by giant organizations, and businesses were in competition in their markets. The foundation had been laid for Japan's postwar economy and society.

WEALTH WITHOUT MILITARY POWER (1952–1965)

By 1956: steel, shipbuilding, electrical machinery, chemicals and other heavy industries were investing robustly in plant and equipment. The Iwato Boom is in full swing. The White Paper on the Economy will soon proclaim the postwar era over.

1952	*March*	The Law for the Acceleration of Rationalization of Enterprises is promulgated. SCAP directs Japanese firms to make armaments. Heavy industries and chemical manufacturers actively begin to import new technologies.
1953		The Anti-Monopoly Law is amended to permit recession and rationalization cartels.
	December	Credit is squeezed as balance of international payments goes into deficit. Many strikes at this time, triggered by corporate cost-cutting.
1954–56		Recession segues into quantitative prosperity. 1956: The Jinmu boom. There is much large-scale capital investment.
1955		The Rightist and Leftist Socialist parties reunite. The Liberal and Democratic parties merge.
1957–59		In 1957, the balance of payments deficit causes a tight money supply. 1958: The nabezoko recession. A sharp recovery in 1959 leads into the Iwato boom. Beginning in 1958, the energy revolution takes hold.
1960	*May–June*	Nationwide demonstrations occur against the U.S.-Japan Security Treaty.
	July	Ikeda Hayato becomes prime minister and announces the Income-Doubling Plan. A trade liberalization program is announced.
1962		The money supply tightens.
1964		Japan signs IMF Article 8 and joins the OECD. Sato Eisaku becomes prime minister. The money supply tightens further.
1965		Securities panic occurs in the midst of recession. The government decides to issue long-term national bonds.

Lecture 5

WEALTH WITHOUT MILITARY POWER (1952–1965)

STATUS OF THE POSTWAR ECONOMY

Before I embark on my main discussion, let me begin by sketching the situation as the postwar disruption drew to a close and comparing it with the situation in the beginning of the Showa era. I have already discussed how, in the late 1920s, about one-half of Japan's population was working in agriculture and of those who were working in industry, a high proportion were employed in traditional industries. When war broke out in China and the Pacific, efforts were made to ensure that workers remained in agriculture in order to maintain the food supply, but commerce, services, and light manufacturing were stripped of their workforces and equipment as the nation mobilized for war.

By the time of the San Francisco Peace Treaty, about six years after the war ended, Japan had changed dramatically. The number of people working in agriculture had swelled from 13 million before the war to nearly 18 million at the end of the war as farm communities temporarily absorbed an influx of population, and although by the time of the peace treaty the numbers had slipped somewhat, they still remained in the region of 16 million. Commerce, services and other tertiary industries, which had been destroyed during the war, were now clearly on the rebound. Wholesalers, retailers, and jobbers had returned to their old occupations, and distribution networks that existed prior to the imposition of price controls had been rebuilt. Light industries made a remarkable recovery, textile products were in short supply, and exports had restarted.

Traditional consumer goods like tatami matting, wooden geta sandals, and soy sauce had revived, and production of miscellaneous household wares that once were destined for the export market, had picked up. It was existing industries and small firms—rather than new industries or big companies—that had absorbed Japan's overabundant manpower supply after the war. By about 1955 an economic structure had been reestablished that resembled that of prewar times. This can be seen in figure 5.1 from the fact that the number of farmers and the nonfarming self-employed (personal business owners and family employees) had increased. (In the late 1950s and early 1960s, their numbers were to plunge again, dramatically.)

In the secondary sector, only heavy industries held a substantially higher percentage of the workforce than in the late 1920s. As I related earlier, this may in fact have been the economic legacy of the war, since heavy industries came through the war with large numbers of technicians and laborers and much equipment. Once

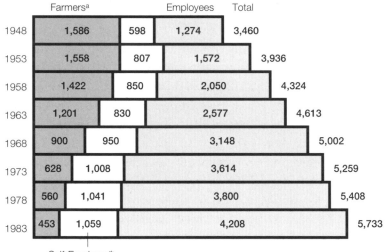

Fig. 5.1 Farmers, Self-Employed, and Employees (in 10,000)

Source: Compiled from Prime Minister's Office, Statistics Bureau. *Labor Force Survey.*
Note: Owing to sampling errors, the sums of the classes do not match the totals.
a Farmers: Self-employed operators of farms or forestry businesses and family-member employees.
b Self-Employed: Self-employed operators of nonfarming or forestry businesses and family-member employees.

the storm of war and its immediate aftermath had passed and a degree of normalcy had returned, this economic picture, not too unlike that which prevailed in prewar days, became the starting point for a new burst of growth.

Consensus for building a wealthy nation

As the occupation drew to a close, a major debate took place about the direction of the Japanese economy. It was generally agreed by all that the future lay in promoting heavy industries rather than light manufacturing. But opinions divided whether to focus on the development of domestic resources or whether, as in prewar days, to concentrate on exporting those manufactured products that Japan produced best and importing those that it was less successful at manufacturing at home. It was a debate on principles between advocates of domestic-oriented development and those who sought to found the wealth of the nation on trade. Nonetheless, the two positions surfaced from time to time in connection with individual industries. For example, it was argued in some quarters that Japan's automobile industry could not be expected to develop rapidly with indigenous technology, and it would be better to take the path of importing.

However, the majority of Japanese in this period wanted nothing more than to restore the Japanese economy to prewar levels. Although the Far Eastern Commission had determined that the prewar period referred to the period from 1930 through 1934, Japan's own Economic Stabilization Board had targeted the average for the period 1934–1936, which marked the peak of Japanese prewar economic prosperity. It was the collective desire of the nation to regain that level that drove Japan's subsequent economic development; without anyone having made any public commitments, a national agreement had emerged that Japan would attempt to become wealthy again without becoming a military power, abandoning the second half of the slogan "A wealthy nation and a strong army" of half a century before. The emergence of this national consensus was, I believe, an important development, and it is reflected, in my view, in Prime Minister Yoshida Shigeru's passionate resistance to American pressure for Japan to rearm. Table 5.1 shows the years in which prewar levels were attained in different sectors of the economy.

Reassessment of occupation policies

From 1951 on, as the deadline for independence approached, the policies and institutions of the occupation period underwent a reassessment. A variety of policies implemented at the direction of SCAP were permitted to be reviewed after MacArthur's dismissal, and an Ordinance Review Committee was set up to reevaluate all directives issued under the terms of the Potsdam Declaration. The nature of the committee's deliberations is still not fully known, but it appears that there were heated arguments by those favoring a return to prewar institutions. For example, almost all the administrative committees were abolished, the Economic Stabilization Board was restructured into the smaller Economic Advisory Agency (forerunner of the present-day Economic Planning Agency), the prerogatives of the ministries and agencies that the board had subsumed were restored to their original proprietors.

Table 5.1 Years When Major Economic Indicators Surpassed Prewar Levels

	Year in Which Item		
	Passed Prewar Level	Attained 200% of Prewar Level	Passed Prewar or Wartime Peak
Industrial Production	FY1951	FY1957	FY1955
Real Gross National Product (GNP)	FY1951	FY1959	FY1954
Real Plant and Equipment Investment	FY1951	FY1956	FY1957
Real Personal Consumption Expenditure	FY1951	FY1960	FY1952
Real Export Receipts	FY1957	FY1963	FY1960
Real Import Payments	FY1956	FY1961	FY1959
Real Per Capita GNP	FY1953	FY1962	FY1957
Real Per Capita Personal Consumption Expenditure	FY1953	FY1964	FY1956
Real Per Worker Productivity	FY1951	FY1962	—

Source: Koza Nihon Keizai (Lectures on the Japanese Economy). Nihon Hyoron Sha. Vol. 1, 1964.
Notes: 1. Industrial production is from the Ministry of International Trade and Industry index.
2. Per worker productivity is real GNP divided by working population.
3. Exports and imports are from national income accounts.
4. National incomes are based on old estimates.
5. Prewar levels are average figures in 1934–1936.

Independence was followed with public calls to revise the constitution and heightened demands for compensation by landlords who had been hard hit by the agricultural reforms. Veterans' benefits were restored. And calls were made to ease the restrictions of the Anti-Monopoly Law on the grounds that these were antipathetic to Japan's economic structure. After the surrender, the pendulum of public sentiment had lurched to the left; now, in the post-independence days it swung back to the right, albeit nowhere as far as in prewar days. Rearmament and the recommencement of arms production were but part of this reversal. Nonetheless the changes that were made were not of such an extent that they undid the principles of the postwar reforms. With the global thaw, many of the occupation reforms, after review, took root. It is safe to say that this was because the reforms and democratization of the immediate postwar period were widely supported across all segments of society.

Favorable international climate

Before I go on to discuss the period of rapid economic growth that was to follow, I would like to remind you that this growth was fostered by a highly favorable international climate. In the period between 1950 and 1965, world economic growth was extremely high: global average GDP growth reached an unprecedented 5 percent. This growth made it possible for Japan's exports to grow steadily and for it to import raw materials. Moreover, as resource development progressed around the world, supplies became more abundant, and crude oil and other raw material prices embarked on a long-term decline. Yet, export prices were high by comparison. Japan was able to make the most of its favorable terms of trade. By contrast, in the late 1920s, the lifting of the gold embargo plunged America and the rest of the world into negative growth that thrust the Japanese economy into deep recession. If the period of the lifting of the gold embargo was analogous to putting the economy on ice, the environment for the postwar economic growth may be likened to a hothouse.

During the period 1950–1965, it is calculated that Japanese export growth stood in a 2 to 1 relation with world imports. If world imports grew 5 percent, Japan's exports tended to grow 10 percent. Yet for all the export competitiveness that Japan had developed, it would not have been able to exploit that competitive edge if the global economy had not been developing so strongly. The Japanese economy was boosted in its growth spurt by this favorable world economic climate.

THE STARTING LINE OF GROWTH

Let us begin with the manufacturing industry up to the mid-1950s. Bottlenecks constrained growth in a number of fields about the time of the Korean War. In particular, manufacturing capacity was low, and without an expansion, economic activity was stymied. Major bottlenecks are often pointed at in electric power, steel, marine transportation, and coal. Electric power was in extremely short supply, and planned power outages were regularly implemented. During evening demand peaks, power would be shut off for a set amount of time—15 or 20 minutes—in each area. Power supplies had to be massively expanded in order to eliminate the outages. In the steel industry, capacity was short, and production processes needed to be streamlined. The merchant marine had been almost entirely wiped out during the war and would have to be rebuilt from scratch. The coal industry, Japan's major domestic source of energy, also needed to boost its capacity, along with upgrading its mining capabilities.

Policy at the time focused on resurrecting and rationalizing these four key industries. Specific manifestations of this policy included the establishment of the Export-Import Bank of Japan to provide long-term credit for exports and the Japan Development Bank, established with the aim of providing funds for capital investments. This latter institution was the reincarnation of the Reconstruction Finance Bank, which was reorganized to supply funds for investment in the four key industries. In the case of shipbuilding, since Japan's merchant ships had been commandeered by the government during the war and had been sunk almost to the last vessel, the government instituted a shipbuilding policy of lending money at low interest rates to marine transportation companies to build new ships. This policy was carried out from 1949 through the early 1980s in one form or another. This, naturally, had a major impact on the revival of Japan's shipbuilding industry.

Figure 5.2 shows how much money the Japan Development Bank lent to which industries during the five-year period from its inception to 1955. Of the ¥253.4 billion in loans made during that period, electric power was the recipient of 46 percent, followed in second place by marine transportation with 25 percent and then coal and steel with yet smaller percentages. All other industries combined accounted for less than 25 percent of Japan Development Bank lending, an indication of the extent to which funding for development was focused on the four key industries.

This period was marked by a series of major hydroelectric power construction projects, including the Sakuma Dam and the Ikari Dam. The last of the series was the Kurobe No. 4 Power Station, after which a lack of potential sites for major hydroelectric projects compelled a shift away from hydroelectric power to coal generation as the mainstay of Japan's power supply.

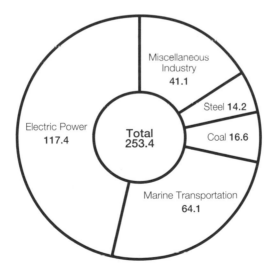

Fig. 5.2. Breakdown of Japan Development Bank Lending (Totals for 1951–1955, in billions of yen)

Source: Compiled from data in *Nihon Kaihatsu Ginko Nijugonen Shi* (A Twenty-Five-Year History of the Japan Development Bank). 1976.

Complementing Japan's nine regional electric power utilities and local power companies, a special corporation, the Electric Power Development Company, was established exclusively for the construction and development of power sources. As can be seen from figure 5.3, power generation capacity climbed steadily throughout the 1950s, enabling power supplies to cover the rising demand for electricity that accompanied the development of manufacturing.

Table 5.2, Japan's Shipbuilding Programs, shows the efforts to reestablish the marine transportation industry. The figures indicate how many ships were built each year and how much government finance was available for their construction.

In the steel industry, two rationalization programs were instituted. The First Rationalization Program, implemented in 1951–1955, focused on the introduction of rolling processes to produce thin steel sheet, an area in which the Japanese steel industry was conspicuously lagging. Strip mills—continuous automated rolling equipment—were introduced in an effort to streamline steelmaking processes, first at Fuji Seitetsu Company's Hirohata

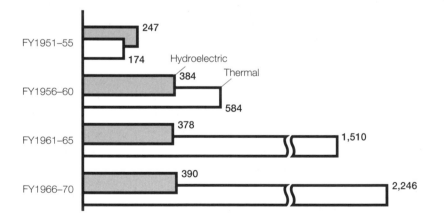

Fig. 5.3. Completion of Electric Power Development Projects (10,000 kilowatts)

Source: From *Nihon Kaihatsu Ginko Nijugonen Shi* (A Twenty-Five-Year History of the Japan Development Bank). 1976.
Note: In addition, 10,000 kilowatts of nuclear power were completed in FY1961–65 and 1,320,000 kilowatts in FY1966–70.

Table 5.2 Japan's Shipbuilding Program

	Number of Vessels	Gross Tons (10,000 tons)	Contract Price for Vessel by Government (¥100 million)	Percent Financed
FY1947–50	164	69.1	581	57
FY1951–55	159	131.7	1,776	44
FY1956–60	140	135.8	1,654	50
FY1961–65	164	449.4	3,129	66
FY1966–70	290	1,135.8	6,921	69

Source: Tallied from figures given in *Nihon Kaihatsu Ginko Nijugonen Shi* (A Twenty-Five-Year History of the Japan Development Bank). 1976.

plant and then elsewhere. This was followed by a Second Rationalization Plan, covering the period up to 1960. The primary focus of investment was in rolling processes, as can be seen in figure 5.4. As a result of the two programs, production capacity was boosted by 12.5 million metric tons for pig iron, 28.2 million metric tons for crude steel, and 140 million metric tons for rolled steel.

The rationalization plans were agreed on in discussions between the Ministry of International Trade and Industry (MITI) and representatives of the industry. But not all companies played along. The president of Kawasaki Steel Corporation in Kobe, Nishiyama Yataro, struck a deal with the government of Chiba Prefecture and embarked on plans to construct a steel plant in Chiba. The company had begun its existence as a spin-off of the steelmaking division of Kawasaki Shipbuilding, buying up pig iron and scrap to make steel. Known as an open-hearth manufacturer, it was not an integrated steel manufacturer—making everything from pig iron to finished steel—of which there were only three in the country—Yawata Steel, Fuji Steel, and Nippon Kokan. Kawasaki Steel, determined to stake its claim on the field, began constructing its own plant in Chiba in the face of much opposition from its corporate rivals and many others.

The project was viewed as adventurism by many. The governor of the Bank of Japan, Ichimada Hisato, was credited with remarking that the factory would be pushing up weeds. But once the plant was completed, demand for steel grew prodigiously, and Kawasaki Steel enjoyed stunning success. It opened the way for

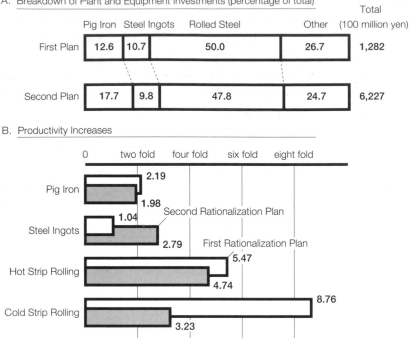

A. Breakdown of Plant and Equipment Investments (percentage of total)

	Pig Iron	Steel Ingots	Rolled Steel	Other	Total (100 million yen)
First Plan	12.6	10.7	50.0	26.7	1,282
Second Plan	17.7	9.8	47.8	24.7	6,227

B. Productivity Increases

Fig. 5.4. First and Second Steel Industry Rationalization Plans

Source: Nihon Kaihatsu Ginko Nijugonen Shi (A Twenty-Five-Year History of the Japan Development Bank). 1976.

Sumitomo Metal Industries, Kobe Steel, and others to enter the ranks of the integrated steelmakers at the time of the Second Rationalization Plan.

Capital accumulation policies

Now that the development of manufacturing had become a national preoccupation, the government actively tried to promote industrial development. The most comprehensive effort of this kind was the Law for the Acceleration of Rationalization of Enterprises, passed in March 1952.

In the previous year, however, the Special Taxation Measures Law was passed, providing incentives in the form of accelerated depreciation for major investments by corporations. Normally, it is assumed that a piece of machinery will last, for example, for 10 years and that its value will decline by one-tenth each year; when that amount is depreciated, the money saved will make it possible to buy a new machine in 10 years' time. The depreciation is counted as a loss to the corporation. In the case of accelerated depreciation, however, the tax law allows 40 or 50 percent of the value of a machine to be depreciated and counted as a loss in the first year or so after installation, even though the machine might be presumed to last for 10 years. So when companies make big investments, their losses increase under accelerated depreciation, and profits decline, with the result that taxes are reduced. In 1951, a system was already in place in which it was possible to make money by reducing taxes through investing in plant and equipment. I believe these incentives to be somewhat problematic from the perspective of "fairness" enunciated in the principles of the Shoup Mission Report, but for a Japan that was newly "independent," the rules were drawn up to favor the accumulation of capital.

In the Law for the Acceleration of Rationalization of Enterprises, drawn up by MITI in 1952, iron, steel, steel rolling, oil refining, metals, chemical fertilizer, soda, and dyes were listed as Designated Industries for the application of the law. Policy measures targeting these industries included subsidies to upgrade technology; loans of government-owned machinery and equipment; shortened depreciation periods for experimental and research facilities; special depreciation provisions for the installation of modern plant and machinery, in particular, 50 percent depreciation of the purchase price in the first year; and reductions on excise on modern plant and equipment. The 50 percent special depreciation provision, together with the reduction of excise on fixed assets, proved particularly effective in stimulating corporate investments.

The Law for the Acceleration of Rationalization of Enterprises also provided for the central and local governments to improve road and port facilities where necessary to streamline industry. Indeed, much construction was undertaken at public expense to build infrastructure as a condition for attracting industries to the more rural regions. There was also considerable central government intervention. One example is the demands to reduce the basic unit of production (for example, the number of tons of coke needed to produce one ton of steel expressed as a percentage). The government collected data from firms and publicized its own targets for reducing the basic unit. Another tool was the assistance provided to local governments to analyze and advise on the rationalization needs of small business. To foster compliance with its programs, the government was empowered to impose reporting requirements and to conduct on-site inspections. During World War II, the government had passed enterprise laws that simultaneously promoted industrial development and tightened government controls; now in the postwar era, it adopted a similar policy to foster industrial development, enlarging the range of industries that fell within the scope of its intervention.

It is safe to say that the Law for the Acceleration of Rationalization of Enterprises played a major role in the postwar development of Japanese industry, and many companies embarked on ambitious programs of capital investment under its provisions. In addition, as can be seen from table 5.3, a variety of policies were undertaken to reduce corporate taxes. For example, there were special exemptions for export earnings, exemptions for production of designated major commodities, and increased allowances for reserves against bad loans. Measures were targeted at specific industries; for example, hydroelectric power suppliers were permitted reserves against drought. Since this was the period in which the government was putting its money on hydroelectricity over thermal power, if there were to be a drought, the argument went, power companies would have to use additional thermal power, pushing up their costs. The program allowed power companies to prepare against such losses. Inducements like this and many others sought to build corporate capital reserves.

During the 1950s, MITI came to the belief that the machine and electronics industries would be particularly important and obtained the passage of two pieces of legislation—the Law for Special Provisional Measures to Promote the Machinery Industry and the Law for Special Provisional Measures to Promote the Electronics Industry—allowing the minister of International Trade

Table 5.3 Increases in Tax-Exempt Income and Corporate Reserves (in millions of yen)

Category	FY1950	FY1951	FY1952	FY1953	FY1954	FY1955	Total for FY1950–1955
Tax Exempt Income							
Special Exemption for Export Earnings	—	—	—	1,379	4,004	8,269	13,652
Tax-Exempt Income from Important Products	1,027	3,628	7,348	10,129	10,748	14,242	47,122
Tax-Exempt Income from Dividends from Capital Expansion	—	—	—	—	3,021	10,962	13,983
Total	1,027	3,628	7,348	11,508	17,773	33,473	74,757
General Reserves and Reserves Against Losses	3,666	11,823	74,096	101,006	110,603	104,311	405,505

Note: Computed on the basis of corporations whose business year finished by the end of January 1956.

and Industry to draw up rationalization plans for these industries secure the funds for their implementation and establish cartels covering the items manufactured, their quantities, and technology. Here again, we find the tradition of the wartime enterprise laws alive and well.

As the Japanese economy developed, economic friction heated up, and Japan's industrial policy often came in for attack from overseas. I believe it was in the 1950s that Japan's policies took their basic shape and were most effective, the classic example being the capital-building policies just discussed.

Impact of imported technology

Technology was another factor. During the war and the early post-war era, Japan was in a state of technological isolation, with little information entering the country about technological advances abroad. In the 1950s, acutely aware of the technological gap, corporations scrambled to bring in overseas technology. The government allocated precious foreign reserves to foster the import of new technology. Technology import numbers are shown in figure 5.5. The strip mills discussed earlier are a prime example of such government-promoted technology imports.

We can cite several examples of closely planned technological innovation that took place during this period. First, the introduction of arc welding techniques into shipbuilding brought major changes to that industry. In the old days, ships where made by placing sheets of steel against each other, opening holes, and punching rivets through them. Newly introduced arc welding techniques were adopted across the board since there was no loss of strength, thus streamlining production processes and slicing costs. Eventually, block shipbuilding was developed in which sections of a vessel are first welded up in a factory and then assembled in the dry dock, a technique that produced even greater efficiency of operations. The shipbuilding industry underwent a rapid recovery, and by 1956 Japan lead the world in the tonnage of ships built and exported.

One imported technology of the time that had a major impact was synthetic fibers. The technology for manufacture of nylon was brought in by Toray and Teijin, and with it, the Japanese textile industry underwent a major transformation. Initially, demand for the fibers was limited to women's stockings and other clothing items, but eventually, the story goes, someone realized that the fibers were ideal for fishing nets, and the market expanded. Another sector that was transformed by imported technology was construction. Dam construction and electric power development entailed the introduction of bulldozers and other large construction equipment, which streamlined construction methods and slashed schedules for large projects. The new technology eventual-

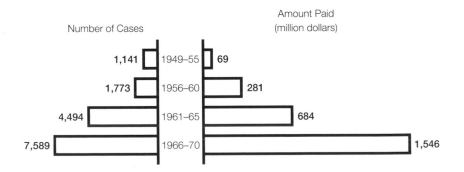

Fig. 5.5. Introduction of Foreign Technology

Source: Science and Technology Agency. *Gaikoku Gijutsu Donyu Nenji Hokoku* (Annual Report on the Introduction of Foreign Technology).

ly led to the emergence of Komatsu and other construction machinery manufacturers.

Not that all imported technologies succeeded. There were a number of egregious failures. For example, new equipment designed to use coal gas instead of hydrogen gas in the manufacture of the fertilizer ammonium sulfate was rendered uneconomical by rising coal prices. Nonetheless, it is true that, overall, imported technology blew new life into industry.

Homegrown technology also advanced. Kuraray undertook its own development of technology to produce vinyl chloride fiber. A market for this was first found in school uniforms, and later a multitude of uses emerged.

Import allotments and the machinery industries
We should also touch on the automobile industry in this period. Domestic production became possible as the result of a combination of protection policies and the introduction of outside technology. The best example of protection policies was the foreign currency allocation system. Since Japan's international competitiveness was weak, there was a major danger of an import surplus, so a foreign exchange account was set up that remained in place until the late 1950s. Every quarter, foreign exchange would be allocated to specific items, and no other items could be imported. It was, in effect, a kind of import restriction.

The foreign currency allocations were used by MITI and other government agencies to protect industries that they sought to have develop. Only a tiny amount was allocated to the import of automobiles. Thus, within Japan, one could only buy domestically produced cars. This was one of the reasons that Japan's car industry developed, but technology also played a role. Toyota had been teetering on the edge of bankruptcy when Toyoda Eiji returned from a visit to a Ford plant in the United States and embarked on a five-year plan to improve production lines introducing modern plant and equipment. In 1956, the first Toyopet Crown rolled off the production line, opening up the way to Toyota's success as an independent car manufacturer. Nissan tied up with Austin, Hino with Renault, and Isuzu with Rooth. Initially they imported and assembled parts, but each eventually progressed to manufacturing their own vehicles domestically.

Electrical machinery was another area in which import quotas played a significant role. In major dam projects like the Sakuma Dam, large numbers of generators were needed, but a foreign currency quota was allocated for the import of only one generator. The imported generator was taken apart and reverse engineered, and Toshiba, Hitachi, Mitsubishi Electric, and Fuji Electric were given contracts to build copies. In this way, different companies gained experience with the technology.

In a similar story, MITI presented a wartime manufacturer of machine-gun parts with a set of designs for the parts of a famous-brand sewing machine and asked it to manufacture them. The country's sewing machine makers then put the parts together for export. Although these were copies, it is also true that they were possible because there already existed the technical know-how to produce such items. Such strategies enabled Japan to catch up technologically.

Amendment of the Anti-Monopoly Law

In 1954, what might be termed the aftermath of the Korean War caught up with Japan. (As I will elaborate later, the period of rapid growth was visited by cyclic fluctuations every three or four years.) As the economic climate turned down, firms got stuck with surplus stocks, and prices fell. Whenever this happened, the pre-war cartels suddenly started to look attractive again. However, the Anti-Monopoly Law was explicit on the subject, so cartels were out of the question. At this point the minister of International Trade and Industry stepped in and ordered a 40 percent cut in textile spinning operations from March–May 1952. Since this didn't involve negotiations among the companies, but was done at the recommendation of the minister, it didn't count as a cartel.

In 1953, the business community demanded, and obtained, a revision of the Anti-Monopoly Law that overtly recognized cartels. With the permission of the Fair Trade Commission, two kinds of cartels became possible. One was a recession cartel that could be invoked in cases where product prices fell below costs, leaving many companies in danger of bankruptcy. The other was a rationalization cartel for industries that were collectively trying to replace antiquated with new equipment in order to streamline their operations. The amended law also eased the restrictions on the cross-holding of shares and cross-directorships. As a result, the Anti-Monopoly Law is reputed to have been gutted, but this is not necessarily the case, since its restrictive force was not lost. The climate of competitiveness in Japanese industries—a climate of competition among small players, undominated by some Gulliver-like corporation—remained intact. In fact, the revisions of the law may in some respects have bolstered competition by creating a sense of security that if recession visited everyone could retreat into the safety net of a cartel.

Administrative guidance

The following may thus be said of the relationship between government agencies and industry. Firms had been hard hit during and after the war, they had undergone postwar reorganization, and were short of capital. Under those conditions, support from government was welcomed. On the other hand, circumstances made it difficult to buck the government. This gave rise to what was known as administrative guidance, in which in informal discussions MITI directed the industries under its jurisdiction and the Ministry of Transportation directed the marine transportation and shipbuilding industries.

In a comparable fashion, the Bank of Japan provided what was known as window guidance, reflecting the growing power of the central bank during and after the war and the relative weakness of the city banks in their reliance on the Bank of Japan for funds. Whenever the economy overheated, the Bank of Japan would seek to tighten the money supply by raising the official lending rate (which would in turn raise the interest rates banks charged on their loans). It would conduct sales operations of its public bondholdings to financial institutions and a little later on would resort to raising the deposit-to-lending ratio. These were all policy measures that utilized the mechanisms of the finance market. However, starting with the credit squeeze of 1954, the Bank of Japan embarked on what became known in the jargon of Japanese economics as window controls or window guidance. This had no basis in law, but instead was moral constraint. The Bank of Japan would designate and enforce a quota for the increase in money lent each month by the head offices and all the branches of the banks. This had immediate impact on tightening the money supply. It was also a form of direct government control that went far beyond the scope of money supply policies employing market mechanisms.

Rise of new industries

As technology imports stepped up, industries emerged that had not existed before the war. The petrochemicals industry, promoted by MITI, came on the scene in the late 1950s. Chemical industries had up until then usually involved the manufacture of a single product, for example, the electrolysis of water to make hydrogen or taking several materials, say hydrogen and nitrogen, and combining them to make ammonia. But the petrochemical industries that were developed in this period were a different breed. They took petroleum gas or crude oil and having cracked these into naphtha then proceeded to create ethylene, methane, propane, butane, and a host of other derivatives, which they then combined to make a variety of products. Compared with the cost of creating a single chemical out of a several ingredients, the process was of course significantly cheaper. Traditional chemical industries could scarcely compete.

In July 1955, MITI proposed a policy of promoting these new petrochemical industries. The policy had the dual goal of securing supplies of raw materials like benzol, phenol, and acetone and in particular of helping Japan become self-sufficient in ethylene derivatives, for which Japan was entirely dependent on imports, and thereby cutting supply costs of major petrochemical-base raw materials for industry and enhancing Japan's international competitiveness. Under this policy, Mitsui Petrochemical Industries, Mitsubishi Petrochemical, Sumitomo Chemical, and eventually Nippon Petrochemical (a subsidiary of Nippon Oil) established petrochemical centers in Iwakuni, Yokkaichi, Niihama, and

Kawasaki, respectively. Associated with these petrochemicals companies, vinyl chloride and other plastics products began to appear on the market in large quantities. I hasten to add that, in the case of petrochemicals, no import restrictions were imposed, and the industries developed wholly in competition with imported products.

In the development of these industries, I believe, is one of the keys to economic growth. The emergence of new industries breeds related other industries, which, in turn, develop rapidly. Table 5.4 shows how as the production of plastics increased, new industries that molded and processed the plastics developed. Plastic kitchen and bathroom equipment, plastic buckets and other household goods, construction materials, and packaging started to appear on the market in large quantities, replacing items that had traditionally been made of metal or wood. New products were invented: for instance, it was discovered that one could make thin vinyl chloride sheets and use them instead of hothouses to accelerate the growth of fruit and vegetables. The industries that manufactured the machinery to process the plastics into these products also developed. It is because these labor-intensive industries grew so rapidly that employment increased along with growth.

Household electrical appliances

The middle part of the 1950s saw the beginning of the mass production of household electrical appliances by Matsushita Electric and then other companies. This was a product area that had been

Table 5.4 Development of Plastic Molding and Processing Industries

	Number of Businesses	Number of Employees (thousands)	Value of Goods Shipped (¥100 billion)
1952	861	11.2	8.5
1957	2,578	47.0	55.3
1962	5,009	127.0	242.3
1967	8,830	189.6	667.4
1972	17,581	294.7	1,810.2

Source: Trade and Industry Statistics Association. *Sengo no Kogyo Tokei Hyo* (Postwar Industrial Statistics Tables). 1982.

ready for takeoff in prewar days, but had never quite made it. Now, electric vacuum cleaners, electric washing machines, and eventually TV began to make their way into Japanese homes. New firms like Sanyo and Sharp came into being, and heavy electrical equipment makers like Toshiba, Hitachi, Mitsubishi Electric, and Fuji Electric joined the bandwagon of this fast-emerging key industry. It was about this time that Sony was born, starting as a small firm with superb technology and expanding from radio and TV manufacture into tape recorders.

About this time, the national desire to regain prewar living standards underwent a gradual modification as these new products emerged. Living standards were rising, and an Americanized lifestyle was being adopted. Japan was fast becoming a mass-consumption society.

Construction of petrochemical complexes

With the emergence of new industries, new industrial areas and petrochemical complexes were built along the Pacific coast. Whether it was a petrochemical center or a frontline steel plant like Kawasaki Steel's Chiba plant, it had to be located on the coast. The fact that the raw materials, be they crude oil or iron ore, all had to be imported meant that plants had to have port facilities. For example, in the case of petrochemicals, the naphtha is cracked simultaneously into ethylene, propane, butane, and other derivatives. So it was decided to build industrial areas, centered on naphtha cracking plants, in which the naphtha products would be piped to other factories that would turn these into products. Examples of such petrochemical complexes include Iwakuni, Kawasaki, Niihama, Yokkaichi, and a little later Goi, Sakai, and Mizushima. Similarly, steel milling areas were established in Chiba, Mizushima, Wakayama, Fukuyama, Sakai, and Kimitsu. The Pacific coast industrial strip was born.

Many new technologies were thus developed or imported in this period, and many new industries emerged. If there is one thing that can be said about this flood of new technology, it is that Japan had the capacity to absorb it. It was this latent strength that underpinned the rapid economic growth of the postwar period.

Finance for growth

How was this growth funded? As we have already seen, the capitalization of Japanese industry deteriorated during World War II. Before the war, about two-thirds of companies' capital took the form of equity capital and savings from past profits. The remaining one-third was other people's money in the form of bonds, loans, and accounts payable. However, as can be seen from figure 5.6, in the mid-1950s, the proportion of self-capitalization had fallen to only one-third, the other two-thirds being supplied by other sources. And the self-capitalization rate falls even further in subsequent years.

To invest in plant and equipment, firms had no option but to borrow. When a firm borrows, however, its interest costs rise. This is not something that a company can do unless its managers have the courage of conviction that it is to the firm's advantage to invest, even at the cost of paying interest. To compete with other companies and raise the standing of one's own company, the manager has to aggressively continue expanding the company. Profits may be substantial, but since even more money is invested in plant and equipment, the proportion of outside capitalization inevitably goes up. This is fraught with risk: if the economic climate takes a turn for the worse, your products don't sell, and your company is

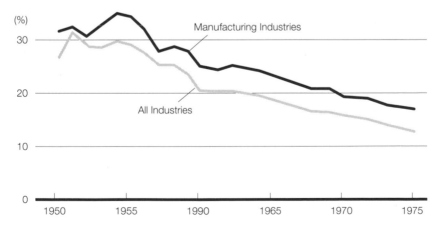

Fig. 5.6. Self-Capitalization in Corporations

Source: Ministry of Finance, *Hojin Kigyo Tokei Nenpo* (Corporate Statistics Annual).

left holding the debts. But in the era of rapid growth, firms ignored that danger in the pursuit of bold expansion. And for the most part, they succeeded.

In the late 1940s and early 1950s, most funds for such investment originated with the Bank of Japan. Banks would borrow from the Bank of Japan and lend funds to corporations. Banks would commonly have more out on loan than they held in deposits (a practice known as overloaning, the elimination of which was not easy). By the late 1950s, however, the sources of money for lending had begun to change. One new lending source was government loans and investments programs in which accumulated post office savings accounts and post office administered life insurance were channeled to industry through the Japan Development Bank, the Small Business Finance Corporation, and the Housing Finance Corporation. Another source was indirect financing from household bank savings, which rose sharply in the early 1950s. The household surplus funds rate (the ratio of surplus household income to disposable income) stood at a mere 2.3 percent in 1951, but had risen to 13.3 percent in 1956 and 19.8 percent in 1961. Since few individuals bought stocks or securities, deposits in banks and other financial institutions soared. It was these funds, lent by banks to companies, that constituted the major source of finance for industry. Figure 5.7 shows the fund surpluses and shortfalls in four sectors: government, corporate, personal, and overseas.

Direct financing takes place when individuals buy stocks or corporate bonds, thus providing direct capitalization to the firms. Indirect financing, on the other hand, places household savings in the hands of corporations through the mediation of banks and lending institutions. As long as business confidence is high, corporate demand for funds generally continues to grow. The pattern in which high household savings, made available to corporations through the banks, complemented other sources of lending became established in the mid- to late 1950s.

As the relations between the banks and corporations drew closer, links spontaneously developed between specific banks and groups of corporations. These included of course the old zaibatsu

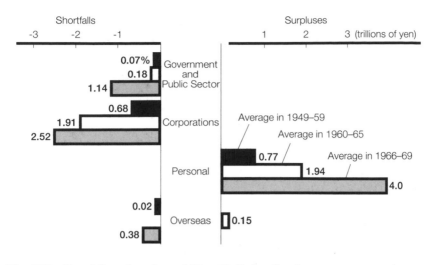

Fig. 5.7. Fund Surpluses and Shortfalls by Sector

Source: Bank of Japan. *Shikin Junkan Hyo* (Flow of Funds Tables).

banks, such as Mitsui, Mitsubishi, and Sumitomo and other, newer groupings, such as those around the Fuji Bank, the Daiichi Bank, and the Industrial Bank of Japan. Many of the newer groupings were based on relations that had been built up under the designated lending institution programs for military supply companies. The member companies of these groups were scattered among many industries and could, if need be, combine forces for new projects. For example, it was common at this time for these groupings to cooperate in the launching of petrochemical plants. Companies in the Mitsui group got together to set up Mitsui Petrochemical Industries, as did the Mitsubishi companies with Mitsubishi Petrochemical. Then Nippon Oil and the old Furukawa zaibatsu companies worked with Fuji Bank and the Daiichi Bank to create the petrochemical complex in Kawasaki centered on Nippon Petrochemical. As Miyazaki Yoshikazu once commented, the big banks each equipped themselves with a complete set of major industries.

Much has been made of the alleged resurrection of the zaibatsu, but these financial groupings were very different from the original zaibatsu. Individual companies within the groups might consult with each other, but the banks, in my view, no longer had the power to direct the companies, each of which was now acting on its own account.

In addition to the government lending programs, there was also cooperative lending. As the new industries emerged, business confidence soared, and companies invested vigorously in plant and equipment. Thus, when the Japan Development Bank lent money to industry, other financial institutions would follow suit, enabling firms to obtain needed funds instantly. In addition, when a firm in one of the bank-centered corporate groups sought to raise funds, the bank would take on the role of coordinating other city banks in consortia to provide the necessary funds. Since the coordinating bank would take the responsibility for the loan, the other banks would cooperate in the project.

It was in the 1950s, too, that financial institutions geared to small businesses were refurbished along the lines of modern financial institutions, the old mutual loan companies (*mujin kaisha*) being reorganized as mutual banks, and the credit unions as credit banks.

THE DUAL STRUCTURE

I have claimed that the early 1950s represent a period in which the economy regained something close to the levels and structure that prevailed in prewar days. Certainly it was true that the big companies lacked the capacity to employ large numbers of people. People who had returned to the farm after the war found themselves unable to leave the land, and even when they did find jobs in manufacturing or commerce, it was frequently only in small businesses.

The labor surplus kept wages generally low. Wages of young workers, just out of school, were especially paltry. In the large firms, wages based on age were reintroduced, and wage differentials according to how long a person had been working for a company rapidly emerged. The gap in wages between big companies and small businesses expanded steadily. In the big companies, it was possible for unions to obtain higher wages, and the age-based pay scales amplified the gap. In small and petty businesses, productivity was lower, and age-based pay scales were not as well entrenched, and many workers satisfied themselves with low wages being preferable to losing their jobs.

Part of this story can be seen from figure 5.8. Only the figures for manufacturing are shown, but it will be seen that if the total value of cash wages in plants with more than 500 employees is calculated at 100, that of firms employing 5–29 persons was 43.6 in 1958. The numbers include bonuses. The gap diminishes somewhat when we count only regular wages, but nevertheless the figures are indicative of a significant gap between big firms and small businesses. In petty businesses, with only a handful of employees, and in take-home piecework, wages were yet lower.

If wages are low, it is possible to use lots of people and low-priced materials to manufacture low-priced products. In the late 1950s, there was an uproar in the United States over Japan's dumping blouses priced at $1 apiece. Even in those days, ¥360 for a blouse was seen as too cheap.

Owing to the labor surplus, the wage gap expanded along parameters of size of company, age, sex, and region. Big companies tried to use low-cost labor in a variety of ways. For instance, temporary workers were widely used during this period. Contracts were for periods of three months or six months, but because of the surplus in young male workers, people had little option but to take what they were offered. Temporary workers were commonly hired

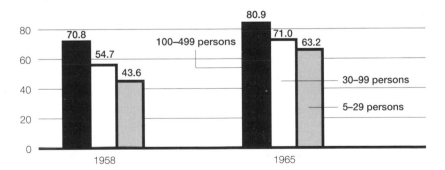

Fig. 5.8. Wage Differentials by Size of Business
       (average for places employing 500 persons or more = 100)

Source: Ministry of Labor. *Maigetsu Kinro Tokei* (Monthly Employment Statistics).

for dangerous or dirty work, and since contracts were short term these workers could be immediately laid off at the slightest economic setback. It was not unusual for temporary workers' wages to be only one-half of those of full-time workers or workers on permanent contracts.

Another practice that ensured low wages was contracting out. Since small businesses paid low wages, big companies would contract the processing of parts or finishing tasks out to these firms. This enabled them to cut costs by indirectly using low-wage labor. Contracting out became widespread in the manufacture of machinery industry parts and in weaving and sewing for the textile industry. It became a common pattern for large companies' plants to be surrounded by a cluster of contracting plants.

Today, the differentials in wages have been significantly reduced, and technology levels have improved, so that a much stronger cooperative relationship now exists between small businesses and big corporations, even though contracting out remains a common practice. In this sense, some significant changes have taken place over the years. During the 1950s, the big companies set up groups of contracting businesses, for which they sought out financing and provided technical assistance to keep them afloat, finding it profitable to utilize these firms despite the need to make such efforts.

As the practice of subcontracting spread, some economists began to argue that the Japanese economy was doomed to a dual structure consisting of an advanced sector, characterized by sophisticated technology and good labor conditions, and a lagging sector, characterized by low levels of technology and low wages. The labor surplus left scant prospect of eliminating the gap. The argument resembled that put forward in the early years of the Showa era, and the debate became heated in the mid-1950s. Even on the eve of Japan's burst of rapid economic growth, prognoses for the future of the Japanese economy remained guarded.

Changes in agriculture

I should not forget to mention agriculture. Although the effects of the earlier land reforms had begun to take root in the 1950s, the farming population stood at 16 million as late as 1955, about 20 percent higher than in prewar years, and the number of farm household units had risen from 5.5 million to 6 million. Since there was no space for the development of new farmland, Japanese farms, which had been small enough to begin with, became even smaller, the average holding being reduced to about 0.8 hectares, or roughly 20 percent smaller than before the war. A growing number of farm operations were simply too tiny to be economically viable. On the other hand, progress was beginning to be made in agricultural technology. Use of agrichemicals and machinery became widespread, as did technologies such as insulated rice seed beds, with the result that farm output surged in the late 1950s. After a crop failure in 1953 that necessitated the importing of rice, rice production soared, and farm incomes began to improve markedly.

The biggest increases were in northeastern Japan, in the Tohoku region. At one time, Nara Prefecture in the Kinki region, central Japan, enjoyed the biggest rice harvest per hectare in the country, but it was later overtaken by Saga Prefecture on the island of Kyushu. In prewar days, the best that Tohoku could manage was a meager 30 kilos a hectare, but now the region was producing a whopping 45–60 kilos. It took only a little over a decade for Tohoku to capture the lead in per-hectare rice yields, the combined result of the land reforms which had motivated farmers to produce and progress made in technology.

Nonetheless, the 1950s were marked by a growing shift to part-time farming. Since farms were largest in the northeast, many farms in that region remained full-time operations, but elsewhere in the country, farmers were finding it increasingly difficult to get by on farming alone. As industrialization gradually spread outside the major cities, farmers' sons and daughters found work in the factories and businesses. On small farms it became normal to make ends meet by combining farm earnings and outside wages. As Japan's rapid economic growth progressed, labor would flow from farming into other industries in a trend whose onset can be observed as early as the mid-1950s.

The labor movement

Another problem of the time was the labor movement. In an earlier lecture I mentioned the beginnings of the postwar labor movement, which can be characterized in terms of two competing thrusts. On the one hand there was the Japanese Confederation of Labor (Sodomei), which inherited the prewar economic unionism of the prewar Labor Federation and was allied with the right-wing faction of the Japan Socialist Party. On the other hand, there was the Congress of Industrial Labor Unions of Japan (Sanbetsu), which was strongly influenced by the Japan Communist Party. Eventually, as occupation policies took on an overtly anticommunist tint, strikes were banned, "reds" were purged from offices and factories, and the power base of the Sanbetsu organization was undermined. Then, in 1950, opponents of Sanbetsu's political focus formed an alliance to democratize the union and negotiated with the Americans to organize the General Council of Trade Unions of Japan (Sohyo).

Eventually Sohyo would revert to overt political activism. In 1952, the year of Japan's independence, a Sohyo racked by internal divisions conducted a series of five united-front campaigns against the newly enacted Antisubversive Activities Law. Sohyo also launched campaigns demanding huge wage increases based on a market basket approach that bore no relation to management realities or labor productivity, and electric power and coal mining unions went on lengthy strikes. A 63-day strike by coal workers left both labor and management exhausted and forced some industries to convert to heavy oil owing to the resultant coal shortages.

When the business climate took a downturn, it was standard practice for management to trim employee ranks by terminating individuals. Since unionists could not stand by as co-workers were fired, the unions would rise in protest at such dismissals. A number of protracted and acrimonious battles occurred between militant unions and companies that saw themselves as defending managerial rights. Prolonged clashes over dismissals had occurred during the occupation days in firms such as Toshiba, Toyota, and Hitachi, but the 1950s were marked by record-breaking marathon disputes with Mitsui Mining, Nissan, and Japan Steel Works'

Muroran plant. Often the union would split during the course of the lengthy dispute, resulting in the birth of a second union and the ultimate defeat of the workers' cause. A dispute at Amagasaki Steel exhausted the resources of labor and management alike and sent the company into bankruptcy.

In 1954, a dispute over human rights erupted at Omikenshi Co., Ltd. over the company's feudalistic policies of demanding standards of deportment for female workers. There were also strikes in unlikely places; for example, department stores and local banks.

In retrospect, the stable relations between management and workers that are seen today had not yet been established. The unions took the position that they were involved in a class struggle, and management resisted on the premise that if they yielded an inch the workers would take a yard. These attitudes resulted in bitter, prolonged strikes that often culminated in tragedy. It was only in 1955–56 that Sohyo's policy of political strikes mobilizing whole families and communities—the line taken by Takano Minoru—finally gave way to a policy of economic action spearheaded by Ota Kaoru and Iwai Akira.

About 1955, the strategy of holding a Spring Labor Offensive, still current today, was adopted. Since individual unions were vulnerable on their own it became the practice for unions in all industries to run a combined wage campaign in the spring. Not that these Spring Labor Offensives were always successful: in spring 1957, for example, steel workers' unions came away empty-handed from a series of strikes.

The 1950s, then, were a period in which Japan's stereotypical pattern of labor relations became established, with the following basic components. First, wages were founded on age-based seniority. Second, there would be lifelong employment—the tacit agreement that companies would not in principle terminate employees, but would retain them until retirement. Third, unions would take the company as their organizing unit; these unions would not only look after workers' rights but would also not eschew efforts to further the development of the company. American economist James C. Abegglen, in a book entitled *Kaisha:*

The Japanese Corporation, argues that these three components—age-based seniority in wages, lifelong employment, and enterprise-based unions—stabilized Japanese industrial relations and merited the envy of other countries. I recollect the shock among Japanese scholars on learning of this view, since the conventional wisdom of the time was that these were indicators that Japan was behind the times and that anything other than industry-wide or skill-based unions was unorthodox.

I believe that the change in relations arose out of a reassessment that took place on both sides after the repeated major disputes of the late 1940s and early 1950s. In the Spring Labor Offensives, for example, it was after 1960 that management ceased to send labor representatives away empty-handed, and unions likewise began to take care not to drag strikes out too long.

Balance of payments crises and the inventory cycle

Let me also touch on the economic fluctuations of the 1950s. Although this was a period of high growth, it was also marked by sharp oscillations. As figure 5.9 shows, Japan was visited by an international balance of payments crisis every three or four years. Trade statistics show repeated import surpluses in 1953–54, 1956–57, 1961–62, and 1963–64. Foreign currency reserves plunged visibly in 1954, 1957, 1961, and 1963 in line with import surpluses. This cycle may be explained as follows. As domestic economic growth continues, rising manufacturing output boosts imports, chiefly of raw materials. At the same time, domestic demand grows because of the improved economic climate, causing firms to slacken their export efforts. The truth is that during these years, export prices were quite a lot cheaper than domestic prices, so as export efforts were throttled back, imports were in surplus, and foreign currency earnings shrank.

When this happened, the Bank of Japan, concerned that foreign currency reserves might shrink, would tighten credit through both standard market tools and its practice of window guidance. Firms would find themselves short of funds and would refrain from new projects. When goods stopped selling, inventories would pile up, tightening credit further. Investments in plant and equip-

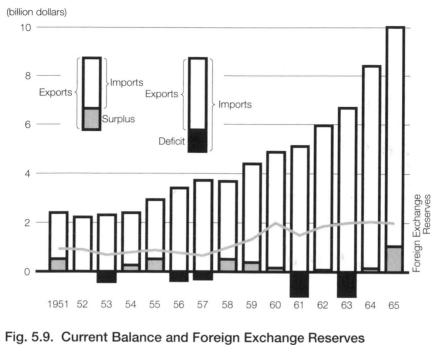

(billion dollars)

Fig. 5.9. Current Balance and Foreign Exchange Reserves (1951–1965)

Sources: Computed in dollars from data in Economic Planning Agency, *Kokumin Shotoku Tokei Nenpo* (Annual Report on National Income Statistics). Foreign currency reserve figures are from Bank of Japan surveys

ment would be canceled or postponed. The upshot was reduced imports and renewed efforts to export products. Since domestic production activities would stagnate, imports would tend to follow suit, sending the international balance of payments back into the black. Then the credit squeeze would be rescinded, output would begin to rise, and companies would resume investing aggressively in plant and equipment. This was the general pattern for short-term fluctuations.

Figure 5.10 shows the growth of real gross national spending (as a percentage increase on the preceding year) for the period after 1955. It is clear that there were good years and bad, depending on the economic climate. The bottoms of the economic troughs were in 1954, 1958, 1962, 1965, and—as I will discuss in my next lecture—1971 and 1974–1975. These are marked by the black dots. Years when the economy performed positively are indicated by white dots: 1956, 1960–61, 1964, a plateau in 1968–70, and 1973. These waves can be explained by the pattern just described in which, up until about 1965, a balance of international payments deficit would trigger a credit squeeze, which would result in fewer goods being sold and an economic downturn. Production would level off, and the growth rate would drop.

These economic fluctuations can be read off any number of indicators, including the trade account and changes in the foreign currency reserve. Figure 5.11A. shows the ratio of product inventories to shipments, a yardstick of how well goods have sold. Manufacturers' inventory ratios bottomed in 1956, a strong year for the economy, and peaked in 1958, a poor year. Again the inventory ratios troughed in 1960, a good year, and peaked in 1962, another bad year. The repeated peaks and valleys replicate the economic climate.

Another indicator, company profit ratios, is shown in figure 5.11B. This, too, exhibits repeated ups and downs, reflecting variations in the economy as a whole. Since in the United States of the

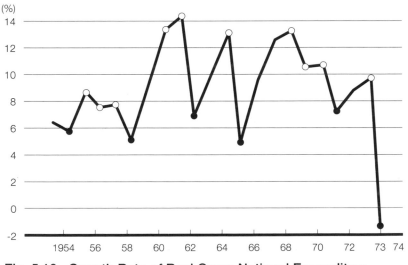

Fig. 5.10. Growth Rate of Real Gross National Expenditure

Sources: Economic Planning Agency, *Kokumin Shotoku Tokei Nenpo* (Annual Report on National Income Statistics Annual). 1976. All figures are based on old UN System of National Accounts.

1950s and 60s and in the Japan of the 1980s, the profit ratio does not drop much, even in an economic downswing, one might inquire why Japan would be the only country in which profit ratios acted so sensitively. The answer is straightforward: Japanese firms invested aggressively in plant and equipment using borrowed funds. Now, if everything goes to plan, the new equipment operates at close to 100 percent and products move in the marketplace. Firms retain profits, even after meeting interest and depreciation charges. But if the plan goes even slightly awry, sales growth brakes, but costs don't go down, so profit ratios plunge.

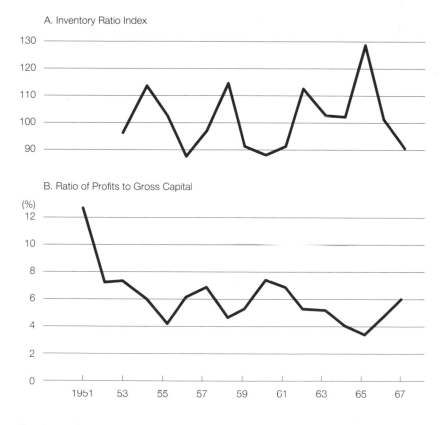

Fig. 5.11. Inventory Index and Profit Ratio in Manufacturing Industries

Sources: A: From Ministry of International Trade and Industry, *Seizogyo Seihin Zaikoritsu Shisu* (Manufacturing Industry Product Inventory Indices). The increase trend in the inventory rates has been eliminated.
B: From Ministry of Finance, *Hojin Kigyo Tokei Nenpo* (Financial Statements by Industry [annual]). Figure for 1960 is an estimate.

At that point, firms hastily desist from further capital investments and resume when the economy picks up. The same aggressive capital investment patterns that brought about Japan's rapid economic growth also left them with little capacity to withstand recession.

The economic growth rate from the early 1950s through to the late 1960s averaged 10 percent, a rate rarely matched anywhere in the world. However, it is not as if the economy grew monotonously for nearly 20 years, since this growth rate was sustained in the face of sharp economic fluctuations. Although with every downturn, pessimists proclaimed the end of Japan's rapid growth, the economy survived the setbacks and found new material to spark a renewal of growth.

The Jinmu boom

Let me say something about the onset of Japan's era of rapid economic growth. Following the boom triggered by the Korean War, 1954 saw a crisis in the balance of international payments. Credit had been tightened, and the public mood was somber, when Shimomura Osamu, an economist in the Ministry of Finance, declared that the balance of payments crisis was over, that the trade balance had recovered, and that the economy would improve. In 1955, the economy began to pick up, and by 1956 a boom was in full swing. The change in the economic climate was dramatic and launched an era of capital investment led by shipbuilding, steel, electrical machinery, petrochemical, and other heavy industries. The people of the time referred to it as the Jinmu boom on the grounds Japan was enjoying its greatest economic prosperity since the mythical emperor Jinmu had founded the nation. The *White Paper on the Economy* for fiscal 1956 confidently declared the postwar era over and announced the arrival of a new era of growth spurred by technical innovation.

However, the Jinmu boom was fueled by the Suez crisis. The United Kingdom had responded to Egypt's nationalization of the Suez Canal with military intervention and had been defeated. Egypt closed the canal for a time. As a result, a major change ensued in the international flow of goods. Shipping costs skyrocketed, as did international commodity prices, setting off a global boom. But once the Suez Canal reopened the following year, the boom abated. Rumors of global shortages spurred Japan to import large quantities of raw materials, plunging its balance of international payments into the red. As a result, financial institutions tightened credit in 1957, and in 1958 a recession was in full swing. Since 1958 was a year of worldwide recession, economic indicators remained flat for a protracted period in what came to be known as the *nabezoko*, or "saucepan bottom," recession (owing to manner in which economic indicators looked as if they were crawling across the bottom of a large saucepan). But at the end of the year, the economy began moving upward, and in 1960–61, the economy was visited by what became known as the Iwato Boom.

The energy revolution
Before I talk about the Iwato boom, however, I must first mention the energy revolution that had taken place. Owing to the development of huge new oil fields in the Middle East, low-priced crude oil was beginning to flow in from what is now Saudi Arabia and also from Kuwait, Iran, and Iraq. This influx of cheap Middle Eastern oil, and a decline in world commodity prices, especially raw material prices, at the end of the Suez crisis, become clearly apparent in 1958 and 1959. In order to ship this oil, tankers became bigger, growing from 50,000 tons to 70,000 tons. In the late 1960s, 300,000 ton tankers would be built, but this was yet to come.

Coal, Japan's principal domestic source of energy, was at a clear price disadvantage vis-à-vis oil, as figure 5.12 clearly shows. Moreover, coal presented other drawbacks. If one burned coal, one had to dispose of the ash, and impurities invariably created problems in coal boilers. Oil didn't present these complications. What is more, miners' unions' opposition to rationalization of the coal industry had the effect of keeping Japanese coal prices up. One notorious labor dispute at the Mitsui Miike mine in 1959 and 1960 was particularly vicious. In the end, the union was weakened

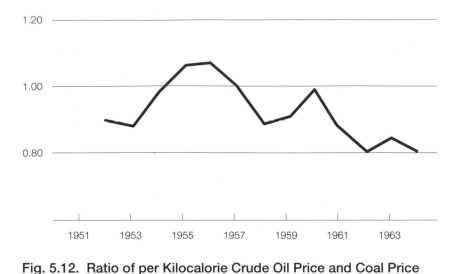

Fig. 5.12. Ratio of per Kilocalorie Crude Oil Price and Coal Price

Source: Computed from Bank of Japan, *Tokyo Oroshiuri Bukka Shisu* (Tokyo Wholesale Price Index).

by a split and vanquished. The Miike dispute marked the end of massive strikes motivated by an ideology of class consciousness.

Electric power companies and other large-scale energy users scrambled to switch from coal to oil in 1958–59, and by the mid-1960s, it was clear that the majority of coal mines could not continue to operate profitably. The government's coal industry policy became a confined unemployment policy and regional policy to deal with the aftermath of mine closures. The progress of the energy revolution is clear in figure 5.13. Oil imports climbed nearly 300 percent in the five years from 1960 to 1965, while domestic coal consumption declined. The total defeat of coal can be safely attributed to price differentials. Oil prices remained relatively low throughout the late 1950s and through the 1960s. It is not unsurprising, therefore, that over 70 percent of Japan's energy consumption should come to be supplied by oil. The later reversal of this trend in the wake of the oil crises of the 1970s can likewise be laid at the feet of price increases. I never fail to be impressed by the power of price mechanisms to transform, sometimes with stunning rapidity, the structure of an entire economy.

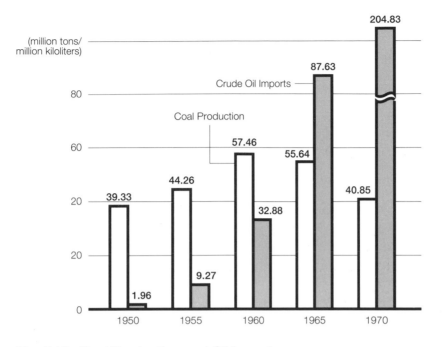

Fig. 5.13. Coal Production and Oil Imports

Sources: Ministry of International Trade and Industry, *Enerugii Tokei Shu* (Collected Energy Statistics), *Sogo Enerugii Tokei* (Comprehensive Energy Statistics).

THE AGE OF INCOME DOUBLING

The Iwato boom

We now come to the peak of the era of rapid growth. On the heels of the recession of 1958, Japan was visited by a frenetic boom that lasted through 1959, 1960, and 1961. This became known as the Iwato boom, on the grounds that it was even bigger and better than the Jinmu boom and that Japan had not experienced such growth since the Sun Goddess was enticed out of her rock cave (iwato)—in other words, well before Emperor Jinmu. The Iwato boom was powered by an across-the-board boom in capital investment. Fixed capital formation by private corporations stood at ¥1.1 trillion in 1955 but had soared to a prodigious ¥4.8 trillion by 1961. Capital investments as a proportion of gross national expenditures (GNP, depicted in figure 5.14) hovered around 12 percent in the late 1940s and 1950s but stood significantly higher than 20 percent by the beginning of the 1960s due to the astounding aggressiveness with which heavy industries and chemical industries had invested in plant and equipment, to the new plants that had been built along the Pacific coast, and to the new industries that had emerged.

In this period, it was machine industries that formed the centerpiece of Japan's industrial development. Any industry, if it invests in plant and equipment, needs machinery. So, naturally, demand grows for machine tools—machines that make machines.

At about this time, I went with Professor Umemura Mataji of Hitotsubashi University to Takaoka in Toyama Prefecture, where we visited a small lathe factory that had burgeoned in just two or three years into a plant employing three thousand people, with young people and housewives being bused in from nearby farms. The general manager of the plant proudly proclaimed that the company intended to capture the entire market for lathes in Japan and that other companies should step aside. The factory went

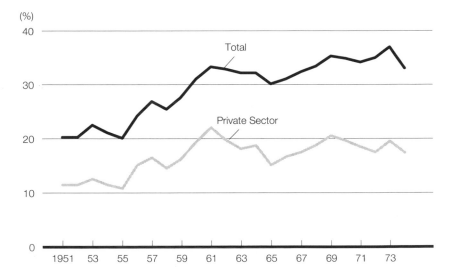

Fig. 5.14. Plant and Equipment Investments as a Percentage of Gross National Expenditures

Source: Economic Planning Agency data.

bankrupt at the first sign of recession in 1962, but its brief success is emblematic of the boom.

Next up to the heavy industry batting plate was automobiles. Although Japanese cars were said to be unable to compete with their overseas counterparts, the 1960s were marked by the emergence of such passenger sedans as Toyota Crowns, Coronas, and Publicas and Nissan Bluebirds, Cedrics, and Sunnys. These were mass produced and sold in the domestic market.

The income-doubling plan

In May and June 1960, violent demonstrations raged in nation-wide opposition to the Japan-U.S. Security Treaty and the Kishi cabinet's pushing of the revised treaty through the Diet. In the end, the revised security treaty passed, but Prime Minister Kishi Nobusuke and his cabinet resigned from office, and in July, Ikeda Hayato became prime minister. Ikeda's trademark was a plan to double Japanese incomes. I believe that what he sought to do was bring Japan out of its politicized climate, represented by the campaigns against the security treaty, into a new season of economics. The National Income-Doubling Plan sought to double either of real gross national expenditures (GNE) or real gross national product (GNP) in the space of a decade. This translates into an annual growth rate of 7.2 percent. In the first three years, it was proposed to achieve 9 percent growth. Since the actual GNE growth, as represented in figure 5.10, shown earlier, hovered around 7–8 percent in the late 1950s, the plan may be viewed as constituting a government guarantee that the economy would continue to grow at the existing rate. Whereas many became pessimistic about the future with each cyclic downturn, and the government had been acting cautiously, Prime Minister Ikeda had in effect declared that current, or even higher, growth levels, remained possible. It was in this public declaration of confidence, I believe, that the real significance of the National Income-Doubling Plan lies.

The plan poured oil on the flames of the already feverish ambitions of the business community. Capital investments stepped up. The *White Paper on the Economy* for 1961 employed the phrase "investment breeds investment" to describe the situation. When companies start building a lot of new factories, machinery factories and steel mills have to be established to satisfy the new demand. Moreover, in order to build a new factory, infrastructure in the form of water mains, sewers, roads, and port facilities becomes needed. These public investments are carried out by central and local governments. In economic terms, large-scale investment was being triggered by vigorous independent investment under the acceleration principle.

Labor shortages

Amid all this, it was suddenly noticed that labor was in short supply. Up until the beginning of the 1960s, many young graduates from middle school and high school had remained on the farm, unable to find outside work. Now, all industries were trying to enlist school graduates, often without success. Companies often resorted to recruiting young workers from stores and other service industries and sallied forth into rural areas to sign up young people in farm families to work in their factories. Since young workers from the now-closed coal mines were also mobilized, unemployment in mining areas was reduced.

The wage gap between big companies and small businesses, shown earlier in figure 5.8, began to shrink. Since the big companies were raising their younger employees' wages, small businesses had to keep up, or to do better, in order to retain their employees. The dual structure of Japanese industry began to break down.

The wave of change began to lap the shores of commerce. The term "distribution revolution" began to be applied in reference to the need to improve distribution mechanisms that linked producer and consumer. The labor shortage also began to have an impact on tertiary industries, as might be expected. In the place of family businesses small self-service supermarkets began to appear on the scene, and traditional Japanese inns (*ryokan*) gave way to hotels.

Liberalization of trade

At about this stage, the liberalization of trade became an issue. Japan had rejoined the world economy in 1949 with an exchange rate set at ¥360 to the dollar, and after the conclusion of the San Francisco Peace Treaty, the country had joined the General Agreement on Tariffs and Trade (GATT) and the International Monetary Fund (IMF). Japanese exports had begun to grow in the late 1950s, and eventually Japan was able to achieve more or less a balance in its trade without relying on U.S. military procurements. Nonetheless, import restrictions, maintained through the foreign currency account, had remained the rule and now came under fire from abroad. Eventually, the liberalization of trade was in principle adopted by the government, to be implemented in a five-year program.

The liberalization program began in 1960, the year of the income-doubling plan. In the past, the government had been in the practice of permitting some items to be imported freely, but these were the exceptions rather than the rule. Now a list was drawn up of items that were to be explicitly restricted. Over a five-year period the number of restricted items was to be reduced until 90 percent of import value was freely imported. The 90 percent liberalization target was achieved ahead of schedule, in October 1962. Car imports, of course, were liberalized somewhat later, in 1965, and electronic calculators and other such items remained on the restricted lists for a long time. A good proportion of agricultural products stayed restricted too, on the grounds that the consequences of liberalization were too dreadful to contemplate. Even the 1980s, two or three farm produce items remain restricted.

That Japan found the courage to embark on trade liberalization at this time is indicative of the country's newly discovered confidence in its ability to compete. The steel industry, for example, at the end of two five-year plans, was now equipped with state-of-the-art steel mills. The machinery, shipbuilding, machine tools, industrial machinery, electronics, optics, and other fields were gradually transforming into export-oriented industries. In the Kami-Suwa region, Nagano Prefecture, camera and electronic organ industries were emerging. And in many leading-edge industries, firms were starting to make their own specialized machine tools (transfer machines) for internal use.

Liberalization of capital

Eventually, the liberalization of capital transactions became an issue. If foreign capital were to enter Japan, overseas companies would be able to set up business in Japan and compete with Japanese industries. What would happen to Toyota or Nissan if General Motors or Ford, for example, were to set up operations in Japan? This threat prompted a bill to be sent three times to the Diet, under slightly different names and with slightly content, in 1962, 1963, and 1964. The bill sought to designate strategically important industries and to force them to merge in the interests of strengthening their management and technology. It failed to pass in the Diet. Its aim would instead be achieved by rationalization plans negotiated between MITI and the industries. Financial institutions were to fund the mergers, and special exemptions were to be admitted to the Anti-Monopoly Law.

What is significant is that this bill, which would have instituted strong protectionist policies, died on its third reading, for one thing because banks objected to the proposition that they should be coerced to lend to projects at the direction of the government. In addition, the bill's failure reflected, I believe, a renewed confidence on the part of industry and a conviction that industry could withstand competition without relying on the ministrations of the government. Industrial policy had functioned most effectively and with the greatest claim to authority during the 1950s, but once Japan entered the era of rapid growth, successful companies began to want a free hand in their own affairs.

Japan became an Article 8 member of IMF in April 1964, committing itself not to restrict trade for reasons of maintaining its balance of international payments. Eventually it would join the OECD so that it could participate in economic development abroad at the same time.

Japan's meteoric progress began to attract international attention. The famous British economics magazine, *The Economist*, ran a series of three special issues focusing on Japan, the first of which, entitled "Consider Japan," appeared in 1962.

Corporate capitalism and the technostructure

The core growth fields were in big firms in heavy industries, including petrochemicals. American economist Kenneth Galbraith's book *The New Industrial State*, published in 1967, describes graphically the role of the big firms in the U.S. economy. I do not believe that one is far off the mark to apply his description to Japanese firms. From a legal standpoint, the highest decision-making organ of the public corporation is the stockholders' general meeting, but that is now a formality. In reality it is teams of specialists within the company who make the decisions. The board of directors may organize the specialists, but once the teams are in place, even the president has only limited authority to affect important decisions. These groups of specialists form what is called the technostructure that is at the core of any major corporation. In Japan, these groups are surrounded by employees and workers trained by the corporation. Thus, the corporation is organized as a set of concentric circles, with the stockholders being the group on the periphery. It is probably true to say that stockholders ask nothing more of the corporation than that it secure them a stable dividend.

Japanese economist Okumura Hiroshi has often employed the term corporate capitalism to characterize another phenomenon that became apparent in this period. As figure 5.15 indicates, ever since the mid-1950s corporations' biggest stockholders have been

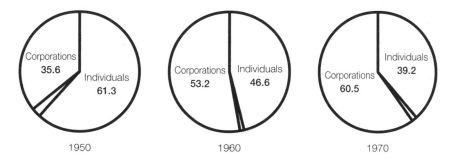

Fig. 5.15. Stock Ownership Patterns in Major Corporations (percentage of total stock)

Sources: Data from Fair Trade Commission and Ministry of Finance; Tokyo Stock Exchange *Kabushiki Bunpu Jokyo Chosa* (Study of Distribution of Stockholding).

other corporations. Big companies hold each other's stock, and the proportion of individual stockholders has dwindled. Almost all directors nowadays are former employees, and not stockholders with significant voting power. Companies that hold each other's stock take their dividends and do not intervene in each other's management unless something major goes wrong. Each company maintains an independent management policy.

In the United States, on the other hand, even today it is far from rare for one company to buy up the shares of another and attempt to take over its management. This is regarded as one way of doing business. If that were to happen in Japan, it would be written up in the newspapers as contrary to public morals. The idea that companies exist for the benefit of the technostructure has generally come to be accepted, a notion that can best be dated to the era of rapid growth.

In this corporate climate, we now begin to see the emergence of the fanatic employee. This individual is entirely focused on company work and thinks of nothing else. He has no hobbies or amusements and only plays golf in order to associate with business colleagues. If the company orders it, he will seek to fulfill its goals even under the most atrocious conditions. It was the role of the third-echelon directors to supervise and lead these zealous personnel, who, one may safely say, were the ones who drove rapid growth.

Rapid growth permeates

The era of rapid growth is ordinarily characterized as an age of development of heavy industries, but it was that and more. Rapid economic growth provided the conditions for a number of individuals to open up new fields of industry.

There is a book entitled *Testimony: Japan in the Rapid Growth Era*, a collection of interviews with representative businessmen by economists (published by the Mainichi Newspaper Ltd.), in which people across a wide spectrum of fields talk about their experiences during that period. The volume includes, for example, a story about the building of Japan's expressways: how the construction of major roadways, an area where Japan was lagging, was undertaken to meet deadlines for the Tokyo Olympics and of how American and German technology was imported to build the expressways, first between Nagoya and Kobe, then between Tokyo and Nagoya, and then in the city centers.

With the construction of the expressways, the significance of road transportation in Japan changed. The mainstay of land transportation had been the railroads. Although there was a large road shipping company called Nippon Express, its main business was small-scale shipping of goods from railroad stations to consumers. Once the expressways were completed, however, it became possible to use large trucks to ship directly from producers to consumers. I am told that a company called Seino Transportation was the first to do so. In no time at all railroad shipments began to be replaced by large trucks. Before anyone knew it the volume handled was greater than that of the railroads.

Another example, also in the field of transportation, was domestic coastal shipbuilding. Small steel vessels of about 500 to 1,000 tons, built during World War II, were already plying Japan's coasts, but with the onset of rapid growth, domestic shipments naturally picked up, so these coastal vessels were in hot demand. As I noted earlier, once arc welding was successfully adapted to the shipbuilding industry, it became much easier to build new vessels. Shipbuilders began a practice called beach shipbuilding: on the coasts of the island of Shikoku in the late 1950s, they would lay railroad tracks on the beach, set ship sections on the rails, and weld the sections together. The era of rapid growth did not just involve heavy industries and big corporations. People emerged to begin new businesses in every field imaginable, and many of them succeeded.

Change in rural communities

The bright side of growth was also matched by darker aspects. One of these was that young people left farm communities to work in the factories in the big city. As a result, the agricultural population plunged, leaving farm communities populated only by old people and children. This we have already seen in figure 5.1.

Many villages became depopulated to the point that they could no longer function as communities.

But if one asks whether agricultural output fell, the answer is a categorical no. In the early 1960s, agricultural output actually grew, and by the late 1960s and early 1970s was climbing at a substantial rate, albeit not as fast as in manufacturing. This growth was partly impelled by a form of agricultural subsidy, rice prices being set by a method that guaranteed producer incomes. In determining rice prices, the government would take into account the wages of the farmers themselves and the wages they paid, but in doing so, these were computed at rates comparable with those of factory workers. Since this was an era in which basic wage rates rose over 10 percent each year in the Spring Labor Offensive, farm households would then receive a commensurate increase.

Another reason was enactment of the Basic Agriculture Law in 1961. With the passage of this legislation, farm products began to diversify, so that farmers began to depend less exclusively on rice for income, and production began to match demand more closely. For example, new production areas were developed for *mikan* (mandarin oranges), apples, and other fruit. Labor shortages were covered by the mechanization of agriculture. Bigger machines came to be used. Combine harvesters became available to farmers, and in the mid-1960s, rice planting machines came onto the scene, so that rice, once the most labor-intensive crop, became the least labor-intensive. Thus, despite the decline in available labor, neither output nor incomes fell. Indeed, it became possible for both to increase.

Traditional industries decline

Rapid growth fundamentally refashioned the structure of Japan's economy. A salient example is the energy revolution that I referred to earlier, in which there were industries like petroleum that made huge advances, while others like coal went into sharp decline. The coal mines of the Chikuho coal field in northern Kyushu almost all closed. This did not just mean that the mines disappeared. The fortunes of the towns that made their living off the mines—names such as Iizuka, Tagawa, Nogata, and Gotoji come to mind—were all affected by the closures, as was the whole region. To take another example, one side effect of the energy revolution was a rapid shift in household fuel. Kerosene stoves became the main form of home heating. As recently as 1955, most homes had been using charcoal. Now the charcoal burners found that they could not make ends meet, and the urban charcoal merchant disappeared to reemerge as a kerosene dealer.

People began to dress more in western-style clothing, so that traditional clothing and footwear merchants were forced to find other lines of business. Sellers of wooden geta sandals had no option but to begin selling leather and rubber footwear. Foodstuff likewise underwent comparable shifts from rice to bread, from fish to meat, from sake to beer and whiskey. More and more small supermarkets appeared on the scene to compete with local retail merchants. Although the number of retail merchants was still increasing on a national basis, in many localities they were finding it harder to do business.

Another major change that took place in this period was that the products of large corporations came to account for a greater proportion of household consumption, while those of traditional industries dwindled. This trend has remained more or less constant to the present day. In western-style clothing, for instance, ready-made suits and dresses made appreciable inroads. Moreover, as mass-production techniques progressed, men's suits began to appear in a rich variety of sizes, so that everyone began buying off the shelf. The craftsman tailor, who sold suits to order, found he could no longer stay in business.

Spread of laborsaving technology

As labor fell generally into short supply, small businesses had to change the way they operated. If they wanted to hire young people, they had to pay them wages that were at least comparable to, if not even higher than, those in the big corporations. Since this would push up their costs, small businesses took the plunge and started to adopt laborsaving technology that meant that they could make do with fewer people. In *Testimony: Japan in the Rapid Growth Era*, there is the story of the operator of a small factory that punched steel plate using a press. In the 1940s and early 1950s, the factory had operated in Osaka, but he had moved it to Tokyo at the behest of the parent company. When he was based in Osaka, he employed 300 people. After the move to Tokyo, he employed at most 70 people, these being middle school graduates (highly valued at the time as productive low-wage employees) that he had brought with him. For the past 15 years, he has been making do with about 20 workers, yet both sales volume and sales value have risen. If they had not increased, it is unlikely that the manager would have been able to meet parent company demands that he cut costs. He says, and I quote, "advances in press machinery and innovations in manufacturing methods together made it possible to improve our productivity several times over."

The big corporations thus had no exclusive monopoly on technological progress. Small businesses succeeded in making technical advances too, and if they had not, it is unlikely that they would have survived. Such undertakings became part and parcel of everyday small business operations. People didn't notice them any more, but that does not mean that nothing was happening. The rapid growth era was one of constant change.

The Spring Labor Offensive as an income distribution mechanism

Finally, I would like to touch on the issue of the Spring Labor Offensive. As I have noted earlier, the labor unions annual wage campaign was not altogether a success at the outset. It was not until the early 1960s, after the announcement of the income doubling plan, that it became clear to workers that if they conducted a Spring Labor Offensive they would invariably win an increase in their basic wages, and a substantial one at that. From about that time on, increases in basic wages in excess of 10 percent became the norm.

On the recommendation of the National Personnel Authority, the salaries of civil servants rose commensurate with the average increase in basic wages gained in each year's Spring Labor Offensive. Similarly, the mechanism for setting rice prices—which guaranteed producer incomes—meant that the going rate in the Spring Labor Offensive affected the price of agricultural products. In other words, a mechanism was instituted during this period by which the going rate of increase in the Spring Labor Offensive was matched by comparable increases for other wage and salary workers and farmers (although limited to rice farmers).

The self-employed were left out of this picture. There was no formal mechanism by which Spring Labor Offensives could directly impact merchants and service suppliers, so it appears to have become normal at about this time for merchants' margins to increase over time. Men's and women's hairdressers, Japanese inns, and other pure service industries followed suit. In agriculture, the prices of vegetables and fruit rose.

It was thus in the era of rapid growth that a mechanism took root by which wage rates agreed on in the spring wage negotiations infiltrated to other sectors of society in the form of higher incomes. However, when farm prices rise, commerce and service industries raise their margins, and the price of a permanent wave or a haircut increases, then all other prices inevitably go up too. In industries where technological advances push costs down, wage increases don't necessarily trigger price increases, since the increase in labor productivity is higher than the rate of wage increases. But the prices of services and agricultural products, where the productivity increase rates are low, have to go up. This was noted at the time as a problem and given a name: productivity differential inflation.

By way of recapitulating what I have just said, figure 5.16 shows that wage increase rates were very low in the late 1950s but climb at a rate of about 10 percent a year in the early 1960s. Later in that decade, the rate of increase tops 10 percent and ranges between 10 and 15 percent. Consumer price indices were relatively stable in the latter half of the 1950s, but, from the early 1960s on, the indices rise roughly 5 points each year, marking the emergence of productivity differential inflation. On the other hand, the index of real wages rose steadily, because wage increases outstripped the relatively moderate increases in prices. Consumption levels thus also improved.

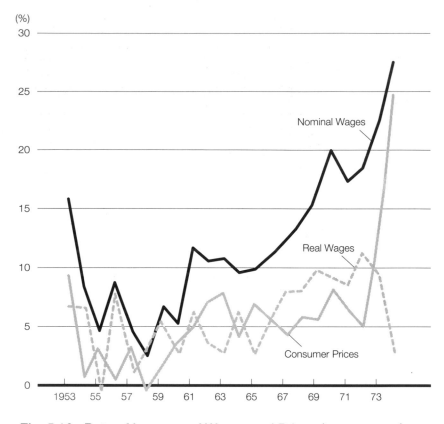

Fig. 5.16. Rate of Increase of Wages and Prices (year on year)

Sources: Wages are Labor Ministry data, prices are based on studies by the Prime Minister's Office Statistics Bureau.

In a social climate like the one I have just described, where incomes rise continuously, living standards advance, and anything resembling social class distinctions gradually erode, nearly the entire population comes to think of itself as middle class. The graph in figure 5.17 summarizes the results of an opinion survey conducted by the Prime Minister's Office, in which subjects were asked to rank themselves by social class. In 1958, it will be seen that 72 percent responded that they were middle class, while 17 percent still claimed to be lower class. Throughout the late 1950s and into the 1960s, however, the proportion of Japanese viewing themselves as middle class rose to 87 percent in 1964 and 88 per-

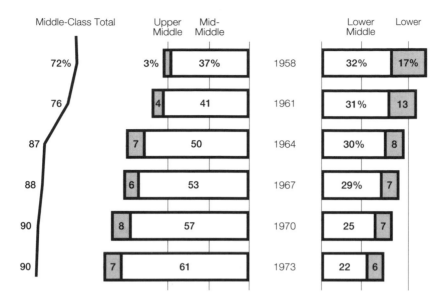

Fig. 5.17 Consciousness of Membership of Social Class

Source: Japan Broadcasting Corporation, *Zusetsu Sengo Seron Shi* (A History of Postwar Public Opinion in Charts and Figures). Second edition, 1982.

Note: Surveys were conducted by the Prime Minister's Office. In 1958 and 1961, subjects were asked to compare their own standard of living with that of the country as a whole. Beginning in 1964, subjects were asked how others would rate their household living standard.

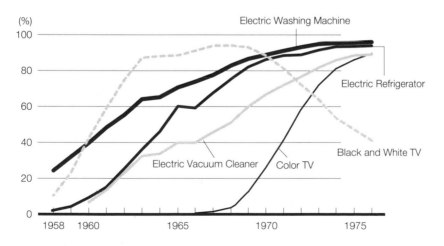

Fig. 5.18. Percentage of Homes Using Electric Appliances

Source: Economic Planning Agency, *Shohisha Doko Chosa* (Survey of Consumer Trends).

cent in 1967, after which the figures settled into the 90 percentile range. More importantly, the percentage of subjects responding "mid-middle class" rose, while that responding "lower-middle" or "lower class" is reduced to insignificance. I find it interesting and suggestive that this change in social perception took place during the era of rapid growth and not at some other time.

Figure 5.18 illustrates how a variety of different household appliances, once thought to be far beyond the ordinary person's means, became widely used in Japanese homes during the decade of rapid growth. In the space of 5–6 years starting with the Iwato boom in 1958, conventional wisdom about the intrinsic shape of the Japanese economy ceased to the case. The conditions had been ripe for major growth that transformed industry, lifestyles, and the national consciousness. That interval, in retrospect, was, in terms of its later impact, the real era of rapid growth.

Recession in the mid-1960s
In the midst of this transformation, economic downturns did occasionally happen. In 1960 and 1961, there was a brief boom triggered by the income-doubling plan, followed in 1962 by a deficit in the balance of international payments and a subsequent economic retreat. After that, the economy started to recover, but as you can see from figure 5.9, the ongoing trade deficit precipitated retrenchment in 1964 and a recession in 1965. Economic performance in 1964 had been relatively weak compared with 1960–61, when the economy had boomed, but now the trough was deep. Some economists argued that Japan had invested too much in plant and equipment and that investment on such a scale would not be seen again for some time. Ongoing liberalization of trade and capital transactions added to a profound sense of crisis among many observers.

The Tokyo Olympics in 1964 had been the symbol of all that had been achieved so far. Roads and, more importantly, a network of expressways had been built for the Olympics, as had the Shinkansen bullet train. Transportation and other modern infrastructure was now taking shape.

But in 1964–65, the economy was marking time. Prime Minister Ikeda took ill and resigned from office and was replaced by Sato Eisaku. Corporate profit ratios continued to deteriorate. Government receipts started falling short, and tax revenues stopped coming in. The situation was sufficiently unhealthy that the government announced it would slash its spending 10 percent. But just at that point, Yamaichi Securities, one of Japan's four biggest securities brokerages, found itself holding some bad investment trusts and was on the verge of bankruptcy. The Bank of Japan, through the offices of the Industrial Bank of Japan, declared it would lend unconditionally to Yamaichi, rescuing the firm from bankruptcy.

To restore public confidence following the securities panic, the government did some rethinking. Deficit bond issues had been prohibited under the Public Finance Law following the bitter experiences of indiscriminate bond issues during the war. Now the government amended the law and adopted a policy of economic stimulation, even at the cost of issuing bonds. This pivotal policy reversal took place in 1965 and was followed by a boom in the late 1960s that marked the final episode in the era of rapid growth.

Lecture 6

EMERGENCE AS AN ECONOMIC POWER (1966–1975)

1965–70		Economic growth of 10 percent is sustained. Trade surpluses become the norm. In the wake of the merger of three companies to reconstruct Mitsubishi Heavy Industry Co. in 1964, a wave of big mergers takes place: Nissan and Prince in 1966, Yawata Steel and Fuji Steel in 1970, and the Daiichi Bank and Nihon Kangyo Bank in 1971. Pollution becomes a serious problem.
1967		The liberalization of capital transactions is announced.
1968-69		Riots and disturbances spread across college campuses
1969		Credit is tightened to control influence of the rising prices of overseas goods. The balance of international payments surplus expands. Sato and Nixon negotiate the return of Okinawa to Japan. Japan-U.S. textile negotiations founder, but an agreement is reached in 1971.
1971	*July*	Nixon visits China.
	August	The government announces a new economic policy and switches to a floating exchange rate.
	December	The exchange rate is set at $1.00 = ¥308. The government takes steps to ease fiscal and credit restraints.
1972		Tanaka Kakuei becomes prime minister and begins to rebuild Japan. Relations with China are restored.
1973	*February*	The yen is floated. During the year, prices begin to rise, and the government tightens credit.
	October	The fourth Middle East War breaks out. OPEC implements its oil strategy. Goods become short in supply, and prices skyrocket.
1974		A powerful program of credit restrictions succeeds in quenching inflation. The era of rapid growth ends.
	November	Miki Takeo becomes prime minister.

Lecture 6

EMERGENCE AS AN ECONOMIC POWER (1966–1975)

ECONOMIC GROWTH TAKES ROOT

In this lecture, I will look at Japan's final spurt of growth up until the end of the 1960s and at the ensuing dramatic changes that drew the curtain on the rapid growth era. To begin, I would like to consider some of the causes of the superrapid growth that occurred in the latter half of the 1960s.

In the late 1950s and early 1960s, Japan was visited periodically by a balance of international payments deficit every three or four years, forcing the government to tighten credit. Once the retrenchment of 1964 and the subsequent economic downturn of 1965 were over, the trade balance stayed essentially in the black. Figure 6.1 shows the accounts for the export and import of goods and services. In 1963 and 1964, the accounts recorded a deficit, but in 1965 the balance switched to a surplus, and apart for a small deficit in 1967, the accounts remained in surplus right up to 1972. This may be read as indicating that Japan's export competitiveness had strengthened as the economy had grown. Under the ¥360 = $1.00 exchange rate, established in 1949 and maintained for over 20 years, Japan enjoyed a superlative competitive edge in exports.

The breakdown of exports had changed, as can be seen from figure 6.2. By 1970, the proportion of textiles and light manufactures had declined, and steel, artificial fibers, ships, automobiles, and light machinery had become the mainstays of Japan's exports. Chemical products also put in a strong showing. It was the products of heavy and chemical industries, and material products in particular, that fueled the initial export expansion, later joined by

229

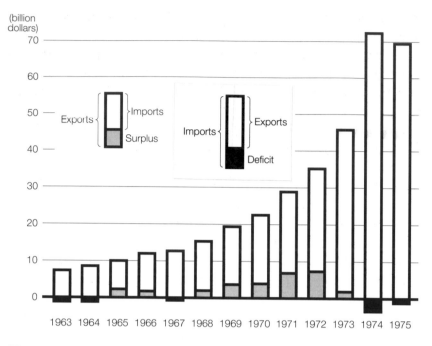

Fig. 6.1. Balance of Goods and Services

Source: Ministry of Finance, *Balance of Payments Statistics*.

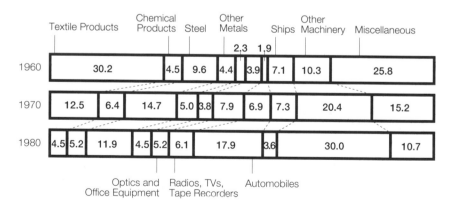

Fig. 6.2. Breakdown of Export Goods

Source: Ministry of Finance, *Clearance Statistics*.

machinery, to generate a trade surplus that pushed the balance of international payments into the black.

If we include capital account data in the balance of international payments picture, we find that the current account had been in deficit ever since the early 1960s and that the figures include a fair volume of foreign bonds, as companies and local bodies issued bonds abroad in order to supplement foreign currency holdings. Since these borrowings were covering the deficit in the current account, Japan's borrowings grew throughout the later 1950s and early 1960s, with the result that overall, the country was a debtor nation, its obligations overseas surpassing debts owed.

From about 1965 on, however, this pattern began to change. As trade moved into surplus, loans were repaid, and companies even began to invest abroad. In 1968, debts to Japan had come to exceed Japanese debts overseas. Japan had become a net lender.

If we look at foreign exchange reserves, given in figure 6.3, it can be seen that these remained stable at about $1.8–2.0 billion for a time in the early 1960s. This was a time, however, when Japan was trying to keep its foreign currency holdings up, even as it increased its debts abroad. After the current account moved into surplus in the late 1960s, foreign currency reserves remained at around $2 billion. Debts that needed to be repaid were paid off, and companies actively invested abroad, but foreign currency holdings were not allowed to rise. The picture is analogous to that of a person who pays off a debt and then boosts his savings but doesn't increase his pocket money.

In 1968, however, foreign currency holdings took off, soaring to $2.8 billion and then to $4.4 billion in 1969. Foreign debts dwindled, and Japanese firms found it hard to find new places to invest their money. Other countries became wary as Japan seemingly turned competitive overnight and unleashed a torrent of exports. This shift, I believe, marked the beginning of Japan's economic friction.

Rapid growth continued apace at over 10 percent into the late 1960s. The year-on-year rate of increase in real gross national expenditures was shown in figure 5.10 [See Lecture 5]. It can be seen that, apart from an exceptionally low 5.1 percent in 1965,

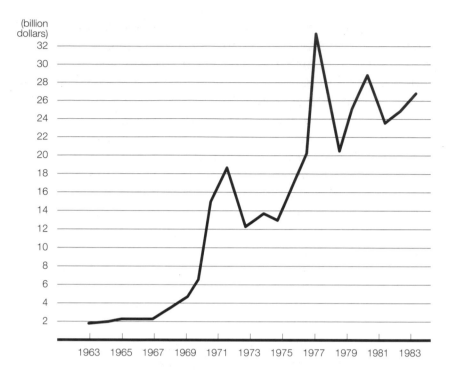

Fig. 6.3. Foreign Exchange Reserves

Source: Bank of Japan.

growth of 10 percent was maintained throughout the period from 1963 to 1970. In 1968, Japan's gross national product emerged as the second largest in the free world. Calculated in dollars at a rate of $1.00 = ¥360, Japan's GNP had outstripped that of West Germany, then in second place. Japan had become an economic power.

Development of heavy and chemical industries

It took a while before the significance of this event began to sink in. People were still thinking in terms of how hard it was to catch up with other countries, but before anyone noticed, Japan had in fact become a major power. I will talk later about how the perception gap concerning Japanese international status gave rise to later economic friction.

Production in steel and numerous other industries put on a sharp spurt of growth at about this time. To secure their raw materials, companies embarked on projects that yoked resource and infrastructure development and imports. Japanese capital was exported to the United States, Australia, Malaysia, Indonesia, and many other countries for the development of mines, inland transportation systems, and large specialized ships to transport the materials. Thus, a pattern of production and trade emerged in which materials would arrive at the piers of the industrial complexes on Japan's Pacific coast, be processed in nearby plants, and then be reloaded on at the piers for shipment elsewhere.

A map depicting the locations of industrial complexes at the time can be found at the beginning of this chapter. Over 20 such complexes had been completed over an area stretching from Tokuyama to Iwakuni to Kashima. If growth centered on heavy industries, including petrochemicals, was to continue to maintain its pace, it was necessary to build at least one new complex a year. Shibushi in Kagoshima, Mutsu-Ogawara, and Tomakomai in Hokkaido were slated as candidate sites for the next big heavy industry complexes.

In the final analysis, the economic expansion of this period was sustained by robust capital investment in heavy industrial complexes and regional industrial zones. Always, the focus was on heavy industry—electric power, steel, machinery, chemicals, and petroleum—where capacity expansions buoyed investment.

But the late 1960s were marked by a number of important transitions in production activity. One major change is to be found in the spectacular growth of the automobile industry. Production of passenger sedans soared from 700,000 vehicles in 1965 to 2.61 million in 1969 and 4.47 million in 1973. At the same time, the quality of Japanese cars improved spectacularly, establishing auto production as an export industry. The number of vehicles exported rose from 200,000 in 1965 to 840,000 in 1969 and 2.09 million in 1973, with nearly half of Japanese automobile output being destined for export.

Another change in the industrial scene was the emergence of the electronics industry. In the late 1960s, people made the switch from black and white to color television. In 1970, the production of color TVs outstripped black and white sets, and this lead widened immediately. Another export industry had been born. A further area exhibiting stunning growth was electronic calculators. In 1965, the annual production of electronic calculators stood at 4,000 units and prices at about ¥200,000. In 1969, production had hit 450,000 units and prices were down to about ¥10,000. By 1973, swiftly improving materials and mass-production techniques had boosted calculator production to 10 million units and sent prices down to a few thousand yen. Manufacturers had also begun to make large electronic computers, although this did not yet have an impact on the United States.

Other typical newcomer industries of this period include aluminum window sashes for homes, gas water heaters, automated vending machines (which spread like wildfire throughout the country), and equipment for everyday use of all shapes and sizes. The background for the emergence of these new industries was a long-awaited increase in housing construction, which emerged as a major source of demand, together with already burgeoning new construction of office buildings and factories.

Changes in smaller business

It was also during the late 60s and early 70s that so-called backbone firms—small companies with their own specialist technologies and management policies—began to come onto the scene in large numbers. According to Nakamura Hideichiro, these are independent companies whose capital is not owned by the big corporations and whose operations are big enough to make the Tokyo Stock Exchange's Second Section. Many component manufacturers, with their own independently developed technologies and perfected production lines, were founded during the peak period of the development of machinery industries. Many of these launched into creative new product areas, defying the conventions of management and technology. Examples include Kashiyama, an off-the-rack clothing manufacturer, and France Bed, which adapted automobile seat production technology to the manufacture of beds. Mass-marketing chain stores, such as Daiei, Jusco, Nichii, and Uni, also came into being in this period.

Another feature of this period was the technological advances in small businesses that came about through their adoption of laborsaving technology. Automated machine tools, numerically controlled machine tools, and a host of other new machines found their way into small businesses. Marketing and inventory management techniques became widespread. Firms found it possible to introduce all these innovations because of quality improvements and price reductions resulting from technological advances.

Tertiary industries, once lagging, now began to venture into new fields. The real estate industry launched itself into housing development and construction of rental buildings. Medium-size apartments, known as *manshon*, began to appear at about this time. Service industries came onto the scene, exploiting the labor shortage by providing businesses with specialized services in security, cleaning, accounting, and advertising and publicity.

Changes in lifestyles

One of the characteristics of the economic growth of this time is that new areas and a much more diversified range of industries began to show expansion. Labor shortages and more equitable income distributions began to change the shape of Japan's domestic industry and the lifestyles of its people. As incomes rose, consumption continued to make headway. The Economic Planning Agency's consumption level indices show gains of 83 percent for urban dwellers in the 13-year span between 1960 and 1973 and a prodigious 150 percent for residents of rural areas. The focus of consumption changed too, from meeting basic needs in food and clothing to housing, automobiles, education, and leisure.

Let me cite two examples of this shift in consumption. One of the changes is housing conditions. Overall, houses and apartments became larger, and the number of rooms and the size of rooms increased. From 1958 to 1973, the average per person space increased from 4.91 standard mats (about 8 square meters) to 6.61 mats (about 11 square meters). The number of rooms per home rose from 3.6 to 4.15. Although not reflected in the statistics, qualitative improvements also occurred: it ceased to be uncommon for homes to have a luxurious lounge, complete with drawing room furniture and piano.

The other example is the change in people's use of time, indicated in figure 6.4, which shows data from a study undertaken by the Japan Broadcasting Corporation. Between 1960 and 1970 a number of noteworthy changes took place. Hours of sleep and recreation, although not directly reflected in the figures, decreased for both men and women, while hours spent on meals and personal chores increased. Hours spent watching television rose, and hours spent on leisure activities on days off increased. Work hours declined incrementally. We may interpret the data to indicate that people were exhausted by work in 1960 but that over time they gained more energy for hobbies and entertainment after work hours. In fact, the percentage of people engaged in sports activities climbed from 24 percent of the total population in 1956 to 60 percent in 1973 and 68 percent in 1979. The percentage of people who took sightseeing trips also increased, from 29 percent in 1957 to 62 percent in 1971. The expansion of leisure formed the backdrop for the growth of tourist hotels and sports facilities, such as golf courses and bowling alleys.

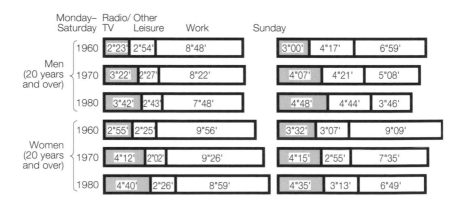

Fig. 6.4 Changes in Utilization of Time

Source: NHK, *Survey on Utilization of Time.*

The spread of the automobile must not pass without comment. As late as 1969, on average only 18 percent of nonfarming households and 15 percent of farming households possessed a car. Then, in the final days of the era of high growth, car ownership skyrocketed: by 1973, 35 percent of nonfarming households and 43 percent of farming households owned a car, with farming households moving into the lead, and by 1984 the figures had climbed to 63 percent of nonfarming households and 78 percent of farming households. Many factors contributed to this explosive growth. The quality of domestic cars had improved, household incomes had risen, and roads had improved as the result of paving and other public works programs. Life in the farm communities around major cities was transformed. The radius of activity, for work or leisure, was suddenly lengthened, and the distance between the villages and the cities shrank. The automobile was crucial in eliminating the lifestyle gap between urban and rural communities.

There is no end to inventory the changes that took place during this period. Rates of advancement to high school and colleges rose. Westernized foods and instant foods became part of the ordinary Japanese diet. The mass-consumption society, to use Rostow's term, matured in Japan at the end of the high-growth era.

Liberalization of capital

It is not the case, however, that the mood of Japan's business community was totally optimistic. The liberalization of foreign capital brought fears that foreign companies might enter Japan, and people began to have second thoughts about the desirability of letting competition heat up so much. To borrow the words of Inayama Yoshihiro, a business leader of the time, it was felt that Japan needed orderly growth.

Attempts were made to bring some order. In 1963, the three companies that had been created when Mitsubishi Heavy Industries was split up under the occupation's deconcentration program merged to become a single company once again. Nissan and Prince merged in 1966. A merger between Yawata Steel and Fuji Steel went through in 1970, but word of the pending move had leaked out several years earlier, prompting economists to voice their opposition to such mergers on the grounds that they would impair the strong competitive climate in the marketplace. One example can be seen in the case of Oji Paper. A trust was formed by the merger of Oji, Fuji, and Karafuto Industries in 1993; after World War II, however, Oji was split into three separate companies—Oji, Jujo Paper, and Honshu Paper—in accordance with the occupation's deconcentration policy. Reflecting the trend at that time, these three companies seriously considered merging again and even signed an agreement to do so. The merger, however, fell through in the end when it was unable to obtain the Fair Trade Commission's blessing.

The banking industry was in a similar frame of mind. In 1969, reports leaked out that the Daiichi Bank and the Mitsubishi Bank were about to merge. The merger collapsed due to opposition within the Daiichi Bank, but in 1971 the Daiichi Bank merged with the Nihon Kangyo Bank to form the present-day Daiichi Kangyo Bank. In 1973, the Taiyo Bank (originally the Nippon Mutual Bank) and the Kobe Bank combined to become the Taiyo Kobe Bank. In 1990 it merged again with the Mitsui Bank to become the Mitsui Taiyo Kobe Bank. In 1992 it changed the name to the Sakura Bank. Despite these mergers, however, competition remained red-hot, and the mergers, in my view, cannot be said to have resulted in the creation of any palpable monopolistic impact.

One reason that competition was so intense during the growth period is that late-starter companies were often competing to catch up with those that had an initial lead. When it became apparent that ethylene costs would not subside unless plants were made bigger, the Ministry of International Trade and Industry issued administrative instructions to the petrochemical industry to the effect that construction of plants of less than 300,000-metric-ton capacity would not be licensed in the future. MITI apparently presumed that by issuing such a directive some companies would abandon production or merge with others. What happened, in fact, was that all eight petrochemical groups ended up building 300,000-metric-ton plants. Similar competition could be seen in the steel industry, where companies competed to build the biggest blast furnace. Sumitomo Metal Industries, in particular, made a major effort, and the competition continued unbridled. Intense competition bred more of the same.

Female workers

To meet the labor shortage that accompanied the economic expansion, a new source of labor was found. The female jobholding rate—the percentage of women over the age of 15 in employment—recorded its lowest point in 1965 but rose thereafter. The reason for the decline up to 1965 is clear: the overall number of people engaged in agriculture had declined. In farm households, women work as a matter of course, especially in peak periods. Thus, the female jobholding rate was directly linked to the percentages of people engaged in agriculture. The early 1960s, however, saw an erosion of the agriculture population and a commensurate decline in the percentage of women in employment.

The year 1965 was a watershed, marking the onset of an upsurge in women's employment that has continued to the present. Again, we may ask why. In former times, it had been the practice in the urban areas for women not to go out to work, and if they did it was usually only for the few years between graduation from school until marriage or childbirth. Thus, a graph of women's jobholding rates by age shows an M-shaped curve, with a trough in the 20s and 30s when women are engaged in child rearing. However, about 1965, companies were scraping the bottom of the barrel for young male labor and began to mobilize females into the workforce.

In the late 1960s, the practice of piecework in the home was revived. Company representatives would go into the housing estates in Osaka and elsewhere and get housewives to perform sewing tasks or engage in simple assembly work. Later, middle-aged housewives began to enter the labor force as part-timers in a development that has attracted much comment in recent years. These trends are clear from figure 6.5, which compares women's jobholding rates in 1956, 1965, and 1982. The spurt in jobholding among women aged 35–50 between 1965 and 1982 and the

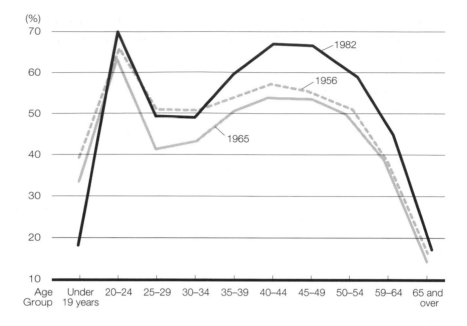

Fig. 6.5. Women's Job Holding Ratios by Age Group

Source: Management and Coordination Agency, Statistics Bureau. *Sangyo Kozo Kihon Chosa* (Basic Survey of Industrial Structure).

shallowing out of the jobholding trough in the 20–35 age group are both manifestations of these new trends.

We can interpret these changes as follows. Companies don't want to increase the number of unionized workers that they hire, since these cannot be laid off when the economy takes a downturn and their wages rise relentlessly. So they start to want workers who will do the job during busy periods and can be terminated during slack periods. Accordingly, firms sought to develop a pool of low-wage workers who could be hired and fired as needed. These were the take-home piecework workers and the part-timers. During the rapid expansion of the late 1960s, housewives began to figure prominently among those employed in this fashion.

The housewives, for their part, started taking these jobs on a temporary basis because they were low paying. But eventually their positions became semipermanent, so that we find part-timers who have been working in the same job for 10 years, who can scarcely be called part-timers any more, and whose households have become dependent on the income so that they cannot afford to quit.

Environmental problems

In the final stages of the rapid growth era, people began to notice the negative aspects of growth, and the economic expansion came to be viewed in a rather more critical light. Four big pollution lawsuits brought during this period—involving pollution claims in Niigata, mercury poisoning in Minamata Bay, cadmium poisoning in Toyama, and asthma in Yokkaichi—are examples. Photochemical smog made headlines. Complaints about air and water pollution and pollution from noise began to be heard, and the government began to undertake serious pollution control measures. Eventually, public opinion forced the government to pass the Environmental Pollution Law, which established the principle that the polluter is responsible for cleaning up. In 1970, the Diet passed 14 legislative bills providing emission standards for individual pollutants and imposing controls on, for example, automobile exhaust gases, especially nitrous oxides.

I remember crossing the Tama River, near Tokyo, one hot day in the early 1960s, observing the river black with pollution and noticing the pungent smell of the methane that rose from its surface. I thought then that we were in trouble. Until about that time the predominant attitude had been that in the interests of industrial development sacrifices were inevitable and that the country couldn't afford to worry about the environment. The late 1960s and early 1970s saw a backing away from economic growth at the expense of everything else and the general introduction of antipollution legislation and initiatives to protect the natural environment and to beautify Japan's cities.

The campus revolution and citizens' movements

In 1968–69, the student rebellion broke out across Japan. How we interpret the student rebellion is an issue that must be left for future scholars. What we can say is that the young people who took part in the rebellion, mostly aged about 20, represented a generation that had known economic growth since they were old enough to remember—a generation that had not known the hardships of war and the early postwar era. Rapid economic growth had granted them stable lives and the faith that things would continue to improve. Yet there seems to have been something in their lives that was missing

Citizens' campaigns in opposition to pollution and a variety of other causes probably reflected a similar lack of fulfillment. Now that improved living standards were a given, people redirected their attention to their remaining misgivings and began to address the less-wholesome aspects of growth. When I saw the *Asahi Shimbun*, one of Japan's leading newspapers, launch a "To Hell with GNP" campaign, I knew that we had embarked on a new era.

Another example of this change of mood, this time on the political scene, was the election of Minobe Ryokichi as governor of Tokyo in 1967 under the slogan of "Blue skies over Tokyo." Minobe, recommended by the Socialist Party, was a vehement critic of growth, which he saw as dangerously inflationary, and of prevailing economic policies, especially the issuance of government bonds to finance the national deficit, which he regarded as the worst possible policy. And he defeated the candidate recommended by the Liberal Democratic Party.

International friction

About the time that growth became a fact of national life and problems began to arise from that growth within Japan, friction with other countries also intensified, generating pressures from abroad that ultimately led to the termination of rapid growth

Let me illustrate these fricative forces from my personal experience. In 1967, I visited West Germany for the first time. I was in Düsseldorf, in the Ruhr industrial belt, the heartland of German heavy industry. Raw materials to feed that industry are off-loaded at Rotterdam, at the mouth of the Rhine, and transferred to smaller vessels of about 2,000 tons for shipment up the river. The finished products are carried back down the Rhine and reloaded onto larger ships. Knowing of Japan's large coastal industrial complexes, alongside which huge ships tie up, I remember thinking, with naive arrogance, that West Germany was behind the times.

Two years later, in October 1969 if I remember correctly, the surplus in West Germany's balance of international payments had grown to the point that a deficit-beset United States had pressured West Germany into revaluing the deutsche mark. Just at that juncture, I attended a symposium on Japan-Germany economic relations in Hamburg. A senior executive of a German shipbuilding company delivered a speech in which he remonstrated bitterly about how Germany had met American demands to revalue the deutsche mark, while Japan was still maintaining an exchange rate of ¥360 = $1.00. We are streamlining our production processes, he said, but no matter how much we do so, we end up revaluing the deutsche mark against the dollar. It is as if we are doing so in order to provide Japan with export markets, he complained, and he demanded to know when Japan was going to revalue the yen.

On my return to Japan, however, I found that no one took such grievances seriously. People would say things like "we're still weak in computers." There was a growing perception gap about Japan. From outside, Japan was seen as some kind of monstrosity, whose government and private sector collaborated to boost competitiveness and assail any and all markets. The Western countries felt threatened. In Japan, however, all attention was focused on the need for Japan to catch up and to make greater efforts to do so. Domestically, discussion of revaluing the currency was taboo, so that the perception gap, a genuine problem, was never bridged. The upshot was that in 1971 the country was stunned by the "Nixon shocks," when the United States unilaterally floated the dollar on international exchange markets.

There was one other problem. Discussions between President Nixon and Prime Minister Sato, at the close of his political career, led to an agreement that Okinawa should revert to Japanese control. The agreement constituted a major political coup for Sato and his cabinet, but in the course of negotiations, Japan was met with demands that it cut its textile exports. It was not as though Japan was exporting great quantities of textiles to the United States at the time. What happened was that during the presidential elections, textile manufacturers in the southern states had come out in support of Nixon, and Nixon, in return, had promised that he would get Japan to restrict its textile exports. It appears that there was a secret agreement that shortly after the reversion of Okinawa, Japan would announce export restrictions, so it is widely joked that Japan traded yarn for *nawa* (rope). However, it took two more years before the Japanese government could impose export ceilings, owing to opposition from Japan's textile industry. President Nixon was angered at the delay, which resulted in cooled U.S.-Japan relations.

THE END OF GROWTH

In 1969, the Bank of Japan tightened credit. I may possibly be one of the minority to hold this view, but I believe that the imposition of a credit squeeze at this juncture was asking for trouble. As I noted earlier, if a tight credit policy is imposed when the balance of international payments is in deficit, domestic demand is held down, inventories grow more than anticipated, and companies step up their export efforts. At the same time, a reduction in domestic demand means a reduction in imports and a recovery in the balance of international payments.

The 1969 credit squeeze, however, was triggered, not by a balance of payments deficit, but by rising commodity prices overseas, and its purpose was to prevent inflation from permeating as a result of increases in the prices of imported goods. Tightening credit under these circumstances will gently brake domestic demand and have the effect of averting inflation, but as domestic demand goes down, exports grow, imports shrink, and the balance of payments surplus is naturally magnified. The problem with credit tightening lay in its deployment in a different environment and for a different purpose from those in which, and for which, such measures had hitherto been employed.

The outcome is shown in figure 6.1. There was already a clear export surplus in 1968 and 1969, but following the Bank of Japan's action, the surplus trend became marked. Exports rose by $16 billion in 1969, $19.3 billion in 1970, and $24 billion in 1971, while imports rose from $15 billion to only about $19.7 billion in the same period. This mounting trade surplus fueled the flames of resentment overseas. The correct strategy would have been a small upward revaluation of the yen. Since the yen prices of import goods would have declined, imported inflation permeation would have been prevented. Exports would have been at a slight disadvantage, imports would have been stimulated, and the trade surplus would have shrunk, or at least have slowed. But domestic opposition rendered such action out of the question. The ¥360 = $1.00 exchange rate had been long established, and it appears that Japan's business community was of the opinion that any other exchange rate would ruin exports. Raising the exchange rate was considered a taboo topic in Japanese government offices.

The "Nixon shocks"
The issue of the textile export restrictions that had been agreed to between Nixon and Sato in conjunction the reversion of Okinawa was still smoldering. Nixon got his revenge in two ways. First, he kept secret from Japan the 180-degree about-face in the United States' policy toward China, that led to the resumption of relations and eventually a visit by Nixon to the mainland. The announcement of the decision on July 15, 1971, came as a major shock to the Japanese.

A month later, on August 15, Nixon announced a new two-thrust economic policy. One component of this policy was a 90-day wage and price freeze along with budget cuts designed to quench America's rising inflation. The other was the import duties to be imposed with the aim of restoring the United States, balance of trade. This latter was, for all practical purposes, a demand that strongly export-competitive countries like Japan and West Germany raise their exchange rates.

Immediately on the announcement of Nixon's new policy, nearly all the Western European countries floated their exchange rates, leaving rates for the market to determine. Japan, however, clung to the old fixed exchange rate until almost the end of August. However, banks and trading companies, figuring that a rise in the exchange rate was inevitable, brought their dollars in hand into the Bank of Japan to convert at the ¥360 = $1.00 rate.

They sold dollars, rather than bought. In the end, Japan switched to a floating exchange rate more than 10 days after other countries, resulting in massive losses for the Bank of Japan.

The yen subsequently rose in value month by month, until eventually a new fixed rate of ¥308 = $1.00 was set at a meeting held at the Smithsonian Institution in Washington, D.C., in December 1971. The new fixed rate survived throughout 1972, a year marked by fiscal expansion and financial easing, with more money in circulation than could be spent.

The impact of the Nixon shocks was serious, at least for a time. The harm may have been more psychological than real, but the business community was badly rattled. As the yen rose in exchange markets, there was outright panic among regional export manufacturers, who feared that they would no longer be able to sell goods overseas. New business halted briefly, although only while exchange rates fluctuated most wildly.

The domestic economy had cooled as a result of the previous year's credit tightening measures. In spring 1971, the economy bottomed out, and then in August, just when things had taken a turn for the better, came the Nixon shocks. As can be seen in figure 6.6, the Sato cabinet, in an effort to regain the domestic economic momentum that it expected to lose in export trade, greatly expanded its fiscal spending and public lending and investment when it drew up the budget for fiscal 1972. Interest rates dropped, the money supply expanded, and the budget ballooned. Public investments showed spectacular growth.

Suddenly there was an excess of liquidity. M_2, for example, shown in figure 6.7, grew at an extraordinary rate, year on year, in 1971 and 1972. M_2 is the sum of all cash currency in circulation, current deposits, and deposits with prescribed terms, and is an indicator of the money supply that feeds demand in the marketplace. It is normally understood that in order to hold inflation down, one adjusts the growth of M_2, that is, the money supply. For example, the growth rate of money supply in 1970 was 17 percent. The money supply, however, grew 24 percent in 1971 and 25 percent in 1972, an extraordinary expansion compared with anything before or since. The issue of banknotes soared. Bank of

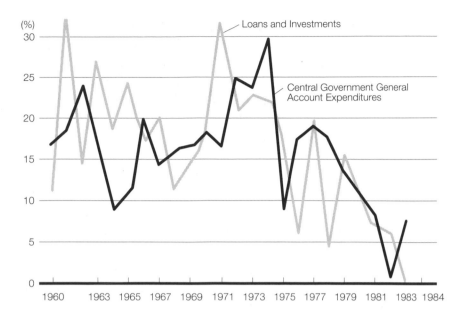

Fig. 6.6. Year-on-Year Increase in Government Expenditures and Government Loans and Investments

Source: Ministry of Finance, *Zaisei Tokei* (Budgetary Statistics).

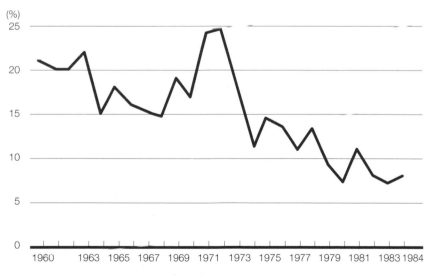

Fig. 6.7. Year-on-Year Growth Rate of M_2

Source: Bank of Japan, *Keizai Tokei Nenpo* (Economic Statistics Annual).

Japan loans rose ¥8 trillion in 1971 and 1972, and loans at banks throughout the country climbed from ¥39 trillion in 1970 to ¥62 trillion in 1972, for an increase of ¥23 trillion.

The government had decisively increased its fiscal spending and channeled large amounts of funds to the private sector in an effort to stimulate a nerve-wracked economy. By overdoing it, it sowed the seeds of huge inflation.

Reconstructing the Japanese archipelago

In July 1972, the Sato cabinet resigned, and a new cabinet was formed by Tanaka Kakuei. Before he took office, Tanaka had published *Rebuilding the Japanese Archipelago*. A native of Niigata, an area that is out of the limelight cast on the Pacific industrial belt, Tanaka was famous for having brought his home region numerous benefits as a politician and thus enjoyed a solid political base in that region. The book proposed, in its essence, to extend to the entire nation the benefits of growth of the kind he had brought to Niigata.

The idea was to redistribute the industrial belt on the Pacific coast throughout the country, constructing industrial cities of 200,000–300,000 that would be linked by expressways and high-speed rail links. Areas that had been left behind in the growth of the 1960s would begin to enjoy growth.

To do this, a high growth rate would have to be sustained over time. Tanaka's plan was predicated on growth of about 9 percent persisting over the next decade and probably represents an attempt to emulate the Ikeda cabinet's income-doubling plan. At any rate, the plan, together with the restoration of relations with China, set off a temporary boom. The problem was that Tanaka appeared on the scene at a time when inflation was rampaging around the world, owing in large part to the exodus of dollars from the United States, which remained bogged down in the Vietnam War. Their foreign currency reserves brimming, countries were adopting growth-oriented policies, with the result that demand soared globally. Prices trended upward everywhere, especially prices of primary commodities.

Global inflation

Oil prices had been slipping throughout the 1960s, despite efforts to the contrary by the Organization of Petroleum Exporting Countries (OPEC), owing to a surplus that had persisted since the beginning of the decade. In 1969 and 1970, however, demand for oil started to rise around the world, tightening the oil markets. Seizing their opportunity, OPEC moved to raise oil prices. In 1971, its members agreed to increase the price of crude oil by $1 a barrel (159 liters) in stages over a five-year period, and in the following year, 1972, they concluded the Ryadh Agreement under which OPEC members would buy up stocks of the major oil companies so that they could benefit from the profits made from the sale of oil.

Another rather unusual event compounded matters in 1972. A grain crop failure in the Soviet Union and the Eastern European countries spurred those countries to buy large quantities of wheat from the United States. Their purchase boosted grain prices around world, and this, as might be expected, had an impact on other prices.

Thus, the Japanese economy was awash with excess liquidity and booming with prosperity owing to the rising expectations triggered by Tanaka's program at a time of global inflation. Companies began to buy up large quantities of real estate throughout the country. This sent land prices skyrocketing and eventually let to speculative buying of other goods, sending their prices upward. The Bank of Japan moved to tighten the money supply as early as the beginning of 1973, but the effects of its response were not immediately felt, and prices continued their upward spiral.

In the United States, President Nixon had adopted a new deflationary policy back in summer 1971. This policy remained in effect for nearly a year, but Nixon, fearing a recession, eventually relaxed the policy, allowing U.S. inflation to return to its former level and resulting in an even larger balance of international payments deficit. In February 1973, Paul A. Volcker, assistant undersecretary for finance (later to become chairman of the Federal Reserve) visited Tokyo to ask Japan to move to a floating exchange rate on the grounds that it was no longer possible to maintain the exchange rates set under the Smithsonian Agreement. Japan promptly floated the yen, which it has continued to do to this day. In the meanwhile, inflation picked up momentum around the world.

The first oil crisis

In Japan, credit was tightened and the yen began to float upward, but the situation was such that the soaring inflation could no longer be leveraged by financial measures or a rise in the exchange rate. The year 1973 is remembered as the year of inflation and the oil crisis; but even if the oil crisis had not occurred, the worst inflation since the Korean War was already in progress. In January and February that year, big companies cornered the market on tuna fish landed at Misaki, a famous fishing port, buying up entire catches at prices of about ¥100 million for a shipload. Stories are told of how every available warehouse was stocked with goods that someone had cornered.

In October 1973, amid inflation in Japan and everywhere else, the fourth Middle East War broke out. OPEC answered Israel's territorial successes by a strategy of using oil as a weapon. This strategy started with talk among the Middle Eastern OPEC nations of banning exports of oil to Arab countries' enemies. At the time, Japan relied on oil for about three-fourths of its energy needs, most being supplied from Middle East sources. Its foreign policy leaned toward the United States', which was sympathetic with Israel. With talk of a ban, there was outright panic in Japan, and the prices, not just of oil and oil products, but even of things that didn't have much to do with oil, started to take off. Sellers withheld goods from the market, and people began stockpiling. Rumors that stocks of toilet paper would soon run out sparked riots in stores, in which a number of people were injured.

Following the toilet paper riots, Tsujimura Kotaro of Keio University conducted a study of household spending in which he looked at demand for toilet paper. He found that households bought abnormally large quantities of toilet paper in and around October 1973, but then for a period of several months bought almost none. He concluded that evened out over a year the amount purchased was the same as in a regular year. When one thinks about it, one is hardly surprised, but incidents of this kind are apt to occur when people panic.

OPEC's oil strategy began with export restrictions, but it seems that the volume of exports did not decrease. Then OPEC boosted crude oil prices fourfold, from $2.8 a barrel to $11. The OPEC countries had succeeded in turning their resources into a strategically useful export item, and the shock reverberated world-wide.

The increase in Japan's oil demand and its oil imports over the preceding decade had been immense. As figures 6.8 and 6.9 show, imports climbed from 87 million kiloliters in 1965 to 175 million kiloliters in 1969 and further to 288 million kiloliters in 1973. Only Japan was buying oil in such colossal quantities from the Middle East. Quite understandably, the prospect of having these imports cut off unnerved Japan.

This was the era of mammoth oil tankers. Tankers had rapid-ly grown in size over the past decade, and huge tankers of 300,000 tons were now being mass produced. Take, for example, Mitsubishi Shipbuilding's Koyagi shipyard. This had been built on an island off Nagasaki that had once been a coal mine. The mine

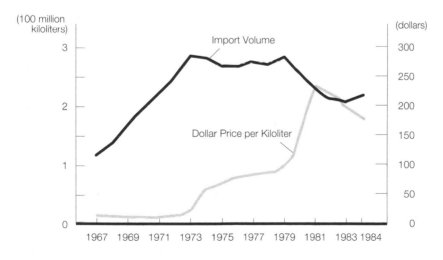

Fig. 6.8. Crude Oil Import Volumes and Prices

Source: Ministry of Finance, *Clearance Statistics.*

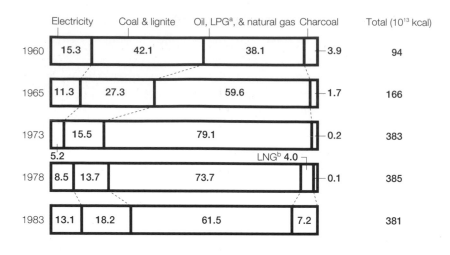

Fig. 6.9. Primary Energy Supply (percent of total)

Source: Agency of Natural Resources and Energy, *Sogo Enerugii Tokei* (Comprehensive Energy Statistics).
[a] Liquefied petroleum gas.
[b] Liquefied natural gas.

was now closed, and a shipyard had been built specifically for tankers. I went once to visit the yard and was taken aback to discover that it was putting 300,000 ton tankers into the water at the rate of one a month.

The shipyard had a monumental dock, 100 meters wide and a kilometer in length, on which it would build two tankers at a time. In the rear, the initial stages were carried out, with the bow and stern of a vessel being constructed separately. When the ship in front was completed and left the dock, the two halves at the rear of the dock would be welded together and moved forward so that the building of another ship could be started in the rear. Sections of a ship, up to half as big as this seminar room, were constructed in a factory, with pipes and electrical wires concealed between the inner and outer walls. These sections would be transported to the dock, where, once the pipes and wiring had been connected, the parts would be welded together to make a 300,000 ton tanker.

As rumors of oil shortages spread, the price of oil and almost everything else jumped sharply upward. As table 6.1 shows, inflation was at its worst in 1974. In February that year, wholesale price climbed an incredible 32 percent on the previous year, and

Table 6.1 Year-on-Year Price Changes (%)

	Domestic Wholesale Price Index	Consumer Price Index	Imported Goods Price Index	Exported Goods Price Index
1969	1.9	5.2	2.0	2.8
1970	3.5	7.7	3.3	4.3
1971	–1.0	6.1	0.0	–1.4
1972	1.6	4.5	–4.2	–3.2
1973	15.7	11.7	21.2	10.2
1974	27.7	24.5	67.8	33.9
1975	2.7	11.8	7.3	–4.1
1976	5.6	9.3	5.2	–0.6
1977	3.3	8.1	–4.5	–4.7
1978	–0.5	3.8	–17.5	–6.6
1979	4.9	3.6	28.7	10.8
1980	14.9	8.0	44.7	8.6
1981	1.4	4.9	1.6	1.2
1982	0.5	2.7	7.9	3.9
1983	–0.7	1.9	–7.8	–6.0
1984	0.1	2.2	–3.4	0.6

Sources: Consumer Price Index: Prime Minister's Office, Statistics Bureau. Others. Bank of Japan.

consumer prices increases topped 24 percent. Reflecting these increases, the basic wage increase in the spring wage negotiations rose 33 percent. This was inflation on a scale not seen since directly after World War II.

Fukuda Takeo justifiably labeled these "crazy prices." As Minister of Finance and later prime minister, Fukuda took the leadership in imposing measures to rein the economy in. He persuaded Prime Minister Tanaka to shelve his grandiose proposals for revamping Japan and swiftly clamped down in the most severe retrenchment program since Dodge imposed his balanced budget program at the end of the occupation. Interest rates and bank reserve requirements were sharply raised. The Bank of Japan undertook its window guidance on lending with a daring and a severity far in excess of anything experienced before.

"Crazy prices" and retrenchment

To extinguish the rampant inflation, the credit squeeze was supplemented by the passage in December 1973 of two pieces of legislation, the Oil Product Market Stabilization Law and the National Life Stabilization Law. The first of these permitted the government to impose rationing and restrictions on the use of oil similar to that in wartime and was, in fact, invoked on a small scale. The second law was readied in order to permit controls on necessities of life other than oil products. It looked as if wartime rationing and controls were about to be reinstituted. Shiina Etsusaburo, vice president of the Liberal Democratic Party, is reported to have remarked that this was the very last thing that anyone should do. That such steps were even contemplated, however, may be taken as indicative of how seriously the crisis was viewed in government circles.

That the controls were invoked only on a small scale is due to the success of the financial retrenchment measures. Until spring 1974, when the 33 percent basic wage increase was announced, the economy was strongly shadowed by inflationary pressures, but from the summer on the economy began to take on the colors of recession. The textile industry, for example, whose products had been moving so fast the factories could hardly keep up, suddenly found itself with surplus stocks piling up in the warehouses and prices slumping. Almost overnight, it seemed the country was plunged into recession.

A nice example of the effect of this sudden change in economic climate is to be seen in the reform of the employment insurance program. Since there had been a labor shortage and not many unemployed up to 1973, the insurance fund was in surplus. The program, however, was problematic. Those unemployed who were receiving benefits were for the most part young people with little intention of taking jobs who would obtain benefits until their eligibility ran out. Moreover, a supplementary month or two of benefits was paid out when people found work early, a feature that led to abuse. (This feature has recently been revived.) Since young unemployed presented problems for the system, and the older unemployed faced poor prospects of regaining employment, the reforms, which had been proposed in a time of prosperity, sought to reduce the payment of benefits for the young and to extend eligibility for older persons, in addition to doing away with supplementary benefits for job takers. The proposals drew the ire of the opposition parties, and debates in the Diet ended inconclusively in spring 1974.

However, the proposed revisions also included an item to the effect that, in the event of a recession, the government could designate industries as being especially hard hit and pay half of the salary of workers from firms that temporarily closed (two-thirds in the case of small businesses), with the money to be disbursed from the reformed employment insurance fund. After the amendment bill was shelved, this provision suddenly became highly attractive to both labor and management, and at the special session of the Diet at the end of that year, the legislation passed within a week. Quite a number of industries gained some respite through this legislation, starting with the textile industry. The rapid passage of the amendment bill is indicative of how the economic climate changed drastically within the space of six months.

I would also like to touch on how consumer anxiety manifested itself at the time of the recession. Common sense dictates that when inflation gets bad, cash and savings lose value, so it is better to convert these into goods. What actually happened, however, is that consumption plummeted and savings rose in 1974, as figure 6.10 shows. I believe that this may indicate a combination of anxiety about the loss of value of existing savings due to inflation and a desire to save because there was no telling what the future might bring. At any rate, consumption growth braked sharply.

The retrenchment measures remained in effect for two years, from spring 1973 throughout 1974 and into 1975. They were finally lifted in March 1975. Stringent retrenchment measures had succeeded in stemming inflation, but they had also brought to an end Japan's era of rapid growth.

JAPAN'S WORST POSTWAR RECESSION

From 1973 to 1975, manufacturing output plummeted. During this two-year period, the index of industrial production fell 18 percent. In fact, when we examine the numbers closely, we find that mining and manufacturing production fell nearly 19 percent in the 15-month period from the end of 1973 to the beginning of 1975.

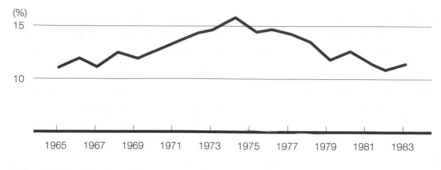

Fig. 6.10. Savings Rates as a Proportion of Worker Household Income

Source: Management and Coordination Agency, *Monthly Report on the Family Income and Expenditure Survey.*
Note: Savings rate = net increase in savings / disposable income

Inventories piled up and companies found they could no longer make ends meet.

Japan's worst postwar recession had arrived. Crude steel production had stood at 119 million metric tons in 1973 but then dropped to just over 100 million metric tons in 1975. Hardest hit was machine tools, which plunged from 212,000 units to 88,000 in a two-year period. Owing to orders in hand, shipbuilding output did not drop sharply until 1975, but over the next three or four years, the number of ships built fell to about one-third of previous numbers.

Although the severest recession since World War II, the economic setback was minor compared with the Great Depression of the early Showa era and presents some interesting contrasts. Whereas the Great Depression had been characterized by falling prices and uncertain production, the recession of 1974–75 was marked by stabilizing prices that showed no inclination to fall and a sharp drop in production. The economy marked time in an inflationary climate in what came to be labeled stagflation. Overseas, too, inflation refused to be reined in, but output stagnated. The only nations that enjoyed any prosperity were the OPEC countries.

Lean management

The rise in prices in Japan was eventually braked by the retrenchment policies, but demand suddenly cooled, and output plunged in response. Companies found themselves in trouble, saddled with too much production equipment and too many workers. The downside of aggressive management policies now came to be felt in the form of mounting interest charges and depreciation costs, which hammered corporate profit ratios down to a nationwide average of 1 percent of total capital, as shown in figure 6.11. The extraordinary extent of the drop is indicated by the fact that the numbers for earlier years averaged 5–6 percent. Nearly half of all Japan's companies reported losses.

As a long-term strategy for dealing with the downturn, companies resorted to what were euphemistically termed employment adjustments—trimming their workforces in installments. The simplest method was not to fill the positions of those who retired. Then there was the strategy of transferring surplus workers to other plants. Workers normally worked at the plant for which they were hired; now they were being transferred to other plants and even other regions, with the result that whole families had to relocate. In other cases employees were sent to work for periods in affiliated companies. Part-timers and other temporary workers

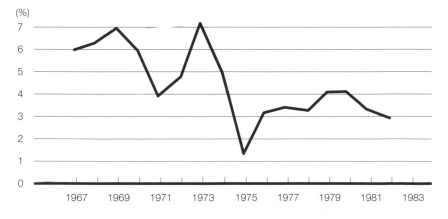

Fig. 6.11. Ratio of Profits to Gross Capital in Corporations

Source: Management and Coordination Agency, *Monthly Report on the Family Income and Expenditure Survey.*

were hired and terminated when their contracts expired. If all these techniques failed to reduce the labor surplus, companies would seek volunteers for early retirement, offering special bonuses as inducements. After several years of labor cutting by every means imaginable, the number of employees in manufacturing industries had been dramatically reduced.

In tune with the personnel cuts, the average gain in the spring wage negotiations also fell sharply. After the record-breaking 33 percent in 1974, the increase remained above 10 percent in 1975 and was about 10 percent again in 1976. But by the 1980s, the increase had dropped into the 5–7 percent range, or just enough to cover the cost of inflation. These outcomes reflect clearly the propensity of company-based unions to place priority on preserving their companies when the continued existence of the workplace is threatened.

To sum up, the oil crisis curtailed company profits. Companies frantically began to use every method available to trim waste from their operations, and the labor unions cooperated in the process. Since prospects for an expansion of domestic demand were slim, companies betted on the export market. This would eventually spark economic friction.

Fiscal deficit

Worse yet, the government was in financial trouble. Direct taxation accounts for an immense proportion of government income, nearly 60 percent of which is derived from taxes on the incomes of individuals and corporations. The recession cut corporate tax receipts to less than 50 percent, and to complicate matters, reforms of the pension system and other social security benefits in 1973 had greatly boosted government fiscal burdens.

If government spending continued to grow, the fiscal deficit would balloon out of hand. For this reason the government hesitated in 1975 and 1976 to expand its spending to stimulate the economy as it had done in the past. The government couldn't boost spending. Consumers were in a saving rather than a spending mood. Companies were overequipped, so except for pollution control measures, there was no grounds to expect an expansion of capital investment. Domestic demand growth had ground to a halt.

Since the logic of the situation dictated that the only potential for economic recovery lay in exports, that is where companies turned their efforts. There was a spurt of export growth. In 1974, Japan had suffered a huge trade deficit; two years later, in 1976, exports outstripped growing imports to generate a trade surplus that continued to expand in subsequent years. This export drive was to have further consequences, as we shall see, in the form of exacerbated economic friction with other countries.

Final accounts on the era of rapid growth

What was the era of rapid growth? I will conclude this talk by drawing together some threads. We can say that it was the age when the efforts for economic growth of the Meiji era, or even earlier, of the later years of the Tokugawa regime, finally blossomed. We can date it from the early 1950s to the oil crisis.

After the war, Japan had reconstructed an economy and society that was not very unlike that of prewar days. This I discussed in my fifth lecture. The rural population was nearly five million higher than in the prewar era, and traditional industries got back on their feet. Heavy and chemical industries expanded on the basis of what had been inherited from the war, but there seemed little prospect of catching up with the levels of Europe or the United States. If Japan were to assume a growth rate of 3–4 percent, there was a danger that the farm villages and urban traditional industries would become a catchment for hidden unemployment. That was the fear in the mid-1950s, manifested in its classic form in the debate over Japan's dual structure.

It was rapid growth that transformed this picture. There is no need for me to go over the process again, so I will just summarize my conclusions. Growth was led by the endeavors of many companies. Its protagonists were the innovators, large and small, who competed to introduce new technology, develop new products, and change the ways in which they operated their businesses. Government policies supported and sometimes overtly assisted these efforts.

Before anyone realized it, economic growth, primarily in heavy and chemical industries, turned a labor surplus into a labor shortage about the time of the Iwato boom in 1959–61. The change was dramatic, like the sudden tilt of a set of scales when a small weight is added to one of the pans. Until then the scales had been static, but now the other pan began to rise.

A population movement to the cities began. A flood of young people poured into the industrial regions, not just school graduates, but young farmers and workers in small traditional industries. The wages of these new workers rose, and soon those of people who were already in employment followed suit. The wage gap between big and small businesses began to shrink. The Spring Labor Offensive functioned as a system for bringing about these changes in the country's wage pattern, and rice prices and the National Personnel Agency's salary recommendations for public employees carried the wage increases into other sectors.

Greater equity of incomes and changes in consumption patterns went hand in hand with these developments. Modernization of homes took place earlier in the rural areas than in the cities, where high real estate prices prevailed, and household durable items and automobiles also became more widespread earlier in the rural areas. The westernized consumption patterns of urban salaried workers, quite unlike Japanese traditional consumption patterns, spread swiftly nationwide. These processes powered fundamental changes in the structure of Japanese society. The notions that Japan could never attain the living standards of the United States or Europe, that it could not shed itself of its outmoded and peculiar social structure—notions that had prevailed from before the war into the postwar era—were overturned by a new reality. If nothing else, the ultimate significance of the era of rapid growth may lie in the way that it dispelled the old sense of inferiority vis-à-vis the West.

True, growth had its attendant problems. Increased incomes for farmers and operators of small traditional businesses brought about a continuous upward spiral of consumer prices that led to public acceptance of inflation and ultimately helped trigger the serious inflationary surge of 1973–74. A degree of gradual inflation and excessively available credit were doubtless inevitable costs of rapid growth, but it is also true that policy makers let slip their guard, albeit only for a while, against the dangers of inflation.

The priority given to industrial development led to many excesses. The overlooking of environmental destruction, for one, was a major sin. It was just before the Tokyo Olympics that the Nihonbashi Bridge, the starting point of the old Tokaido highway, was plastered over by an expressway, an act of stunning historical insensitivity. From around 1965, intersections in the big cities were redesigned to give priority to vehicles; many pedestrian crossings were done away with, and foot traffic was relegated to trudging over pedestrian bridges. It was not until the late 1960s that the government finally began to deal with pollution, and it was only after 1970 that controls were instituted. Much of natural and cultural value was already scarred.

It was in 1973, under the amended Employment Security Law, that fullfledged social welfare programs finally became a reality after lagging significantly behind such programs in Europe and the United States. Until then, welfare programs had been centered on health. It was after the law was passed that old-age pensions began to increase. It was in ways such as this that the era of rapid growth changed Japanese society.

Keynesian policies under fire

In closing, I would like to say something about the thinking behind the policies that formed the backdrop to this growth. It is safe to say that whether in the United States, the United Kingdom, or Japan, the primary focus of postwar economic policy was the achievement of full employment and higher standards of living. In the United States, in the Kennedy administration in the early 1960s and in the subsequent Johnson administration, Keynesian economists with Democratic Party affiliations stood at the helm of policy making, and the dominant views leaned toward the creation of a welfare society through expanded government spending. The economic function of government permeated every corner of national life. In Japan, too, public investments were used to sustain economic growth and eventually, toward the end of the era of high growth began to be directed toward improving the lives of the people. Construction of public housing, increased loans by the Housing Loan Corporation, bold improvements in social welfare benefits—these all came in the early 1970s.

I think it is safe to say that the dominant view up until the beginning of the 1970s was one that said it is a good thing for big government to implement a variety of economic measures to secure jobs for the people and to improve welfare. This was a view that claimed that economic fluctuations can be minimized and stable growth achieved by the right mix of fiscal and financial policy.

The United States, however, became embroiled in the Vietnam War. U.S inflation increased, and when it did, economic growth rates slowed. Under those conditions, public faith in the efficacy of economic policies that traced their roots to Keynes eroded sharply. What was criticized was Keynesianism in the broad sense, not just Keynes' ideas, but also the contributions of those who followed after. Criticism of Keynesian growth policies rose stridently around the world, and Japan was not immune from the new current. Japan was ready to enter a new age.

Economic Globalization
(1975–1988)

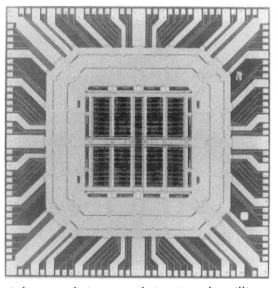

A large-scale integrated circuit, only millimeters across. Technological innovations in microelectronics and other fields drove much of Japan's economic growth after the 1973 oil crisis.

1975		Japan suffers its greatest postwar recession. Mining and manufacturing production drops 18 percent between the end of 1973 and the start of 1975. Female part-timers are dismissed in growing numbers. Management fat trimming begins.
1976		The Lockheed bribery scandal forces Prime Minister Tanaka out of office. Fukuda Takeo becomes prime minister.
1977		The yen strengthens sharply at the beginning of the year owing to a huge trade surplus. Export industries a slump. Emergency measures are taken to boost government spending.
	December	The Anti-Monopoly Law is amended.
1978		The yen continues its climb, reaching ¥170 = $1.00 in October. The second oil crisis breaks out at year-end.
1979		Fiscal and credit retrenchment forestalls inflation. Budget reform becomes a major political issue.
1981		Exports surge, expanding areas of economic friction, while imports stagnate.
1983		Inflation begins to subside.
1985	*September*	The Plaza Accord sends the yen soaring past the ¥200 = $1.00 mark.
1986	*December*	The yen hits ¥150 = $1.00
1987		The Bank of Japan's official lending rate begins a two-year period at an all-time low of 2.5 percent.
	October 19 (Black Monday)	Stock prices plunge around the world.
1989	*January*	The Showa Emperor dies. A new era, Heisei, is declared.
	December	The Nikkei stock index hits its historical high of ¥39,000.
1990		The bubble starts to deflate. Stock and land prices begin to slide.
1994		The exchange rate breaks the ¥100 = $1.00 mark.

ECONOMIC GLOBALIZATION
(1975–1988)

THE TRANSITION TO STABLE GROWTH

During the dollar crisis of February–March 1973 that overtured the oil crisis, Japan switched from a fixed exchange rate of ¥308 to the dollar to a floating exchange rate. Although this was not publicly announced at the time, it had earlier been agreed with the United States and the countries of Europe that the yen would be revalued 17–20 percent to about ¥257–264 to the dollar. Indeed, shortly after the yen was floated, the exchange rate jumped to more or less that level.

In October 1973, however, came the first oil crisis. Japan, the world's largest importer of oil, plunged into a deficit on its international accounts. The yen exchange rate softened for a time, hovering at about ¥300 to the dollar through 1975 and into 1976. Thereafter, the Japanese economy was to be heavily affected by exchange market fluctuations.

The post-oil-crisis recession was severe. According to the *Corporate Statistics Annual*, corporate profits plummeted to 1 percent of gross capitalization. Nearly half of Japan's firms chalked up losses, as we have already seen.

Energy conservation and streamlining of production

The issue for the Japanese economy in the latter half of the 1970s was how to return to a growth track. The key to doing this was corporate efforts to trim waste through energy conservation and the rationalization of production processes. To give an example of what I mean, during the mid-1970s I visited a Bridgestone Tire plant at Kurume. What the people there told me was in a sense

265

quite elementary. The factory was an old one built in 1933, and the machinery was all steam powered. Steam pipes ran through the factory, but the pipes were bare and made of iron. The staff told me that by wrapping the pipes in insulation to keep the heat in, they were able to cut energy use nearly in half. It appeared that previously they had not even attempted anything so simple as installing insulation, so that was where the cost cutting started. In the steel, cement, and other energy-intensive industries, far more serious technological efforts were made to cut energy consumption. In the steel industry, waste heat was recovered for use in other processes, waste gas from blast furnaces was utilized to generate electric power, and continuous molding technology was developed to its acme. In the cement industry, kilns were redesigned to reduce energy input.

Efforts to trim labor costs flourished too, of course. One of the major features of the late 1970s was that it became the general practice for companies not to replace retiring workers. When firms had to hire, as much as possible they hired part-time and temporary workers, almost all of whom were middle-aged housewives.

Total quality control

Total quality control, which had been around for some time, became actively practiced during this period. Quality control techniques had originally been introduced from the United States and had started with random sampling of products. In Japan, all the workers on each factory floor would be involved in discussing how to improve product quality and production processes. Efforts to eliminate unneeded processing steps, economize on raw materials, or otherwise produce more efficiently were evident in every factory I visited at this time.

When workers came up with proposals for streamlining operations, companies would take up the better ideas and reward the proposer with a certificate of appreciation. Some individuals would frequently come up with ideas on the factory floor, while others never produced ideas, so in a very Japanese twist to personnel relations, the more inventive would let the less inventive turn ideas in as their own. That way, everyone would get a turn at receiving an award.

Strategies to avoid layoffs

While rationalization efforts were carried out at the factory level, from the viewpoint of the company as a whole, the task was how to trim the workforce to the absolute minimum needed. Nonetheless, from the perspective of Japanese labor management, they could not abandon the principles of lifelong employment and age-based salaries. Some companies recruited volunteers for early retirement, but most avoided this if they could. Large companies would transfer workers to other locales, as, for example, did Hitachi, which moved workers from its Ibaraki plant to Gifu. Since this involved uprooting entire families, it was not something that ordinarily happened to factory workers, but at any rate this was the kind of length to which firms went to secure employment for their workers. Another option was to transfer workers to subcontractors and affiliate companies, with the parent company making up any difference in salary or fringe benefit. In this manner, firms managed to avoid layoffs and dismissals.

Part-time hirings rise

Another theme of the time was the use of part-timers. Employment statistics for this period very clearly show that although the number of part-timers initially drops for a brief period, around 1976 and 1977 there is a rapid spurt in part-time hirings, indicating that at about this time companies began hiring female part-time workers on a large scale instead of full-time regular company employees. At the same time, although the numbers are much smaller, part-time student workers began to be used quite extensively in certain industries, mostly it seems in commerce and service industries. The numbers of students employed in these jobs were to rise sharply.

Another change that took place in the period 1976–77 was that companies tried to shed their bank debts. During the period of rapid growth, companies had regarded borrowing to finance capacity expansions as the natural thing to do. As growth slowed, however, Japanese firms found themselves gasping under high interest burdens, and, in the face of a sudden slowdown of growth in production, began trimming their borrowings in an effort to raise profits. These debt-trimming efforts were largely successful.

However, laggard growth in capital investments proved a major stumbling block to economic recovery. During the preceding period of rapid economic growth, huge industrial belts had been developed on the Pacific coast and elsewhere. In these locations, major oil refineries, steel plants, and other projects were constantly in progress. I think the last of these mammoth projects was Nippon Kokan's steel plant at Ogishima in Kawasaki. That was a project to move an existing plant in Kawasaki and did not involve a net increase in production capacity.

Domestic consumption and exports fuel growth

Plant and equipment investments per se continued thereafter, but as the structure of industry changed, these investments ceased to be on the colossal scale of the past. The driving force for economic growth in the era of rapid growth had been capital investments; now the weight shifted to domestic consumption and exports.

This can be seen from the graph in figure 7.1, which shows how much of the real GNP growth rate was contributed by

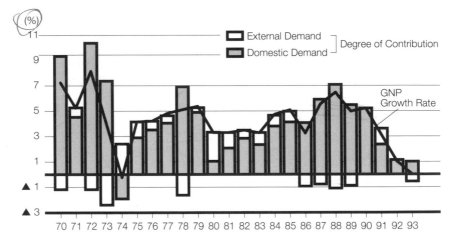

Fig. 7.1. Contributions of Domestic and External Demand to Real GNP Growth Rates (year on year)

Source: Economic Planning Agency, *Annual Report on National Accounts.*
Note: Sum of external and domestic contributions shows real GNP growth rate.

domestic demand (indicated by the shaded portion) and how much by overseas demand (indicated in white). According to the standard definition of GNP, the following relationships hold: GNP = domestic demand + (exports – imports) = domestic demand + the difference in the current account. I will define the current account difference as external demand, which is shown in white. The data starts from 1970. Around about 1973, you will see that the white portion is sticking far into the negative side of the scale, indicating how much the current account difference was in deficit. We can see that this acted negatively on GNP growth.

From 1974 until 1977, however, the white portion is all coming out on the plus side, and it is clear that economic growth was aided by the current account surplus together with domestic demand, mostly consumer demand. As I will discuss later, this pattern was to be repeated in the period from 1980 to 1985. The relatively sluggish growth of domestic demand from the latter half of the 1970s into the early 1980s was thus offset by the international balance of payments surplus, something that became a factor in economic friction.

Exchange rates begin to rise

The years 1975 and 1976 marked a period in which export-driven economic growth had already begun. During this time, apart from minor fluctuations, the exchange rate stood at roughly ¥300 to the dollar, a situation in which it was easy for export industries to make a profit. The problem was that Japanese exports surged ahead while the United States and the countries of Europe were still suffering trade deficits owing to the impact of the oil crisis, which naturally attracted unfavorable attention. In 1977, criticism of Japan began to be voiced in the United States. Michael Blumenthal, secretary of the Treasury at the time, argued that Japan's trade surplus was so large because the low yen rate facilitated exports and that the yen ought therefore to be higher. I'm not sure that his remarks set anything off, but in 1977 and 1978, the yen soared on exchange markets. Figure 7.2 shows how the exchange rate, which started at about ¥300 to the U.S. dollar, began to rise sharply at the

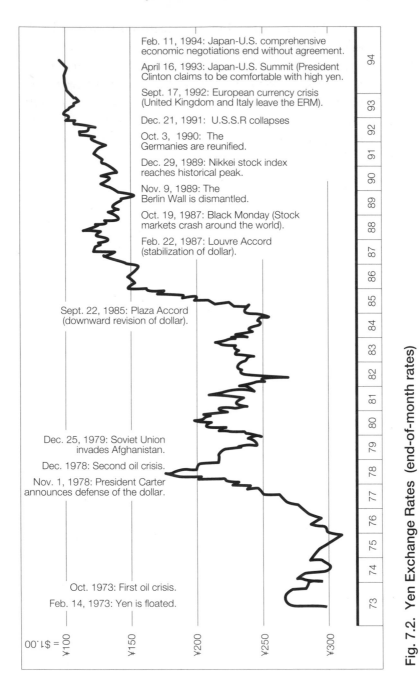

Feb. 11, 1994: Japan-U.S. comprehensive
economic negotiations end without agreement.

April 16, 1993: Japan-U.S. Summit (President
Clinton claims to be comfortable with high yen.

Sept. 17, 1992: European currency crisis
(United Kingdom and Italy leave the ERM).

Dec. 21, 1991: U.S.S.R collapses

Oct. 3, 1990: The
Germanies are reunified.

Dec. 29, 1989: Nikkei stock index
reaches historical peak.

Nov. 9, 1989: The
Berlin Wall is dismantled.

Oct. 19, 1987: Black Monday (Stock
markets crash around the world).

Feb. 22, 1987: Louvre Accord
(stabilization of dollar).

Sept. 22, 1985: Plaza Accord
(downward revision of dollar).

Dec. 25, 1979: Soviet Union
invades Afghanistan.

Dec. 1978: Second oil crisis.

Nov. 1, 1978: President Carter
announces defense of the dollar.

Oct. 1973: First oil crisis.

Feb. 14, 1973: Yen is floated.

¥100 = $1.00   ¥150   ¥200   ¥250   ¥300

94 93 92 91 90 89 88 87 86 85 84 83 82 81 80 79 78 77 76 75 74 73

Fig. 7.2. Yen Exchange Rates (end-of-month rates)

Sources: Bank of Japan, Annual and Monthly Report on Economic Statistics.

beginning of 1977 and continued to advance until October 1978, when it recorded a peak of ¥170 = $1.

Noting the serious problem of poor economic performance around the world, Laurence Klein of the University of Pennsylvania wrote an article in which he observed that the only countries with any economic power were the United States, West Germany, and Japan. These three countries needed to improve their domestic economies, he argued, and thereby stimulate global trade. Japan needed to become one of the three locomotives pulling the global economic train.

As the yen rose, export industries found themselves utterly unable to break even, and in autumn 1977, they were howling. Although I don't believe the exchange rate was the only reason, there was much talk of recession, and in some regions, especially those with shipbuilding or steel industries, there were severe localized slumps.

The J-curve effect
Moreover, the J-curve effect kicked in, so that while exports computed in dollars continued to grow, those computed in yen showed only sluggish growth or declined. The J-curve refers to a phenomenon in which the yen increases in value, dollar-denominated export prices rise, and exports calculated in dollars increase for a period, triggering a further rise in the price of the yen.

Ultimately the exchange rate was to remain high right up to autumn 1978, when the cabinet of Prime Minister Fukuda Takeo embarked on a bold program of economic stimulation through public investment and came up with a fairly large supplementary budget, in the region of ¥6 trillion. The yen subsided when the International Monetary Fund, West Germany, Switzerland, and Japan agreed on a powerful package of measures to restore the U.S. dollar on November 1, 1978.

The exchange-rate driven recession left scars that took a long time to disappear. Around about 1975, the budget had been thrust heavily into deficit by the loss of tax revenues following the oil crisis. Since the government had attempted to restart the economy by floating government bonds, public bond issues increased sharply. This was to have major consequences some years later.

Changes in industrial structure

Thus high yen exchange rates and increased prices of crude oil and other imported raw materials had willy-nilly the effect of transforming Japan's industrial structure. Figure 7.3 shows indices of

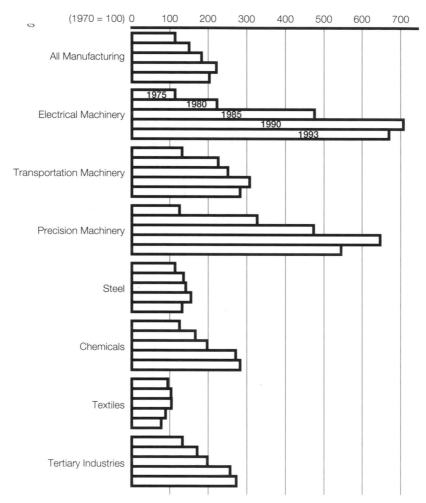

Fig. 7.3. Indices of Industrial Activities

Source: Based on the Ministry of International Trade and Industry's *Annual Report on Mining and Manufacturing Industries.*

industrial output for 1975, 1980, 1985, 1990, and 1993, with the 1970 levels as 100. We can read off figure 7.3 the rapid changes that took place after the oil crisis. Electrical machinery did not make a big showing in 1975, but by 1980 its index of production was more than twice that of 1970. Putting in similar performances are precision machinery and industrial machinery. The main reason that the growth of transportation machinery is less than the others is that automobile production had already undergone significant growth in the years up to 1970.

The next largest area of expansion is precision machinery. This would be largely due to growth of clocks and watches, cameras, and medical equipment, the expansion being greatest around 1980. On the other hand, one industry that did not show as much growth was steel. At its peak, steel output was only 30 percent higher than 1970 levels, after which it marked time. Then there is chemical industries. Petrochemicals were flat, and fine chemicals and pharmaceuticals, with relatively high value added, show growth. A bigger problem was textiles, which never went significantly beyond 1970 levels and have more recently beaten a retreat. Overtaken by developing countries owing to high wages within Japan, the surviving firms have taken to producing overseas.

Turning to tertiary industries, which I will need to talk about shortly, we find that although their growth performance was generally not as stellar as electrical machinery and precision machinery, tertiary industries have continued to advance overall right up to the present day.

Bearing this overall picture in mind, we can now look more closely at the problems of specific industries. One group that we should be concerned with is the depressed industries. These included steel, shipbuilding, petrochemicals, and synthetic fibers, which had sustained Japan's earlier rapid economic growth under large-scale importation of crude oil and raw materials at very low prices. Aluminum, too, had been smelted domestically owing to the availability of cheap electricity. However, rising prices for imported raw materials and low prices for the end products during the late 1970s thrust all these industries deep into crisis. In the case of shipbuilding, the industry had two years of orders on hand at the time of the oil crisis, but once those orders were filled, the shipyards fell silent.

Rationalization cartels

The Ministry of International Trade and Industry and the Ministry of Labor were the primary agencies responsible for helping these industries out of their plight. MITI obtained passage of the Law for Temporary Measures for Designated Depressed Industries, which allowed for the creation of rationalization cartels and the industry-wide junking of equipment. The Ministry of Labor came up with a series of measures that aided workers who were laid off, extended the period of unemployment insurance benefits under the Law for Temporary Measures for Separated Workers in Designated Depressed Industries, and provided measures for workers and industries in areas dominated by such industries under what was informally called the Company Town Law. This legislation was amended and strengthened after the second oil crisis. One example of the extreme lengths to which industries went to survive was in shipbuilding, which scrapped more than 35 percent of its capacity at the beginning of the 1980s. In petrochemicals, a sizable number of plants did away with their ethylene manufacturing facilities.

Over an extended period of falling profit ratios, the depressed industries cut their workforces, diversified their operations, and set up business overseas. In 1978, I went to visit the Nippon Steel Tsurusaki plant, in Oita Prefecture. Just about that time China was planning the Baoshan steelworks near Shanghai and wanted to use the Tsurusaki plant as a model, which would be copied exactly. I remember being told that Nippon Steel was greatly pleased and had begun work on the Baoshan project. However, the project suffered setback after setback before it could be brought to completion. In another famous case from around about this time, Mitsui Trading Company and Mitsui Petrochemical, which had teamed up to build a petrochemical plant in Iran, were forced to withdraw from the project owing to the Iran-Iraq War.

The microelectronics revolution

The economy continued to expand quite satisfactorily despite all these difficulties owing to the spectacular development of fields in which materials costs constituted only a small proportion of sales and in which value added could be raised through high levels of technology. The best example of this is the electronics industry, whose progress I would like to trace briefly. During the late 1970s, the "microelectronics revolution" was a buzzword in Japan. Above all, this meant the use of semiconductor elements. The technology to incorporate semiconductors into integrated circuits stabilized during this period. By the end of the decade, Japanese firms excelled at this technology.

With microelectronics, a slew of new products began to hit the market. From the outset, videotape recorders (VTRs) were manufactured with both the domestic market and the export market in mind. This is something that comes out very clearly in the production statistics. About 80 percent of the units produced in the early days were exported, suggesting that this was a field that developed initially as an export industry. In the early stages, a high percentage of VTRs were U.S. bound, but as more firms began to produce locally in the United States, exports to that country declined and the emphasis shifted to exports to the European Community and Asia.

The role of corporate research and development

Figure 7.4 shows numbers for research and development activities. The left-hand columns are research spending, the right-hand columns are numbers of research personnel. Beginning in 1970, it is very clear that research spending grew extensively, with a very large jump from 1980 to 1985. The momentum has carried into the 1990s and up to the present. If we ask where the growth took place, it is overwhelmingly in the corporate sector. Regrettably, the universities have come in for budgetary restrictions, with the result that major growth of any sort has been ruled out. The work of research in technology has now moved into the companies. This is true both of research spending and personnel.

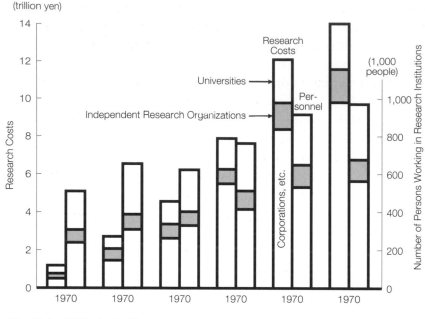

Fig. 7.4. R&D Activities

Source: Science and Technology Agency, *Kagaku Gijitsu Kenkyu Chosa* (Survey of Research in Science and Technology).

One interesting observation may be made in this connection. There is a book, by Kikuchi Makoto, entitled *Forty Years of Semiconductors in Japan.* This is not a field that I am deeply familiar with, but I read this volume with a great deal of interest. Dr. Kikuchi spent many years in MITI's Electrotechnical Laboratory and then moved to Sony's central laboratory at the invitation of its director. He relates how they were developing a charge coupled device camera (an electronic camera that doesn't use film). For a long time, all they could produce was a cloudy image, obscured by countless flecks of "snow" on the screen. Eventually, the snow was reduced to 10–20 dots, at which point, Sony's president, Iwama Kazuo, showed up at the lab. After looking everything over, he spoke privately with Dr. Kikuchi and told him that he was moving the entire project to the Atsugi plant. Dr. Kikuchi was surprised to find that of the 40 people working on the project, over 30 were transferred to the factory in the space of two weeks. The product had some defects, but the decision had been made in their tête-à-tête to go ahead with production, and the research was transferred to the factory. It is because Japanese firms are able to act so decisively that they are able to launch one new project after another.

Also emerging at this time were word processors and personal computers. Robots, too, had already been developed and were assigned to the factories. In Japan, robots were introduced on a bold scale. I visited West Germany at the end of the 1970s to find that companies had introduced robots but had not done so wholesale on the grounds that it eliminated jobs. I guess it reflects the strength of German labor unions. In Japan, the unions were cooperative, and once developed, robots were brought into the workplace in large numbers.

The emergence of mechatronics

Another theme of the times is the emergence of mechatronics, best represented by numerically controlled machine tools. By directly tying computers to industrial machinery, work that was once performed with the intuition and touch of a skilled worker was now carried out by a machine. If something of a special shape had to be turned on a lathe, the shape could be recorded in the computer as numerical formulas, and the cutting could be done automatically. It was in the 1970s that numerically controlled machine tools with these capabilities appeared on the factory floor in large numbers. Developed primarily by the electrical machinery industry, these new machine tools brought machinery and electronics together. The ground-breaking introduction of mechatronics propelled Japan's machine industries to the forefront of the world.

Changes in export structure

One clear example of this leadership can be seen in the pattern of growth of Japanese exports. Figure 7.5 shows graphs of Japan's export/import structure. Since the graphs begin in 1970, we can obtain a very clear picture of how the export structure changed. In 1970, metals—steel and nonferrous metals—foodstuffs and textiles, and chemical products accounted for over 40 percent of the total. Meanwhile, four categories of machinery—general machin-

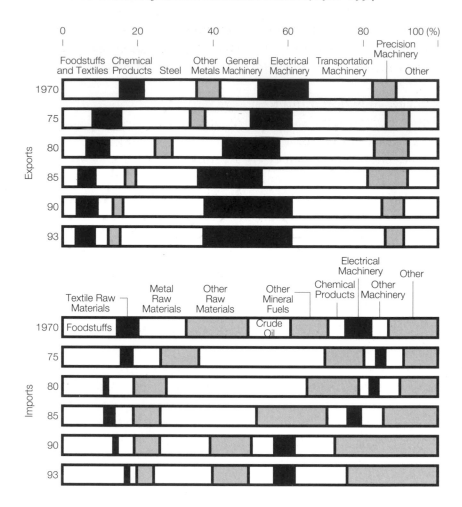

Fig. 7.5. Structure of Exports and Imports

Source: Ministry of Finance, *Foreign Trade Statistics.*

ery, electrical machinery, transportation machinery (a substantial percent being shipbuilding), and precision machinery—already accounted for a massive 50 percent of total exports in 1970.

Subsequently, however, in the period from 1975 through 1980, steel and other metals, the mainstays of the rapid growth of earlier years, declined as a percentage of total exports, while transportation machinery, especially automobiles, advanced, and electrical machinery and precision machinery began to put in a bigger showing. This trend has continued right up to the present, with the result that the four machinery categories have recently come to account for nearly 80 percent of all exports.

Changes in import structure

The import structure, meanwhile, displays the clear impact of the oil crisis. In 1970, there was no hint of a coming oil crisis, and Japanese imports centered on raw materials for metals and materials for textiles. When we count crude oil and coal, we find that raw materials constituted roughly 60 percent of Japan's imports, with other goods accounting for only a minor share. Machinery imports were a small proportion of the total. Also noteworthy is foodstuff, which accounted for a large percentage. After the oil crisis, however, crude oil expanded to about 40 percent of imports and remained that way for some time. This was one of the more problematic effects of the oil crisis.

The line indicating crude oil prices in figure 7.6 gives a very good indication of how rapidly oil prices rose during the first and second oil crises. In 1971, the crude oil price was roughly $2 a barrel (on a customs-clearance basis), but from the end of 1973 into 1974 the price jumped from $2 to $11. The price remained roughly flat at that level until 1978 then soared during the oil crisis of 1979 through 1981 to an all-time peak of $34. It is safe to say that these price swings were largely responsible for the growth of crude oil as a component of imports on a value basis. The volume imported, on the other hand, peaked at 288 million kiloliters in 1973, after which it remained almost flat until the second oil crisis, at which point import volume tumbled to 200 million kiloliters as the second oil crisis spurred the introduction of new energy saving technology.

The late 1970s were a period that saw the development of new products, such as cancer drugs and other pharmaceuticals and new ceramics and other new types of materials. Later, biometrics would emerge as a new field, although it has not become particularly big. The industry in which most growth was concentrated was electronics, which used semiconductors in applications across a wide spectrum of fields.

As I noted earlier, the development of tertiary industries transformed the structure of the economy in the late 1970s and early 1980s. The changes first became visible in commerce in the 1970s, as supermarkets and somewhat smaller self-service stores, such as convenience stores, made rapid inroads during this period. In 1972, I spent some time in Washington, D.C., and the large supermarkets there had no counterpart in Japan: there were a few small supermarkets scattered here and there, but supermarkets that sold precooked foods and everything else imaginable were not to be found, even in Tokyo. My wife escorted a visiting journalist, who was in the United States to write about consumer issues, to one of these large supermarkets; this individual was delighted and promptly wrote about the experience in an article. At the beginning of the 1970s, supermarkets in Japan were still in their infancy, but within a few years they were to put on a huge spurt of growth.

Falling somewhere between service industries and commerce come things such as family restaurants. It was during the 1970s that large chains of these restaurants began setting up business in suburban locations that were readily accessible by car.

Emergence of tertiary industries

The development of commerce and services went hand in hand with another theme of the 1970s. The gap between urban and rural incomes closed even more during this period, and after the first oil crisis, urban consumption patterns generally flooded into the rural areas. Although spending on plant and equipment and other investments had slumped in manufacturing, the growth of tertiary industries offset this decline during the late 1970s.

The types of service industries were as many as they were varied. Pachinko (pinball) salons, golf courses, cram schools, and culture centers (adult education centers) began to increase substantively at about this time.

A variety of services directed at corporations also developed at about this time. Advertising and think tanks had long flourished in Japan, but now they were joined by building management firms that undertook security, industrial waste disposal, and cleaning services. Companies had formerly delegated such services to their own internal divisions, but now they suddenly began to contract them out. With the spreading use of office computers, the so-called information industry began to develop at about this time to handle companies' software needs.

The second oil crisis

Finally, I need to touch on the second oil crisis. After the first oil crisis, the oil-producing countries had been awash in so-called oil money, which they had applied to their modernization. In Iran, modernization had taken place at too rapid a pace, and in 1978 the Shiites had risen in a revolt that forced the Shah to abdicate and go into exile. With this, the tide of modernization began to be reversed, and foreign technicians and engineers left the country, causing Iran's oil production to drop. In the following year, 1979, war broke out with Iraq and quickly became a quagmire. OPEC, seeing an opportunity, reverted to its oil strategy, citing reduced oil output and resource conservation as the reasons for its action. Oil prices skyrocketed nearly threefold, from $12 a barrel to $34.

What concerns us is how this impacted on Japan. The first oil crisis left a profound impression on Japan. When one mentions oil crisis to Japanese today, it is the 1973–74 crisis that first comes to mind. At a time of severe domestic inflation, oil prices had risen five- or six-fold, setting off a round of massive inflation.

In terms of the magnitude of increase, the price rise in the second oil crisis was far greater—a jump from $12 to $34, as opposed to from $2 to $12 the first time round. But during the second oil crisis, the Japanese government swiftly modified its policy, minimizing the impact of oil price increases. As I noted earlier, 1977–78 was a period of high yen exchange rates, as a result of which economic stimulation measures were taken during those two years. Then, in 1978, the Iranian revolution took place. So OPEC invoked its oil price increases shortly after Japan had launched its stimulation package.

Thus, just as the domestic economy was beginning to look up, large oil price hikes began to loom on the horizon. Japan's fiscal and financial authorities switched from stimulation to policies designed to avoid another round of inflation. The Bank of Japan set about raising interest rates, and the Ministry of Finance curbed fiscal spending. For a brief period in 1980, the Bank of Japan's official lending rate stood at 9 percent, on a par with that during the first oil crisis. I think it is true to say that during the first oil crisis, the retrenchment was more severe. The official lending rate was capped at 9 percent, but the window guidance was more restrictive. The upward momentum of inflation was so powerful that it had to be stopped even if it meant sacrificing Japan's rapid growth. By contrast, 1978–79 retrenchment kicked in at a time when prices were not rising—at a time when, if anything, import prices had dropped owing to the high yen rate, and prices were thus subsiding. This allowed Japan to keep the impact of the second oil crisis relatively small. Figure 7.6 does not show it, but the increase in consumer prices was held to about 8 percent, with the result that most of the public did not feel threatened by inflation.

Toward the top of figure 7.6 is a line indicating the wholesale price index. You will see that in 1977–78, when the yen was high on the exchange markets, gross average domestic prices were almost unchanged, while imports and export prices had clearly moved downward. The year 1978 marked the nadir of both import and export prices. Subsequently, however, when oil prices spurted, import prices also lifted sharply, in 1980 through to 1982. Gross average domestic prices were dragged up by rising import prices until 1979, but after that they remained completely flat for five years. Export prices showed some increase under the impact of import prices and devaluation of yen, but at far lower rates of advance. It seems a fair assessment of the policies of the time to say that they succeeded in holding price increases to the minimum possible. Overall, Japan's policy management in the late 1970s merits a pretty good grade. On the negative side, however, as the growth rate fell, the export drive stepped up.

Overseas the stagflation that started with the first oil crisis persisted until well after the second. As output stagnated, unemployment grew, and inflation continued unabated. The stagflation may be attributed to the fact that in many countries retrenchment to deal with the oil crises was not thoroughgoing

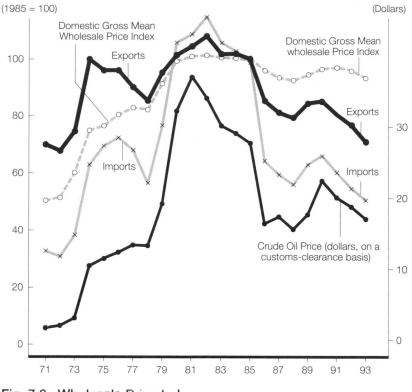

(1985 = 100)

(Dollars)

Domestic Gross Mean Wholesale Price Index

Exports

Domestic Gross Mean wholesale Price Index

Exports

Imports

Imports

Crude Oil Price (dollars, on a customs-clearance basis)

Fig. 7.6. Wholesale Price Index

Sources: Bank of Japan, *Wholesale Price Indexes;* Ministry of Finance, *Foreign Trade Statistics.*

enough out of concerns for domestic unemployment, and credit was eased too quickly at the first sign of inflation subsiding. West Germany did comparatively well, but it relaxed credit quite early on, opening the country up to a bout of stagflation. Labor unions' wage demands intensified as prices rose, especially in the United Kingdom, the United States, and France, where stagflation was particularly evident in the 1970s.

FINANCIAL DEREGULATION

Change of government bond market

In 1975, the Japanese government's tax receipts plunged as direct taxes, especially corporate taxes, were hit by the post-oil-crisis recession. Given that government spending had nowhere to go but up owing to snowballing social security spending and other commitments, government bond issues ballooned. This picture is clear from figure 7.7, which shows the cumulative figure for bond issues. Not only did bond issues rise, their management became more difficult. Prior to the first oil crisis, financial institutions in government bond underwriting syndicates had been required to keep bonds, issued at fairly low rates, for a period of one year. The practice had been for the Bank of Japan to buy up the bonds after one year, with the result that the bulk of the issues would ultimately end up in Bank of Japan vaults. This practice changed substantially with the increase in bond issues. I will omit the lesser details, but if you would look at the chronological table in table 7.1, Deregulation of Finance and Exchange Markets, you will see that beginning in 1978, a tender system was introduced in which underwriting syndicates became able to buy bonds keyed to the anticipated final market interest rate. Even earlier than this, 1976 saw the emergence of a brisk, publicly conducted secondary market for so-called *gensaki* transactions with short-term buyback agreements. Such measures resulted in a large expansion of the government bond market.

The distribution market for government bonds was further liberalized so that underwriting syndicates were free to sell off their

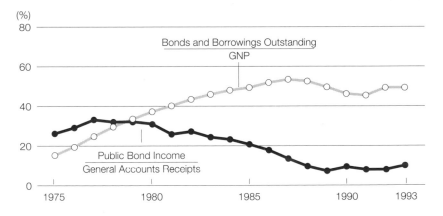

Fig. 7.7. Cumulative Government Bonds

Source: Computed on the basis of the Ministry of Finance's *Fiscal Statistics.*

Table 7.1 Deregulation of Finance and Exchange Markets

1975		The large-scale flotation of government bonds begins.
1976	*March*	Secondary market *gensaki* transactions (with short-term repurchase agreements) are initiated.
1978	*January*	Measures are announced to deregulate foreign exchange markets.
1978	*May*	The Ministry of Finance introduces tenders for government bonds.
1979	*April*	Call money official quotation rate is abolished (the beginning of interest rate deregulation).
1979	*May*	City banks begin to issue negotiable certificates of deposit. Ministry of Finance relaxes restrictions on foreign capital (short-term impact loans, etc.).
1979	*December*	The new Foreign Exchange Law introduces a shift from regulation in principle to liberalization in principle.
1981	*April*	Underwriting syndicate bondholding terms eased to three months.
1981	*June*	The Bank Law is completely rewritten. Banks and securities firms become able to enter each others' territory.
1982	*April*	Foreign firms are allowed membership on the Tokyo Stock Exchange. Financial institutions begin selling government bonds over the counter.
1984	*June*	Restrictions on yen convertibility are abolished.
	July	The issue of yen-denominated bonds by overseas borrowers (*samurai* bonds) is deregulated.
1985	*March*	Money Market Certificates, tied to market interest rates, are introduced (initial minimum deposit of ¥50 million, this abolished in 1992).
1985	*March*	The Committee on Foreign Exchange and Other Transactions reports on the internationalization of the yen (recommends deregulation of Euroyen transactions and the establishment of a Tokyo offshore market).
1985	*October*	Interest rates on large fixed-term deposits (minimum ¥1 billion) are deregulated (floor abolished in June 1992).
1987	*November*	A commercial paper market is launched (subject to the Bank of Japan purchasing operations beginning in November 1989).
1988	*March*	Overseas futures options transactions by financial institutions (currency, cash, bonds, stocks, etc.) are deregulated.
1988	*April*	The ban on the issue of commercial paper by nonresidents is lifted.
1989	*August*	The Tokyo financial futures market is established.

bondholdings after a three-month waiting period. The yield on government bonds began to function as the standard for setting long-term interest rates. One may reasonably conclude that once-strict regulation of interest rates had to be relaxed as a result of the increase in government bonds. In 1979, the call rate was deregulated.

Focus on the money supply

Another important change that took place in this period was that the Bank of Japan began to adopt policies that focused on the money supply rather than interest rates. The rate of year-on-year increase of M_2 or, alternatively, M_2 + Certificates of Deposit (CD) became the standard index for financial policy making in Japan. M_1 is cash currency in circulation + current deposits, M_2 is M_1 + deposits with prescribed terms. Certificates of deposit are negotiable certificate of deposits, and over ¥500 million worth were issued in 1979, when they were first instituted. In the United States M_1 is considered to be the key indicator, but in Japan policy makers have monitored growth of M_2 + CDs. In the past, interest rates had been the key indicator for determining financial policy, but this had changed in the 1970s as the advance of inflation made interest rates unserviceable. An interest rate of 6 percent a year is tantamount to a low rate of 1 percent if the expected inflation rate is 5 percent and to a negative rate if inflation is higher than 6 percent, in which case the more one borrows the better. For that reason, the money supply, which is not affected by anticipated inflation rates, was adopted as the indicator by which to determine financial policy.

Internationalization of finance markets

One further feature of this period was that Japan's finance markets, which had in many respects been cut off from overseas markets, became more closely tied to foreign markets. In May 1979, the Ministry of Finance lifted many of its restrictions on the inflow of funds from short-term foreign impact loans. I hasten to add that there had been influxes of foreign assets prior to this. When the ministry wanted to obtain foreign currency to handle the international balance of payments deficits, as happened at the time of the first oil crisis, it eased restrictions. When there was a balance of payments surplus, it would tighten restrictions. Tuning of this kind had been standard practice since the beginning of the 1970s, but now the government had begun substantially eliminating its restraint mechanisms.

Shortly after, in December 1979, the new Foreign Exchange Law was enacted. Previous to that date, all foreign exchange transactions that had not been specifically permitted were banned. Now, all exchange transactions were in principle permitted. Although some restrictions remained in place, Japanese companies now became able to raise funds in Japan and abroad, wherever interest and other conditions were most favorable.

A complete revision of the Bank Law was carried out in June 1981. Up until then, ordinary banks, trust banks, long-term credit banks, and securities companies had each worked in defined fields that were regulated by the Ministry of Finance. Under the newly revised law, banks became able to conduct business that had hitherto been the territory of the securities industry and vice versa.

International demands for easing of restrictions formed a constant backdrop to the developments of this period. One of the best-known examples was the Tokyo Stock Exchange's extension of membership to foreign corporations in April 1982. Also in 1982, financial institutions became permitted to sell government bonds over the counter to customers. These institutional changes were to have a profound impact in the latter half of the 1980s.

Flow of investment funds

Turning now to Japan's economic relations with the United States in the period from the end of the 1970s to the beginning of the 1980s, we can identify two major issues. The first was the constant flow of investment funds from Japan, the other was economic friction. Economic friction has had much press, but the former in my view is the more fundamental problem. The culprit behind the influx of funds from Japan was the United States' twin deficits—the budget deficit and the current account deficit. In Economics 101, the equivalency of investment (I) and saving (S) is assumed to hold when computing the national economy. However, if one divides the national economy into a government sector, a private sector, and a foreign sector, savings and investment are not necessarily equivalent within each sector. In Japan in the late 1970s and 1980s, the government was constantly in a state of high investments and low savings (I > S), resulting in fund shortages. The private sector, on the other hand, had a savings surplus, with savings outstripping investments (I < S). If we treat the foreign sector as if it were a domestic economic sector, we find that in Japan, the foreign sector always had an investment surplus (I > S).

If we apply this framework to the twin deficits of the United States, we can say something like the following. One of the features of Reaganomics—the economic policies espoused by the Reagan administration—was the implementation of a tax cut. Some economists argued that a tax cut would eventually boost tax receipts by raising incomes, but that was not the way it worked out, and the United States government, already deeply in debt, found itself facing massive deficits in the first half of the 1980s. The private sector may have had a surplus of savings over investment, but the margin of surplus was small. As a consequence, the foreign sector filled the gap in the federal budget with its savings surplus, thus allowing the equation I = S to hold. To put it another way, from the perspective of the foreign sector, the United States current accounts deficit was offset by an outflow of funds from the foreign sector, that is, the foreign-sector savings surplus. Viewed from inside the United States, the picture inevitably had to be seen as one in which the United States was suffering both federal budget and trade deficits, one of which was being met by purchases of treasury bonds from countries like Japan, which were racking up trade surpluses.

For the United States, there could be no balance of savings and investment, and the domestic cycle of funds would remain disrupted as long as funds flowed in from Japan and West Germany to cover the federal budget deficit. Moreover, there was considerable resentment at Japan's huge trade surplus, shown in figure 7.8, which led to trade friction. I don't propose to go over the issues in detail but, for example, trigger prices were set for steel, and Japan became required to export at prices higher than those set by the United States government. In the case of automobiles, voluntary restraints were imposed on the number of cars exported from Japan. Or in the case of beef and oranges, Japan was pressured to liberalize imports; initially it eased quantitative ceilings and later lifted all restrictions.

Thus, on the one hand, the United States was unable to finance its federal budget without a constant influx of funds from Japan (or West Germany), yet, on the other hand, trade friction was perennially arising between the United States and Japan. Serious

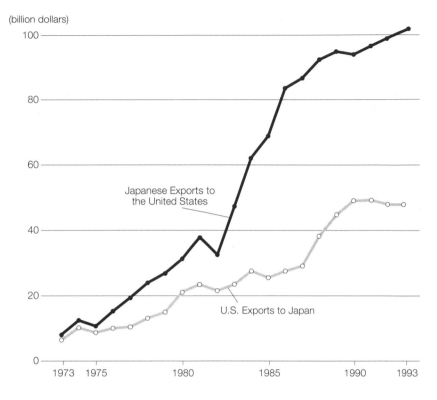

(billion dollars)

Japanese Exports to
the United States

U.S. Exports to Japan

Fig. 7.8. The Japan-U.S. Trade Imbalance

Source: Based on U.S. Department of Commerce data.

negotiations took place on these issues on repeated occasions from the beginning of the 1980s throughout the decade.

One of the conditions that fostered the influx of Japanese investments into the United States was the constant gap between Japanese and U.S. interest rates, the former being consistently 3–4 percent lower than the latter. Naturally, Japanese funds flowed overseas.

As part of the process of soothing the economic friction, foreign exchange transactions were deregulated. As I noted a few minutes ago, the revised Foreign Exchange Law liberalized the markets so that all transactions that were not explicitly prohibited became permitted in principle. In 1984, the Japan-U.S. Yen-Dollar

Committee report came out, as a result of which Japan relaxed the last of its major remaining restrictions.

If you look at the chronological table of deregulation (not to clear from table 7.1), you will note that restrictions on the yen convertibility of Eurodollars and other Eurocurrencies were abolished in 1984. In July that year, the Ministry of Finance lifted restrictions on the flotation of yen-denominated bonds by foreign concerns. The Commercial Code was revised to permit the issue of warrant bonds, that is, bonds convertible to new stock issues. These and other major changes occurred in the middle of the 1980s.

Deregulation of interest rates

Far-reaching steps to deregulate interest rates began to be undertaken in 1985. Interest rates on large deposits were deregulated, and before that Money Market Certificates, linked to market rates, had been introduced. Although I won't go into the details, the minimum deposit limits for MMCs and other instruments were successively reduced over the next few years. In the first half of the 1980s, the overseas financial transactions of Japanese corporations and financial institutions were rapidly deregulated. This had the effect of stimulating corporate fund-raising and investment overseas.

To end this section, let me make one final observation. The outset of the 1980s was still characterized by global stagflation. However, the stringent retrenchment policies of President Reagan in the United States and Prime Minister Thatcher in Great Britain pulled those countries out of the doldrums at the beginning of the 1980s, terminating the global stagflation that had persisted since the 1970s and setting growth rates on an upward track around the world. In 1984 and 1985, Japan began to show considerable signs of recovery, with real growth rates hitting almost 5 percent.

INTERNATIONALIZATION AND THE STRONG YEN

A further feature of the United States economy in the early part of the 1980s was that despite the country's huge budget and trade deficits, the Americans did nothing about the overvaluing of the dollar vis-à-vis the yen and the deutsche mark. For a period in the early 1980s, under Treasury Secretary Donald Regan, the monetarists that dominated the Treasury Department held that the yen and mark should weaken and the dollar strengthen. President Reagan himself was heard to announce that a strong dollar was a good thing. The attitude only began to change after Howard Baker's appointment as Treasury secretary after the abandonment of the policy of benign neglect.

In figure 7.2, the yen is seen moving upward in the first half of 1985. On September 22, 1985, the G5 nations reached the so-called Plaza Accord under which the yen and mark were to be revalued and conversely the dollar down priced. At the time, the yen was worth about ¥240 to the dollar, but the Japanese indicated that a range of ¥210–200 would be acceptable, and this was actually agreed upon. These events are vividly described in Paul A. Volcker and Gyoten Toyoo's book *Changing Fortunes: The World's Money and the Threat to American Leadership*.

The rising yen
Once the yen had got up some momentum, it proceeded to strengthen on its own. The exchange rate broke ¥200 to the dollar and continued to rise to ¥150 = $1.00 by the end of 1986. To deal with this sudden show of strength by the yen, the Louvre Accord was reached in February 1987 extolling the virtues of stable exchange rates. However, this had little effect, and after a few months' hiatus, the yen proceeded to rise again, attaining ¥120 to the dollar in the beginning of 1988.

The question is what brought on the yen's upsurge. If you look at Japan's trade figures in figure 7.9, you will see that the dollar-based figures behave quite differently from the yen-based figures. Exports calculated in dollars rise consistently throughout. Imports calculated in dollars if anything tended to fall for most of the 1980s and started to move upward in 1988. However, Japanese exports show a rapid decline after 1985 when computed in yen. The falloff lasted about four years, and it was only in 1992 that exports retook their 1985 levels.

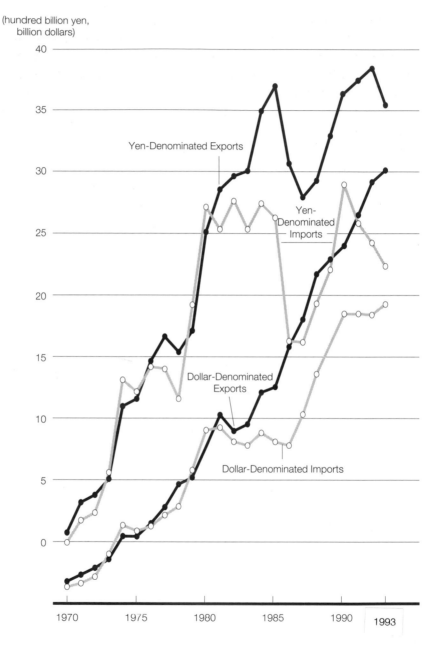

(hundred billion yen,
billion dollars)

Yen-Denominated Exports

Yen-Denominated Imports

Dollar-Denominated Exports

Dollar-Denominated Imports

Fig. 7.9. Japan's Exports and Imports

Source: Ministry of Finance, *Foreign Trade Statistics.*

Overseas production

Japan's export industries were hard hit by the strong yen, and efforts to resolve the crisis took many forms. In addition to cutting their internal costs, they demanded that their contracting companies cut their unit costs and moved their production of components to overseas plants. In the automobile and electrical machinery industries, firms began local production overseas as an alternative to exporting. This is clearly visible in figure 7.10, where overseas production of automobiles begins to advance after 1985. Honda had already been producing overseas for some time, but now even the more conservative Toyota and Nissan began to put an effort into local production.

Figure 7.11 shows the proportion of household electrical products produced by Japanese companies in overseas factories. In the case of radios, color televisions, tape recorders, and other simple consumer electronics, overseas production levels top 50 percent and in some cases stand in the region of 60–70 percent. About 20 percent of videotape recorders are made overseas. Even when electrical machinery is actually made in Japan, more and more firms are moving their production of components to Thailand, Malaysia, and other parts of Asia. Together with increasingly stiff demands on contracting firms and suppliers, the drive to produce overseas is emblematic of Japanese corporations' frantic efforts to deal with the stronger yen.

The government responded to the exchange-rate-triggered recession with fiscal and policy measures. The Bank of Japan's official rate at which it lends funds to other banks was cut substantially from 1985 through to 1987, which time the official lending rate had reached an unprecedented low of 2.5 percent.

Recession ruled unremittingly until March or April 1987, but by the beginning of spring 1987, there was a discernible turnaround across the board. Falling prices of imported materials were visibly generating profits in electric power, gas, and other industries that provided goods and services within Japan. These profits had begun to show up at the beginning of the high exchange rate period, but as the yen continued to advance, raw material and fuel

(million vehicles)

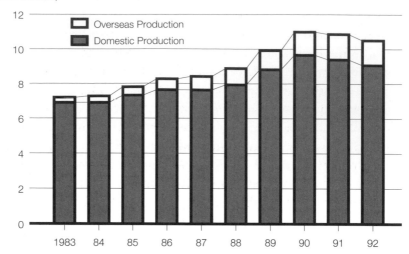

Fig. 7.10. Domestic and Overseas Production by Japanese Automakers

Source: Japan Automobile Manufacturers Association, Inc., *Annual Bulletin on Automobile Statistics.*

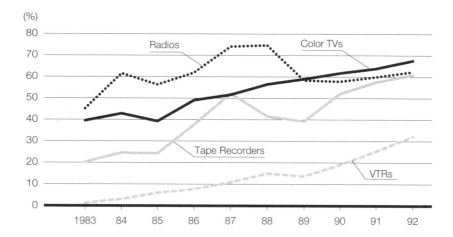

Fig. 7.11. Overseas Production of Major Household Electrical/ Electronic Products (percentage made overseas)

Source: Electronic Industries Association of Japan, *Minsei Yo Denshi Kiki Deta Shu* (Data on Civilian Electronic Equipment).

Note: Percentage manufactured overseas = $\dfrac{\text{Overseas production volume}}{\text{Overseas production volume} + \text{domestic production volume.}}$

prices fell even further, with the result that profits spurted in the latter half of 1986.

Returning to figure 7.6, it is clear that import prices dropped after 1985, with yen-denominated imports plunging to nearly half their 1985 level by 1987. The falloff can be partly ascribed to the strength of the yen but more importantly to the impact of the drop in the price of crude oil, Japan's most crucial import, which fell below $20 a barrel. The mean domestic price index also fell, but consumer prices remained flat despite the rapidly strengthening yen, as profits from the fall in import prices all ended up in the pockets of manufacturing and distribution firms, so that the impact was not felt by the ordinary public. This, I believe, raises serious questions about the Japanese economy.

Falling export prices
Be that as it may, wholesale prices fell across the board. Export prices dropped more than 20 percent—not as much as imports, but a drop nonetheless. Since overseas prices were relatively steady, firms could not shift the burden of the stronger yen by raising prices overseas but had to cut prices by streamlining their operations and by producing more abroad. The fact that manufactured imports, which stood at one-fourth of all imports in 1985, jumped to nearly one-half the total by 1987 reflects an upswing in component imports. Even though the yen had risen in value, Japan's exports, as calculated in dollars (not export volumes per se), spurted even more than before, partly because of the J-curve effect. The export surge sparked further recriminations in the United States and prompted threats to invoke the Super 301 section of the 1988 Trade Act to impose a 100 percent retaliatory tariff on imports from Japan.

When calculated in yen, on the other hand, exports slumped heavily, as we saw earlier. However, the rapid recovery in capital investments and other sectors of the domestic economy plainly set economic growth on a domestic demand driven track beginning in 1985. Returning to the relative contributions of external and internal demand shown in figure 7.1, we see that external demand substantially sustained growth up to 1985, but that from 1986 on external demand impacted negatively on growth, and that the recovery was sustained by domestic demand alone.

The improvement can be seen in figure 7.12. In 1985 and 1986, sales turnover and ordinary profits of big corporations plunged, but in the period from 1987 through 1990, a rapid improvement may be observed. These figures only cover corporations listed on the country's stock exchanges, but they provide a good indication of the rally that came in 1987 and thereafter. The boom sparked an expansion of capital investments, not only in the expected automobile and electrical machinery industries, but also in tertiary industries, such as commerce and services. One of the features of this time was a burst of housing investments and construction of office buildings, boosting demand for the construction industry, which had languished in the doldrums in the late 1970s and early 1980s.

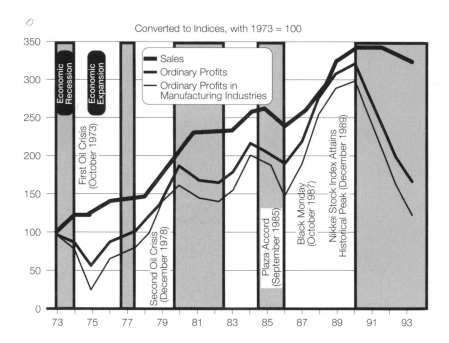

Fig. 7.12. Sales and Ordinary Profits of Listed Companies

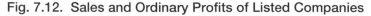

Source: Statistics prrepared by the *Nihon Keizai Shimbun* (Japan Economic Journal) on companies listed on the stock exchanges of Japan.

Economic prosperity and growth thus revived on the basis of domestic demand; the fly in the ointment was financial policy. I mentioned a moment ago that the Bank of Japan official lending rate hit its historical nadir at the end of the two-year period from 1985 to 1987. The problem was in the fact that this low interest rate of 2.5 percent was sustained for two years until 1989. As figure 7.13 shows, land and stock prices showed a clear upward momentum as early as 1985. Although general prices fell owing to the drop in import prices, stock and land prices, having no linkage to import prices, remained high. This indicates that credit had become too easy. Whereas a year-on-year rate of increase in M_2 +

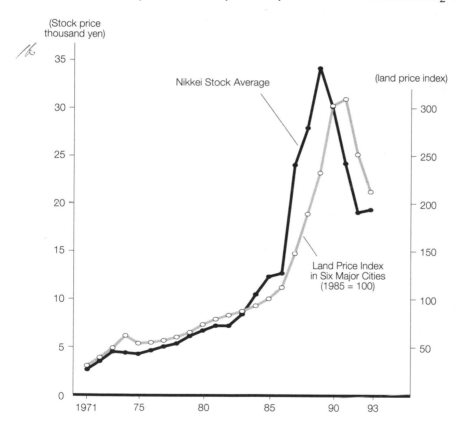

Fig. 7.13. Sales and Ordinary Profits of Listed Companies

Source: Figures on stock prices are based on averages prepared by the *Nihon Keizai Shimbun*. Those on real estate are based on *Urban Real Estate Indexes* prepared by the Japan Real Estate Research Institute.

CDs of 7 percent is held to be optimal, for nine months in the period from April 1987 to October 1990 the year-on-year increase of M_2 + CDs was in excess of 9 percent. The period of easy credit lasted for over three years, and the necessary tightening measures were implemented a year too late.

Black Monday

One reason for the delay in tightening lending was the plunge on global stock markets that followed Black Monday, October 19, 1989. Stocks fell on the Tokyo Stock Exchange for a time, while foreign stocks remained in the doldrums for a long time thereafter. I believe that the Bank of Japan may have mistimed its raising of the official lending rate because of the interest gap that existed between Japan and the United States, causing Japanese funds to flow into that country. Suzuki Yoshio, formerly of the Bank of Japan, reflects on these events in his book (*Japan's Financial Policy*)* with a curious turn of phrase that suggests that in terms of the impact on other countries, the Bank of Japan timed the correction too late. Doubtless there was much debate within the central bank, but it maintained its stance of keeping interest rates low, a position that surely contributed to the "economic bubble," that was to follow.

Nikkei index hits ¥39,000

Japanese stock prices continued to soar in the late 1980s, with the Nikkei index hitting its all-time peak of ¥39,000 at the end of December 1989. Since the starting point in 1985 had been about ¥12,000, this represents a tremendous advance in stock prices. Figure 7.13 presents a graph of the Nikkei stock price index and the index of real estate prices in six major cities. The peak stock index price of ¥39,000 is not shown, since the graph gives only annual average prices, that for 1989 being ¥35,000. You will see from the graph that the real estate price index rises at approximately the same pace as stock prices. Although ordinary prices were relatively stable, the Bank of Japan should have moved

---

*Suzuki Yoshio, *Nihon no Kin'yu Seisaku* (Japan's Financial Policy) Iwanami Shoten, 1993.

quickly to tighten credit in view of the abnormal increases in stock and real estate prices, but these did not enter significantly into central bank calculations.

One of the things that enabled stock and real estate markets to soar to such heights was the ease of raising funds. Figure 7.14 shows firms' sources of funds in capital markets. It can be seen from the graph that a major change in Japanese corporate fund-raising practices took place between 1985 and 1986. The figure shows the numbers starting from 1977; domestic funding sources predominated in the 1970s, but in the 1980s, foreign fund sources became more conspicuous owing to the deregulation of foreign exchange. The "etc." part of "convertible bonds, etc.," in the Ministry of Finance data refers to warrant bonds, which firms found extremely advantageous when raising funds overseas. Throughout this period, almost no stocks were issued abroad, the

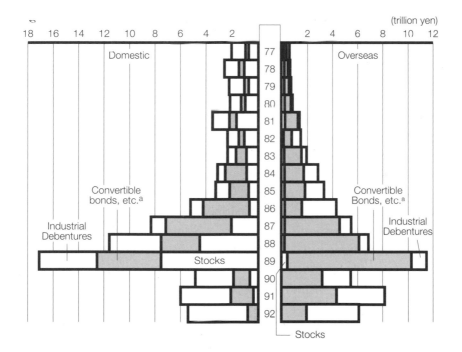

Fig. 7.14. Corporate Fund-Raising in Capital Markets

Source: Ministry of Finance, *Shoken Kyoku Nenpo* (Securities Bureau Annual Report). 1993.
[a] Convertible bonds, etc., includes warrant bonds convertible to new stock.

bulk of overseas fund-raising taking the form of convertible bonds and warrant bonds. To give some indication of the huge amounts firms were able to procure, in 1987, about ¥9 trillion was raised domestically and nearly ¥6 trillion overseas, and 1989, at the peak, domestic fund procurements totaled ¥17 trillion, with those overseas at nearly ¥12 trillion yen. Firms even found it profitable to place funds raised at low interest rates in large-scale time deposits.

Securities investments

It was often said during this period that firms could, if they played their cards right, end up paying negative interest on the funds they raised overseas. Convertible bonds and warrant bonds during this period had very low interest rates in anticipation of rising stock prices in Japan. These were typically long-term bonds, due in 10 years. Firms had to forecast the exchange rate at the payback time, but when one took into account the likely strengthening of the yen in the interim, the payback amount in yen at the end of 10 years turned out, quite surprisingly, to be less than the amount of money raised. Such conditions spurred Japanese corporations to raise huge sums of money at advantageous terms, from both within Japan and abroad.

Although firms had enough of their own to invest in plant and equipment, they went on to raise further funds primarily in the quest for the capital gains to be derived from manipulating financial investments. One example of this can be seen in figure 7.15, which shows the year-on-year gains in negotiable securities investments by large manufacturing corporations. There is a spurt, beginning in 1987, that peaks in 1990 at a rate of increase of 25 percent over the preceding year. Similar large investments were also made in real estate. Huge profits fueled yet more investments. Even private individuals found themselves able to afford expensive cars and art objects, paid for from their capital gains. Most of the increase in bank lending went to commerce, real estate, and non-banking services, while loans to manufacturing did not increase, a fact that may be interpreted as indicating that these other sectors were actively borrowing from banks for investment in stocks and

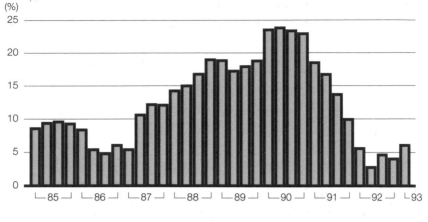

Fig. 7.15. Investment Securities Outstanding in Major Manufacturing Companies (year-on-year change)

Source: Ministry of Finance, *Financial Statements of Corporations, by Industry* (Quarterly).

real estate, while big manufacturing firms had access to other more advantageous financing arrangements and did not have to rely on the banks.

The numbers in figure 7.16 show Japan's overseas direct investment by region and industry for 1980, 1985, 1990, and 1993. Since these numbers are tallied from reports filed by investing corporations with the Ministry of Finance and do not include investments that were later withdrawn, they are somewhat overblown. Nevertheless, they are informative. Global investments by Japanese firms rose from about $80 billion in 1985 to over $300 billion in 1990 and more recently, in 1993, topped $400 billion. The 1990 figures show that recent direct investments have been carried out in an immense range of fields. Manufacturing remains the largest area of investment, but investment in foreign real estate, services, finance and insurance, and commerce have all attained formidable levels. Some of the more prominent examples include Sony's purchase of Columbia Pictures and the Seibu Saison Group's acquisition of Inter-Continental Hotels. Sumitomo's purchase of the RCA Building when the boom was at its peak in 1988–89 is an example in the real estate field.

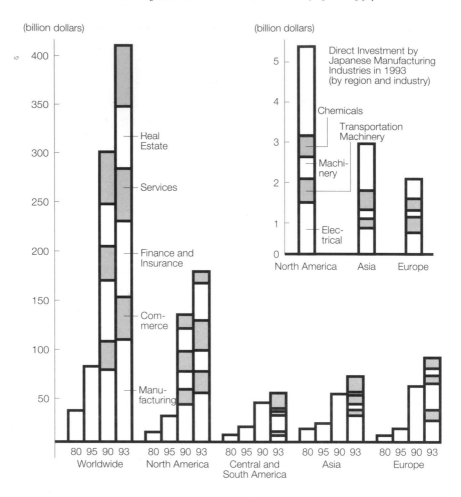

Fig. 7.16. Japanese Direct Investment (by region and industry, in billion dollars)

Source: Data from Ministry of Finance, International Finance Bureau.

What is interesting are the differences in the regional distributions of direct investment by industry. In Asia, a high proportion of investments were in manufacturing. By way of contrast, manufacturing accounted for a relatively small proportion of overall investments in Europe and elsewhere, with finance and insurance accounting for relatively large proportions.

The insert shows direct investment in manufacturing by industry and region in 1993. The largest field, not unexpectedly, is electrical machinery, followed by transportation machinery, which in this case really means automobiles. In Asia, the largest proportion of direct investments went into electrical machinery, with chemicals putting in a surprisingly strong showing.

Thus, as the bubble grew within Japan, direct investments overseas also became brisk, growing continuously in the period after 1985.

Growth of overseas assets

Figure 7.17 shows Japan's assets and liabilities overseas. Ever since the end of the 1960s, assets have outweighed liabilities, and Japan has been a net lender nation. The problem has been the rapid rate at which assets grew in the late 1980s. Japan had already chalked up a fair amount of foreign assets by the first half of the 1980s, but these began to swell sharply in 1986 and continued to do so for the remainder of the decade. At the same time, Japanese corporations were busily raising funds overseas, so that liabilities also grew, resulting in the bell shape that you see in figure 7.17. Once again, this can be attributed to the deregulation of foreign exchange.

Net overseas assets—that is, the difference between overseas assets and overseas liabilities—increased steadily during the same period, as shown in the insert in figure 7.17, from $10.9 billion in 1980, to $130 billion in 1985 and $328 billion in 1990. More recently the figure has topped $600 billion, in an increase in net assets that is nothing short of stunning.

Table 7.2 compares Japan's net assets with those of other countries. Since the latest figures are for 1991, they don't quite match those in figure 7.17. Japan saw increases in both assets and liabilities between 1986 and 1991, resulting in the growth of net assets, but the United States, which had a surplus of assets over liabilities in 1986, had negative net assets by 1991. Japan's surplus matches almost exactly the U.S. deficit in net assets in 1991. The United Kingdom's net assets have also been declining, and Germany's surplus was almost the same as Japan's in 1991. I might add parenthetically that Germans I have met recently have stressed that country's trade deficit. A short-term deficit is unlike-

Table 7.2 International Comparison of Overseas Assets and Liabilities (billions of dollars)

		1986	1991
Japan	Total Assets (A)	72.7	200.7
	Total Liabilities (B)	54.7	162.3
	Net Assets (A–B)	18.0	38.3
United States	A	150.8	20.7
	B	139.9	248.9
	A – B	10.9	–38.2
United Kingdom	A	106.3	177.8
	B	91.6	174.8
	A – B	14.7	3.0
Germany	A	50.2	115.3
	B	40.5	81.0
	A – B	9.7	34.3

Sources: Bank of Japan, *International Comparison of Statistics between Japan and Other Countries,* 1992.

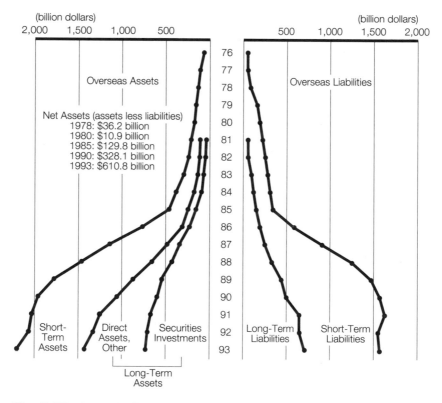

Fig. 7.17. Japan's Overseas Assets and Liabilities

Source: Ministry of Finance, International Finance Bureau, *Balances of Overseas Assets and Liabilities.*

ly to prove a problem for Germany, but its economic interests are likely to be focused on the former East Germany for some time to come.

The bubble was born out of the complex interaction of financial deregulation and internationalization and the current account surplus triggered by the strengthening of the yen. It constituted the single greatest reality of the latter half of the 1980s, with the boom reaching its peak in 1988–89.

The Showa Emperor died on January 7, 1989. Thus, the Showa era, which began with the bank panic in the 1920s and passed through depression and war, came to a close as Japan became the world's largest net asset holder.

Epilogue:
The Bubble Bursts

It was only after the bubble reached its maximal expansion that the Bank of Japan stepped in with tighter credit. However, neither stock prices nor land prices responded readily. It took until 1990 for stock prices to begin to fall, and real estate prices continued their upward spiral until 1991 (possibly because the index uses six cities as its base). In 1990, the Ministry of Finance notified banks that they should curb their lending for real estate, at which point real estate prices finally began to subside. The real estate price rises started in Tokyo, spread from there to Osaka and Nagoya, and finally to the other regional cities; the price drop began in Tokyo, and followed the same path into other regions.

Credit tightening began in 1989 and was followed by restrictions on real estate lending in 1990. Then, the bubble burst. The process took place along the following lines, although it is not something about which I have any firsthand experience. The value of one's stock or real estate holdings begin to slide. Slowly and unremittingly, their value creeps downward. If one has paid for the assets out of one's own pocket, one might grin and bear it, but the assets were purchased with borrowed funds that one went out on a limb to obtain, so the price decline directly reduces the value of the company's assets, and you are still having to pay heavy interest charges. For the same reason, customers and suppliers are seeing their asset values fall; they may not go bankrupt, but it gets harder to recover loans and accounts receivable. The number of firms saddled with these latent losses increases. Moreover, stock and real estate values do not fall all at once but edge slowly down over a three-year period beginning in 1991.

Thus the latest recession has been characterized by ever deepening wounds as asset values slipped and the number of bad loans gradually mounted. What the Economic Planning Agency initially regarded as a mild economic setback has been surprising in the length of its duration, the breadth of its impact, and its severity.

In the meantime, the dirty linen started to show: banks and other institutions had lent too easily during the bubble era, and some, it was now learned, were beset by huge latent losses. It also became known that securities companies had illegally guaranteed customers against investment losses. Financial institutions had to write off a substantial amount of bad and nonperforming loans, and securities companies chalked up heavy losses. Companies and individuals alike were hard put to deal with their change in fortunes. The writing off of losses peaked in 1993, and at the beginning of 1994, the economic climate began to revive.

The recession, however, had boosted exports in dollar terms, while keeping import growth sluggish. The upshot was a large trade surplus. The yen, which had subsided for a while, began to gain new strength just before summer 1993. Export industry profitability deteriorated, so that companies were forced to trim their operations. The recovery within Japan was thus delayed, and it was only in spring 1994 that the outlook began to become a little brighter.

Once the bubble collapsed, banks became circumspect about lending: there had been a number of scandals involving financial institutions, and it had been revealed that capital-asset standards in Japan did not generally meet the standards mandated by the Bank for International Settlements. The Japanese economy was forced to enter a new phase in which these problems had to be dealt with. Economic stimulation measures were introduced, and the official lending rate has been cut to a historical low of 1.75 percent, but corporations remain leery of committing themselves to new plant and equipment investments. The one ray of hope is the pickup in housing investments by individuals.

Changes in lifestyles

Before I conclude, let me touch on how Japanese lifestyles and living standards have changed. Figure 7.18 tells us that Japanese consumers' lifestyles have undergone a number of gentle but irreversible changes in the period beginning in the late 1970s. One of these is the growth of services as a component of the consumption structure: consumer lifestyles have shifted from the purchase of goods to the purchase of services, the key areas being travel, education, and recreation. Services have recently accounted for 40 percent of consumer spending. This may not seem like much change on the 30 percent in 1977, but with the stronger yen, overseas travel has boomed—some 8 percent of Japan's population travels overseas for tourism every year.

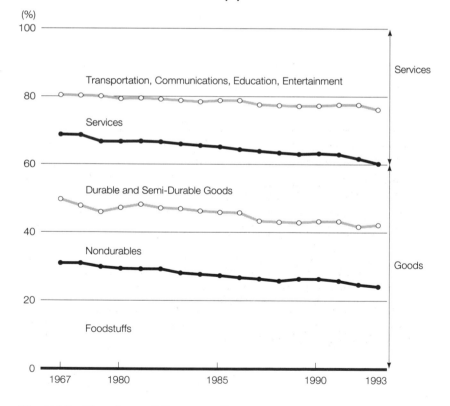

Fig. 7.18. Structure of Consumption

Source: Management and Coordination Agency, Statistics Bureau, *Annual Report on the Family Income and Expenditure Survey 1993.*

Spending on foodstuff and other necessities has consistently fallen as a proportion of the total. On the other hand, Japan's notoriously bad housing conditions have improved substantially in recent times. Overall, the number of homes has increased, but more importantly, their size has also increased. Back in 1973, the average home had 7 mats (approximately 14 square meters) per person; more recently the figure was close to 10 mats (approximately 20 square meters) per person. Since this latter figure is for 1988, the situation has presumably improved since then.

The rise in real estate prices put on hold for many Japanese the long-standing dream of owning one's own home. As you can see from figure 7.19, the proportion of resident-owned homes has remained stable ever since the 1960s. There was a slight increase around 1983, but by 1988, the proportion had dropped somewhat. It is likely that soaring real estate prices around this time truncated the growth of resident ownership.

Although overall Japanese living standards have made headway over the years, housing conditions remained a problem even

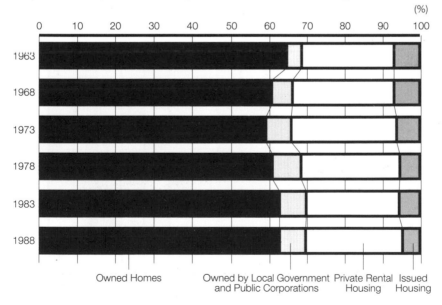

Owned Homes   Owned by Local Government Private Rental Issued
               and Public Corporations   Housing   Housing

Fig. 7.19. Housing Units by Owner-Occupant Relationship

Source: Management and Coordination Agency, Statistics Bureau, *Japan Statistical Year Book,* 1993, 1994.

in the late 1980s. More recently, the fall in real estate values and low interest rates have spurred a burst of housing starts, so in that respect the present recession may help improve the percentage of owned homes.

Aging population

One further observation that I could tack on here is that the Japanese population is aging dramatically. Figure 7.20 shows how the percentage of the population aged 14 years and under is rapidly shrinking, down to about 20 percent recently. The percentage

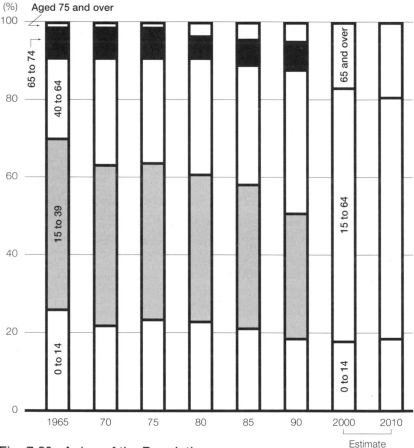

Fig. 7.20. Aging of the Population

Source: Management and Coordination Agency, Statistical Bureau, *National Census and Monthly Estimates on Census.*

of those in older age groups, on the other hand, is rising fast. In 1990, the percentage aged 40 and under fell below 60 percent, while those aged over 40 topped 40 percent for the first time. These figures support the prediction that the population of elderly will increase in the future. When that happens, rising social welfare costs are likely to prove a major burden.

The recession that arose in the wake of the bubble's collapse is still with us. Despite the cutting of interest rates to extraordinarily low levels, things have only just started to hint at looking up. The growth of the money supply has been very low. M_2 + CDs slipped into negative growth for a time and have only just returned to a small degree of positive growth. Financial institutions remain wary, but it is also true that little in the way of new demand for funds is arising. The influx of funds from overseas does not now appear to have the momentum that it once had. The yen continued to strengthen in 1994 and has now broken the ¥100 = $1.00 mark, so export industries will unquestionably be hard hit.

At the same time, a new issue is beginning to arise. The growth in automobiles, electrical machinery, and precision machinery—Japan's leading industries over the past two decades—has gradually slackened. When one thinks about it, these industries, above all electrical machinery, have released a constant stream of new products on the market. As the growth of one product has waned, another has been developed to take its place. Over the last 20 years, the electrical machinery industry has expanded overall by producing a series of products, first televisions, then a slew of products incorporating semiconductors and integrated circuits: videos, word processors, personal computers, and most recently portable telephones. But of late it seems that new products are not coming forth in comparable numbers. Word processors and personal computers no longer exhibit the rapid growth that they once did. Similarly with automobiles: although it remains possible that cars will continue to sell well owing to production overseas, production within Japan has declined for the last three years or so, and the old momentum is no longer visible.

When leading industries cease to grow, the question is where new industries will emerge to replace them. What one may be able to say is that at the moment there is nothing on the horizon to take the place of electrical machinery or automobiles as major growth industries. A great many small industries are emerging, but it seems questionable to me whether these can replace the old leading industries.

I will take a stab at making a prediction. I would like to take note of the bold discount merchandising that has recently sprung up in the retail industry. In a wide range of fields, companies have begun high-volume marketing of merchandise at much lower prices than in the past, combining overseas mass production with high-volume purchasing. This trend is likely to shake the Japanese business community, which has hitherto enjoyed a great deal of price stability owing to the relative power of the producer to determine prices oligopolistically. The question is whether the sales receipts of such operations will continue to grow with sales volume, since unit prices are reduced in the short term. It should be remembered, however, that discount merchandising is a new phenomenon that is closely tied to deregulation. If these new retail industries really do reduce prices to consumers so that they boost real consumption, they offer a new possibility, I believe, for further economic growth.

The U.S. budget deficit and Japan's role in the world

To conclude my talk, I would like to add a few final remarks about Japan's status in the international community. Japan's international assets and liabilities, as shown in figure 7.17, should give one food for thought. Today, the world's leading nation is still unquestionably the United States. In the 1960s, the United States was a power, equipped with economic and military might, but now its international assets are outstripped by its international liabilities. It can hardly be described as having all the economic strength of a world leader, and whether or not the U.S. economy will regain its former luster is a question for the future. For the present, the U.S. economy cannot function unless Japan and Germany cover its budget deficit. The United States that threatens Japan with economic sanctions is the same United States that cannot function without the supply of funds from Japan. We cannot say that we don't want to buttress this mercurial, egotistical superpower; rather, we have to take active steps to buoy it. For if we don't, the problems of the global economy will become far more serious than they already are. By bolstering the United States, Japan is placed in a position where it must contribute to the totality of the global economy.

Japan, moreover, is an Asian country, and we must consider what Japan can do to further the development of the other countries of Asia. There is a major problem if we think we can get away just with making direct investments. The newly industrializing economies of Asia are doing fine, but there are many other Asian countries that are far worse off. To those countries, Japan must provide Official Development Assistance and other aid. But Japan's own budgetary problems do not give it much margin to do so, something that may be hard for people in other countries to understand. The Asian countries would not be sympathetic if the world's largest international net asset holder were to scrimp on its ODA on the grounds that it was suffering fiscal difficulties of its own. Since the end of the 1980s, Japan's global responsibilities as an economic power have weighed all the heavier on its shoulders.

INDEX

The LTCB International Library Foundation
Statement of Purpose

The world is moving steadily toward a borderless economy and deepening international interdependence. Amid this globalization of economic activities, the Japanese economy is developing organic ties with the economies of individual nations throughout the world via trade, direct investment, overseas manufacturing activities, and the international movement of capital.

As a result, interest is growing in many countries about Japanese politics, economy, and social fabric, and also about the concepts and values that lie behind Japan's socioeconomic activities.

However, the overseas introduction and international dissemination of works originally written in Japanese are presently insufficient. Such works are not sufficiently well known or actively utilized outside of Japan. One main reason for this is that the high costs involved in translating and publishing materials written in Japanese hinder the undertaking of such activities on a commercial basis. It is extremely important to overcome this barrier to deepen and broaden mutual understanding.

Therefore, we have founded the LTCB International Library Foundation to address this pressing need. Our primary activities are to introduce and disseminate information about Japan in foreign countries through the translation of selected writings in Japanese concerning social sciences, such as Japanese politics, economy, society, culture, and other fields, into English (and other languages) as well as through the publication and distribution of these translations. To commemorate the completion of The Long-Term Credit Bank of Japan, Ltd.'s new headquarters and the Bank's fortieth anniversary, LTCB has provided the LTCB International Library Foundation with an endowment.

We sincerely hope that the LTCB International Library Foundation will serve to promote international exchange, and that the Foundation will undertake substantial activities that shall contribute to increased mutual understanding.

March 1, 1994

The Founders of the LTCB International Library Foundation